The BYTE Guide to CP/M-86

The BYTE Guide to CP/M-86

The BYTE Guide to CP/M-86

by
Mark Dahmke

McGraw-Hill Book Company

New York St. Louis San Francisco Auckland Bogotá Hamburg
Johannesburg London Madrid Mexico Montreal New Delhi Panama
Paris São Paulo Singapore Sydney Tokyo Toronto

Library of Congress Cataloging in Publication Data

Dahmke, Mark.
   The byte guide to CP/M-86.

   Includes index.
   1. CP/M-86 (Computer operating system)   I. Title.
QA76.6.D3325   1984   001.64'25   83-19613
ISBN 0-07-015072-9

1234567890   DOCDOC   89876543

ISBN 0-07-015072-9

Printed and bound by R.R. Donnelley and Sons, Inc.

The BYTE Guide to CP/M-86

by
Mark Dahmke

McGraw-Hill Book Company

New York St. Louis San Francisco Auckland Bogotá Hamburg
Johannesburg London Madrid Mexico Montreal New Delhi Panama
Paris São Paulo Singapore Sydney Tokyo Toronto

Library of Congress Cataloging in Publication Data

Dahmke, Mark.
  The byte guide to CP/M-86.

  Includes index.
  1. CP/M-86 (Computer operating system)   I. Title.
QA76.6.D3325   1984   001.64'25   83-19613
ISBN 0-07-015072-9

1234567890   DOCDOC   89876543

ISBN 0-07-015072-9

Printed and bound by R.R. Donnelley and Sons, Inc.

To Robert Vassell, who planted the seed.

Table of Contents

Preface

CP/M has become the de facto standard operating system for the 8080, 8085, Z80, and 8086/8088 microprocessors. "De facto" does not necessarily imply best. CP/M on the 8080 or Z80 has its particular problems. CP/M-86 (the subject of this book) carries forward some of those problems. For the most part, CP/M has been a positive influence in the world of microcomputers because it has helped to standardize software. It is now possible to buy any of hundreds of "CP/M compatible programs," load them, and realistically expect them to work.

One of the major drawbacks to CP/M-80 (the 8080, Z80 version) was the lack of good documentation. The manuals supplied by Digital Research were hopelessly inadequate, so many user's guides like this one were published to fill the information gap. CP/M-86 comes with manuals that are harder to compete with. They are well organized and cover all operational aspects of the operating system, with one exception—they neglect to explain *why* you need an operating system. Their manuals assume that you understand this. The *BYTE Guide to CP/M-86* explains each part of the operating system and and each program or utility that comes with it in terms of its use and why it needs to be discussed at all.

Such an approach makes this book more than just a reference manual. It is compatible with my previous book *Microcomputer Operating Systems*, although this book stands on its own.

An appendix is included that lists references and sources for further reading. I have also listed books that may not relate directly to CP/M-86, but that might be interesting to the reader who wants to learn more about operating systems.

Appendices III and IV contain complete listings and descriptions for several public domain programs written in the 8086 instruction set for use on any CP/M-86 system. The first is a sample program that performs some of the functions of the DIR built-in command in CP/M. The purpose of the example is to demonstrate the use of many of the BDOS function calls.

Appendix IV includes a full description, flow charts, and listings for Char-io, a set of subroutines that simulate disk-oriented character input and output. Since it is often necessary to filter a text file for special characters, it is desirable to read the file a character at a time, rather than a record at a time. The rd-char and wr-char routines allow a file to be transferred as a stream of characters, with all disk access being handled transparently. The listing for a library file including these routines is given, with two examples for its use. With the examples, readers should be able to use char-io for any purpose, without much trouble.

Acknowledgments

I would like to thank Digital Research in general, and Susan Raab in particular, for their support. Bruce Roberts, Ed Kelly, Chris Morgan, and Steve Ciarcia were the instigators behind the project, and I would like to express my appreciation for their efforts.

The BYTE Guide to CP/M-86

1

Introduction: What Is CP/M-86?

1.1 INTRODUCTION

CP/M stands for "Control Program for Microcomputers." It was first developed for an Intel 8080 microcomputer system by Gary Kildall, founder of Digital Research. The acronym CP/M means little to the uninitiated user. All digital computers require programs or sequences of instructions to operate on. These programs or instructions are referred to as software. The actual computer is referred to as the hardware. The hardware may consist of the central processor, memory, disk drives, and so on. The central processor is responsible for executing the instructions that you give it. The problem is that the instructions it wants to read are not very human readable. That is where computer languages such as BASIC or Pascal come in.

A language such as BASIC reads English-like commands and converts them into commands that the computer can understand. This is referred to as compiling or interpreting a program. Even a language like BASIC needs help when it wants to read data from a disk or write characters to a video display terminal. CP/M, the operating system, is a control program that can be called upon to carry out menial chores in a generalized fashion. For example, suppose you have a BASIC interpreter and a word processor program written in some other language. If every program or every language went its own way, reading files from disk and communicating with printers or terminals as it pleased, there would be no standardization in the computer.

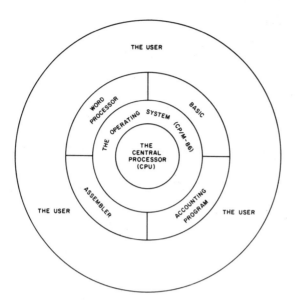

Figure 1.1: The relationship between the microprocessor, operating system, applications, and users.

The control program or operating system acts like a traffic cop who makes sure everyone obeys the conventions of the system, or, if you like, the "rules of the road."

Note: CP/M-86 is one of the control programs developed for the 8086 and 8088 microprocessors. It is derived from the 8080 version of CP/M (now referred to as CP/M-80, or CP/M 2.0). CP/M for the 8086 or 8088 is always referred to as CP/M-86. In this book, we will assume that all references to "CP/M" refer to CP/M-86, CP/M for the 8080, 8085 and Z80 microprocessors will be referred to as CP/M-80.

1.2 FEATURES AND FACILITIES

The purpose of an operating system is to provide a common environment for programs to run in. This can mean many things. All microcomputer systems have the following characteristics: input and output devices, main memory, a central processor, and mass storage. (See Figure 1.2.) The problem is that many manufacturers have their own ideas about how these building blocks should go together and have built products that can run CP/M, but are all different in some respects. For example, the disk interface may use different circuitry or may store information on the disk in a different fashion. Alternately, the video display terminal might be connected to the central processor differently.

To take all these minor variations into account, CP/M was de-

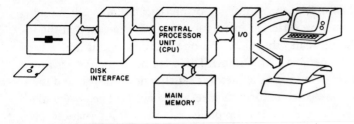

Figure 1.2:   Microcomputer system organization.

signed with a customized section that must be set up by the manufacturer of the computer. This section is called the basic input/output
system (BIOS) and is the lowest level of the CP/M operating system.
CP/M calls upon this section to accomplish its needs.

Because the BIOS is the only portion of CP/M that changes from
one manufacturer's computer to the next, the user need not be aware of
any differences in the actual operation of CP/M. To get around the
problem of incompatible software, CP/M supports logical devices that
are indifferent to the actual hardware. Such devices include a console or
video display terminal, a printer, disk drives, and perhaps a modem or
telephone line interface. All software, whether it be BASIC, a word
processor, or a program written by the user, must use the logical devices
provided by CP/M. If this is done, any program should be able to run
on any CP/M system, regardless of who wrote it or what system it was
developed on. This portability of software implies that anyone running
CP/M can trade software with anyone else running CP/M.

Note that CP/M-80 programs should run on any CP/M-80 microcomputer, and CP/M-86 programs should run on any CP/M-86 microcomputer. However, as stated earlier, due to differences in instruction
sets, a CP/M-80 program will not run directly on a CP/M-86 system,
and vice versa.

Another feature of CP/M is that it provides built-in functions that
would be tedious to recreate if the programmer were forced to supply
them. Functions such as open disk file, search disk directory, and compute file size are easy for CP/M to do, but would take a programmer a
long time to figure out.

1.3 THE ENVIRONMENT

CP/M-86 requires a certain environment to operate in. The most
important element of the environment is the microprocessor. As the
name implies, CP/M-86 was designed to operate on an Intel 8086 16-bit
microprocessor. The 8088 will also work since it uses the same instruction set as the 8086 and operates identically.

The type of microprocessor is important because many different microprocessors have different instruction sets. This means that the instruction code for "call subroutine" on one microprocessor may mean "store data into memory" on another. Different microprocessors are developed by different manufacturers for different purposes, and the instruction sets are often tailored to meet those needs. The 8086 and 8088 are newer, more powerful components, and their instruction sets have been enhanced from previous generation microprocessors. Specifically, the 8086 is an outgrowth of the incredibly successful Intel 8080. The 8080 was introduced in the early 1970's and has been the most popular of the microprocessors. It addresses memory in 8-bit wide chunks called *bytes*.

A *bit* is a *b*inary dig*it* and can be either a one or a zero. A byte is a group of eight bits. Since each bit can be either a one or a zero, the range of numbers possible with an 8-bit microprocessor is: 00000000 to 11111111 or, in decimal, 0 to 255. For many applications, an 8-bit computer is more than adequate. However, the 8080 (and most 8-bit machines for that matter) can only address memory with a 16-bit address, allowing for 64K bytes (65535 in decimal). The *K* after the 64 is short for *kilo*. One kilobyte is not 1,000 bytes but 1,024 bytes. Since computers use a base 2 or binary number system, 2^{10} or 1024 is more convenient than 1,000, so 64K is $64 \times 1,024$ or 65,535 instead of 64,000.

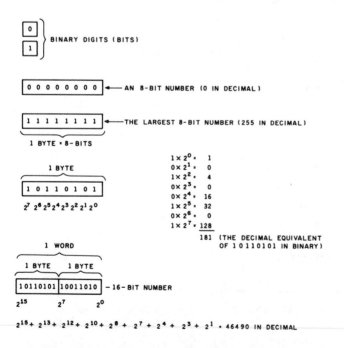

Figure 1.3: 8-bit and 16-bit binary numbers.

The 8086 is called a 16-bit microprocessor because it addresses memory and operates on data in 16-bit chunks called *words*. A word is two bytes long. When the 8086 reads data from a memory location, it gets two bytes at a time instead of one. This means that the 8086 runs faster and is more efficient in handling data.

In order to run CP/M-86, the microcomputer system must have at least 56K bytes of main memory. The memory, or the address space, of the 8086 is a continuous sequence of words, in which each word is 16 bits long. Although the 8086 can operate on 16-bit words, it is still convenient to speak of the amount of memory in bytes. If a particular system has 64K words of memory, it would be correct to say that it has 128K bytes of memory. The 8088 microprocessor is functionally identical to the 8086, but addresses memory in bytes instead of words. Thus, for those who wish to upgrade their 8080 or other 8-bit computer to an 8086, it is sometimes possible to replace the old circuit card with one that has an 8088 processor. Note that the 8088 addresses memory in bytes, but it operates on 16-bit words just like the 8086. Instead of loading a word of memory in one operation, the 8088 requires two loads of one byte each to accomplish the same thing.

The 8086 microprocessor allows the user to address up to one megabyte of memory because it generates a 20-bit memory address. Note that 2^{20} is 1,048,576. If this number is divided by 1024 to convert to kilobytes, we find that a megabyte is equal to 1024 Kilobytes. Since all the 8086 internal registers are 16 bits long, the 20-bit memory address must be generated indirectly. The 8086 uses a memory addressing technique called segment addressing, as shown in Figure 1.4. When a program is loaded, it is placed into memory at an address designated by CP/M-86 at load time. The program is treated as if it were located at address zero in memory, but is actually at a higher address. In the example in Figure 1.4, the program is loaded at 34FD0H (the H stands for hexadecimal notation or base 16) in absolute memory. The code segment register is loaded with the top 16 bits of the start address. The program counter currently holds 0045H, the address of the next instruction to be executed. The 8086 shifts the code segment address to the left 4 bits, making it into a 20-bit number. Notice that only the top 16 bits were stored in the first place. This means that programs can only start on 16-byte boundaries. The shifted code segment is added to the program counter, and the result is used to access the instruction in the program.

With the segment scheme, it would appear that programs cannot be larger than 64K bytes (!) and that no more than 64K bytes of data may be addressed. Actually, the programmer has complete control of the segment registers and can set up as many data or code areas as desired. Several machine instructions are provided to make this easy.

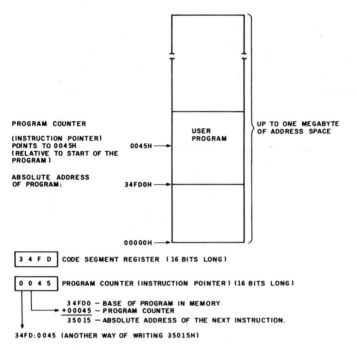

PROGRAM COUNTER

(INSTRUCTION POINTER)
POINTS TO 0045H
(RELATIVE TO START OF THE
PROGRAM)   0045H →

ABSOLUTE ADDRESS
OF PROGRAM: 34FD0H →

00000H →

| 3 4 F D | CODE SEGMENT REGISTER (16 BITS LONG) |

| 0 0 4 5 | PROGRAM COUNTER (INSTRUCTION POINTER) (16 BITS LONG) |

3 4FD0 — BASE OF PROGRAM IN MEMORY
+00045 — PROGRAM COUNTER
35015 — ABSOLUTE ADDRESS OF THE NEXT INSTRUCTION.

34FD:0045 (ANOTHER WAY OF WRITING 35015H)

USER PROGRAM

UP TO ONE MEGABYTE OF ADDRESS SPACE

Figure 1.4: Addressing memory with the 8086.

Since the program and data areas can be separately addressed in the 8086, the user has several options for organizing a program in memory. Three memory models are provided in CP/M-86: the Small model, the Compact model, and the 8080 model. Normally, the user does not need to be aware of these memory organizations, but they are mentioned here to show that memory must be managed and that CP/M-86 performs that function. Chapter 5 discusses memory management in detail.

1.4 DISKS AND DISK FILES

Almost all modern microcomputer systems have floppy disk drives or a hard disk drive. Floppy disks have become the industry standard for software storage and distribution.

Floppy disks are circular, flexible sheets of mylar with a magnetic coating. They come in two sizes: 8 inches and 5.25 inches in diameter. A typical 8-inch disk can hold 243,000 bytes of information in single-density mode, 486,000 bytes in double-density mode, and 1,200,000 bytes in double-density, double-sided operation.

Information is recorded on a floppy disk in tracks and sectors (see

Figure 1.5). A track, or concentric circle, is divided into sectors. Some disks are hard sectored (not to be confused with hard disk). Hard-sectored disks have ten or more holes cut around the inner part, each hole indicating the start of a sector. Most disks in use now are soft sectored—meaning that the sector layout is determined by software, not hardware (holes in the disk).

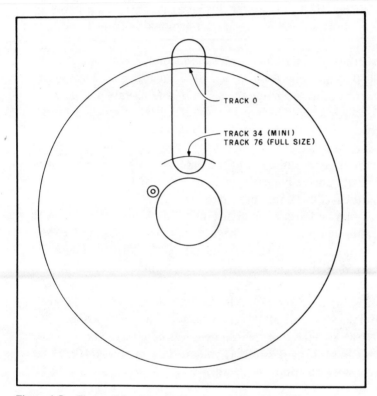

TRACK 0

TRACK 34 (MINI)
TRACK 76 (FULL SIZE)

Figure 1.5: Floppy disk geography.

Standard 8-inch single density disks have 77 tracks, each divided into 26 sectors. The CP/M standard (following the IBM 3740 disk format standard) stores 128 bytes per sector. Therefore, each track can hold 26 × 128 bytes or 3328 bytes. Since there are 77 tracks, a total of 256,256 bytes or characters can be stored on a disk. CP/M normally reserves two tracks for the operating system, or loader program, and the directory. A normal single-density disk directory has room for 64 entries. Each directory entry contains the file name, file type, and location information of each file on a disk. The directory for a given disk is unique and restricted to that disk. Only files on a particular disk may have directory entries on that disk.

1.5 COMPATIBILITY WITH CP/M-80

CP/M-80, developed for the 8080 microprocessor will also run on the 8085 and the Z80 microprocessor. As mentioned earlier, the instruction set of the 8080 is not compatible with that of the 8086 or 8088. However, the 8086 was designed to be upward compatible with the 8080. This means that it is possible to translate an 8080 program (at the instruction mnemonic level) into the 8086 instruction set. A program exists that can do this for standard Intel mnemonic assembler programs.

For programs that have been translated from CP/M-80, CP/M-86 offers an 8080 memory model in which all segment registers are set to the same starting address, giving the effect of all program and data areas overlapping. This environment most accurately duplicates the architecture of the 8080. For more information on the 8080 model, consult Chapter 5, Section 5.11.

If you are transferring a BASIC or Pascal (or other language) program, you would normally recompile it on the CP/M-86 system. This is not always the case, but under most circumstances, it is possible.

All disk files and disk formats from CP/M-80 are compatible with CP/M-86, although program files have a file type of .COM in CP/M-80 and .CMD in CP/M-86. Also, command (.CMD) files have a header record in CP/M-86 that contains allocation information for the four segments (among other things). Since command files from CP/M-80 are not executable on CP/M-86, this change is not a problem. Source text files and data files are all directly transferrable to CP/M-86.

The CP/M-86 operating environment was designed to be as compatible with CP/M-80 as possible. If you are an experienced CP/M-80 programmer, most functions of the operating system will already be familiar to you.

1.6 OPERATIONS

When you start up your microcomputer system for the first time, it is necessary to take some safety precautions. The most important one is to make a back-up copy of all the diskettes supplied with the system. Disks don't last forever, and you may need to go back to the original disks if one of your daily working copies is damaged or loses data.

The COPYDISK program supplied on the master disk will make the back-up copy for you, but first, you will probably need to format the blank disk you intend to use. Most manufacturers supply a program called FORMAT or FMT or INIT with their computer. It will clear off a new disk or reformat an old one. This is necessary because disks often have garbage data on them that the microcomputer could not properly read.

After formatting a disk, run the COPYDISK program (described in the next chapter), following all the instructions it provides. Then put the master disk in a very safe place, preferably in another room. It is wise to make several back-up copies of the master disk.

1.7 THE CARE AND HANDLING OF FLOPPY DISKS

Floppy disks are just flexible sheets of very strong mylar, and they do bend. The name "floppy" infers a certain vulnerability. Each disk is enclosed in a more rigid envelope that has holes cut in it. The center hole allows the disk to come into contact with the disk drive spindle, much as a phonograph record must touch the turntable to rotate properly. The long narrow holes allow the disk read/write head (similar to a tape recorder head) to touch the surface of the disk. The head is not always touching the disk—only when it is actually reading or writing data. The small round hole is used by the disk drive to detect the index hole in the disk. The index hole tells the computer when the disk has started each revolution.

Important: never touch any of the exposed surfaces or allow them to get dusty or dirty. Disks should always be returned to their paper pouches or envelopes when not in use.

Most disks have labels on them, with written messages indicating the contents of the disk and the last update—in human readable form. Always use a felt tip pen when writing on a label, and never press too hard. Permanent damage could result if too much pressure is applied to the disk.

If you start to notice wear or scoring on the exposed surface of the disk, it is time to copy all the files to a new disk. It is better to throw away a worn disk than to risk losing valuable information.

Never leave a disk in a hot place, such as on a radiator, on the dashboard of a car in the sun, or even on top of a computer. The heat will warp the disk and the protective housing. Never store disks near magnets, fans, or any high voltage equipment. The electromagnetic interference can cause information to be lost. Airport metal detectors use X-rays which won't hurt disks, but the large electromagnets in the metal detectors can. It is always wise to opt for hand inspection of disks.

Most microcomputer systems act erratically when power is turned on or off. It is best to pop open disk drive doors, letting the disk come part of the way out of the drive before powering up or down.

1.8 GETTING STARTED

All microcomputers that use floppy disks have more or less the same start-up procedure. To start up a system, you must load a copy of CP/M-86 into main memory from disk. If you are loading from floppy disk, insert the system disk (or your back-up copy, after the first time) into disk drive A (see the instructions for your particular computer). Some systems will load CP/M automatically after you insert the disk. Others will require that you press the reset button or hit a key on the keyboard. Please check with the start-up instructions for your computer.

You can usually tell if the system is loading by the noises made by the disk drive or by an indicator light on the disk drive. If CP/M has loaded correctly, the message:

```
CP/M-86      Version X.X
Copyright (c) 1981 Digital Research Inc.
A>
```

should appear on the video display screen. The Version X.X tells you the major and minor version levels of your copy of CP/M-86. Generally, Digital Research informs all registered users when new versions become available, so you can order an upgrade copy on disk.

The last line of the message, A>, tells you that CP/M-86 is logged in to disk drive A and that it is ready to accept your commands. Being logged in to a disk means nothing more than that it is the default disk. If, when entering commands, you do not specify the disk drive to operate on, CP/M will assume you mean the default disk. It is merely a convenience feature.

1.9 ENTERING COMMANDS

CP/M will perform tasks based on the commands you give it from the keyboard. When you see the command prompt, you may enter a command line. Every command consists of a command keyword and a command tail. The keyword identifies the built-in command or transient program that you wish to execute. The command tail is optional and may contain extra information to be passed to a program, such as a file name or parameters for the program.

Only one command can be entered at a time, and the command line must be terminated by entering a carriage return. The carriage return may be labeled RETURN, CR, or ENTER on your system.

As you begin to enter a command, the characters you type on

the keyboard will appear in sequence on the screen, just after the A> prompt. If you make a mistake, you may use the backspace key or the delete key to step backwards character by character. Some keyboards don't have a backspace key, so the control key (abbreviated CTRL) may be held down, and the H key can be pressed. The short hand notation for this is CTRL-H.

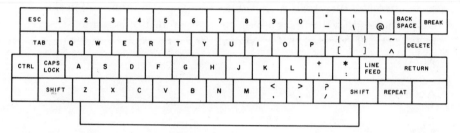

Figure 1.6: A typical keyboard layout.

CP/M doesn't care if you use lowercase or uppercase letters on the keyboard. The CP/M command line editor (not the ED editor though) converts all lowercase letters to uppercase as you type them in, and you may mix them as desired. This is not the case with other programs such as a word processor—uppercase and lowercase letters are passed to the program unchanged. Only in the command editor (the console command processor or CCP) are they converted to uppercase.

When you type in a command, you will normally begin in the first character position after the prompt symbol, but CP/M does allow you to enter spaces at the beginning of a command line.

1.10 COMMAND LINE EDITING AND SYNTAX

One of the biggest problems newcomers to computers have is distinguishing between form and content. Computers are very unforgiving of errors and are not very intelligent in terms of understanding what you mean. If a space is put in the wrong place or one is left out, the meaning of a command can change completely. In this section, I will try to show the difference between the form of a command and the content of a command.

One frequently used command in CP/M is STAT, which means display the status of the specified disk or of specified files on the disk. If the command is entered with no options or command tail, the STAT program will list the amount of disk space left on the default disk.

A > STAT

Remember, after entering the command, you must type RETURN to execute it. Otherwise CP/M will not know when you are finished entering it. If you accidentally entered:

A > STATUS

CP/M would search the disk directory for a program called STATUS.CMD (the .CMD is called the file type extension, and in this case indicates that the file is a built-in command). If it is found, it will be loaded and executed. If CP/M can't find a program by that name, it will return:

A > STATUS

STATUS.CMD?

which tells you that it couldn't find a file by that name.

If STAT is correctly entered, the following message will be displayed:

A: RW, Free Space: 100K

This line tells you that disk A is defined as read/write, and 100K bytes of free space still exists on it.

Detailed information can be retrieved about any file on a disk. For example, if we want to know how big the file MYFILE.CMD is, the following command could be entered:

A > STAT MYFILE.CMD

This would return:

Drive A:		User 0	
Recs	Bytes FCBs	Attributes	Name
32	18K 2	Sys RO	A:MYFILE.CMD

Total: 18K   2

A: RW, Free Space: 100K

If the same command had been entered without a space between the command and the commnd tail, the following error would result:

A > STATMYFILE.CMD
STATMYFILE.CMD?

because CP/M would not know where the command (STAT) ended and where the command tail (MYFILE.CMD) began.

1.11 OTHER EDITING FUNCTIONS

CP/M allows several other line-editing functions in addition to backspace. Table 1.1 lists them. The most useful of these is backspace, but the next most useful command is CTRL-X because it essentially kills the current command line and returns you to the beginning of it, without executing what you had entered. This makes it easy to start fresh, without having to backspace repeatedly to return to the left.

CTRL-E   This command moves the cursor to the beginning of the following line without erasing the characters already entered in the buffer.

CTRL-H   This command is identical to Backspace. It moves the cursor back one space and deletes the last character entered.

CTRL-I   This command is identical to Tab. It enters an actual tab character, but CP/M displays it by moving the cursor to the next tab stop (every eighth column).

CTRL-M   This command is identical to Return. It enters the command line to CP/M (it is the line termination character), then moves the cursor to the start of the next line on the screen.

CTRL-R   This command will retype the current input buffer. It is useful if many deletions have been made in the command line. It displays a pound sign (#) at the end of the current line, moves to the next line, and retypes the current contents of the command buffer.

CTRL-U   This command causes the command line to be reset to empty. All characters typed so far (on the line) will be discarded. A pound sign will be displayed at the end of the discarded line, and the cursor will be moved to the start of the next line.

CTRL-X   This command is the same as CTRL-U above, except that it moves the cursor back to the first column of the current command line, rather than moving down to a new empty line.

CTRL-S   This command causes the display to stop, for viewing purposes. It is used primarily when a long listing is being displayed on the console. Any key will start the output again after it has been stopped.

CTRL-C   This command (if it occurs as the first character in a line) will cause the current program to abort, and will return control to the Console Command Processor (CCP) and perform a warm start. If you are. already within the CCP, then it will cause CP/M-86 to perform a warm start.

Table 1.1:   These control characters [typed by holding down the CTRL or Control key and simultaneously depressing the specified alphabetic key (e.g., CTRL-I)] are used for line editing purposes in CP/M-86.

1.12 DISK FILES

Each disk may have a collection of files stored on it. Files are simply a long sequence of bytes or characters that contain information that can either be a program or data that may be used by a program.

All files on disk must have a unique file name, so the user or program can address the file without confusion. All file names are stored in the disk directory, as discussed earlier. If a file is on a particular disk, it must have a directory entry on that disk to be locatable. Without the file name, the information would be forever lost, even if it were actually recorded somewhere on the disk. File names on one disk can never refer to files or data on other disks. Each disk is isolated from all others.

As previously mentioned, files can contain either programs or data. Programs are sequences of machine language instructions that can be executed by the 8086 microprocessor. The microprocessor cannot execute a file that contains the source statements for a program, nor can it execute the data for a program. A program such as the CP/M-86 Assembler will convert an assembler source file into an executable program, assuming that the program has no errors in it that would prohibit execution.

Compilers also create program files from source files. Many versions of BASIC will compile programs into executable instructions. Interpreters (some other versions of BASIC) don't actually convert commands into executable instructions to be stored in a file; they execute the commands directly. Thus the program runs, but no program file is created.

1.13 FILE SPECIFICATIONS

Every file must have a unique name. The name is composed of three parts: the drive specifier, which is optional; the file name portion, which can be up to eight characters long; and the file type, which can be up to three characters long. Only the file name portion is required. The format for file specification (filespec) is:

D:FILENAME.TYP

The file name and file type portions can be made up of letters, numbers, and some special characters. The following characters should not be used as part of a filespec because CP/M recognizes them as delimiters or separators.

[ ] * < > . , ; : = ?

The disk drive specifier and the colon in the example are used to tell CP/M which disk drive to look on to find the file. If the file is on the default disk, the specifier is not needed.

File specifications can be very short, or longer and more descriptive. The following filespecs are all valid:

MYPROG	MYPROG.BAS
M	A:MYPROG.BAS
STAT.CMD	A:M.CMD

If a program file is to be executed as a command, the .CMD file type must be part of the filespec, or CP/M will not be able to load and execute it. Also, the drive specifier (A:) is not stored on disk in the directory. You only need it when you are referring to a disk other than the default drive.

1.14 FILE TYPES

The file type field is used to organize files into families or groups for the convenience of the user. Table 1.2 shows the established file types used on many CP/M systems.

```
CMD          8086 or 8088 machine language (object code) program.
BAS          CBASIC source program.
$$$          Temporary file.
A86          ASM-86 source file.
H86          Assembled ASM-86 (or other compiler) program in
             hexadecimal format.
SUB          Submit file (contains a sequence of CP/M (CCP level)
             commands to be executed in order by SUBMIT.
```

Table 1.2: The file types listed here are established families of files. Many programs, including ED, SUBMIT, ASM86, and DDT86 expect files to have these file types.

1.15 USING WILDCARDS TO ACCESS FILES

Some CP/M utilities such as STAT allow the user to select more than one file at a time. Wildcards are single characters in the file name or file type fields that allow any character or group of characters to be specified at once. The two wildcard characters allowed in CP/M are: * and ?. The question mark is used if only one character in the file name or file type is to match all directory searches. The asterisk affects the entire file name or file type field. For example, if you want to display the status of all files with the file type of CMD, the following command could be entered:

A > STAT *.CMD

which will cause all files with the CMD file type to be listed in the status display. Alternately, the same function could have been performed with:

A > STAT ????????.CMD

because eight question marks will match all eight characters of every file name.

Similarly, all files with the file name of MYPROG could be listed by entering this command:

A > STAT MYPROG.???

or

A > STAT MYPROG.*

because the three question mark wildcards are equivalent to a single asterisk, which affects the whole filetype field.

This feature can be carried to its extreme case, listing all files on the disk:

A>STAT *.*

or

A>STAT ????????.???

which would match all files on the disk.

Other examples of wildcards are shown here:

A??.CMD   matches all CMD files with three character file names starting with A.

A*.CMD   is the same as: A???????.CMD

???.*   would match B.CMD, BB.BAS, BBB.A86.

Wildcards are not allowed in the drive specifier field.

1.16 CHANGING THE DEFAULT DRIVE

When CP/M is loaded, the command prompt A> is displayed, indicating that drive A is selected. This drive is referred to as the default drive, and all file specifications not including the drive specifier automatically imply the default disk. Most microcomputer systems have two or more disk drives. CP/M allows you to change the default disk to another drive. The format is:

A>D:

where D is the drive specifier. The colon tells CP/M that the preceding character is not a file name, but a drive specifier. If it weren't present, CP/M would try to find a file on disk called D.CMD. The drive specifier can be any alphabetic character from A to P, although you cannot address a drive if it doesn't exist on your system. For example, on a two-drive system, the disks would be addressed as A and B. If you selected C, your system would probably respond with the error message:

A>C:

BDOS ERROR ON C:

because the disk drive doesn't exist. If this occurs, you may have to type RETURN to get back to the command prompt. Some systems may lock out if you enter a drive specifier that doesn't exist. If this happens, try depressing CTRL-C. If this doesn't work, you will probably have to reset the system and start again.

To change back to the original default drive, enter:

B > A:

1.17 CHANGING DISKS

Many people use the A disk drive as the system disk, which contains all the utility programs and perhaps their word processor or accounting program. The B disk is used as a work disk that contains all the data files. This keeps data and program files separated, and makes the data files easier to back-up by themselves.

Another common method of organizing files to keep projects separate from each other is to put one application or project on each work disk. One disk could be for correspondence, one for payroll, one for reports, and so on. This technique keeps files from one project out of the way of others and helps to organize information. It also protects you from losing too much information if a disk is damaged.

During daily operation, it might be necessary to change from one project disk to another quite frequently. This is easily done under CP/M. Before actually taking the disk out of the drive, be certain that no files are in use at the time. If a program is running that uses data files, terminate it before removing the disk. Even if the program is supposedly finished, it is best to terminate it from the keyboard. This is necessary because sometimes the last record or block of information written to the disk has not been actually transferred to the disk yet. It may still be in an internal memory buffer. The close file function in CP/M causes all remaining data to be written to a file before the file is closed. If a file is written and not closed properly, unexpected results can occur—to the point of rendering a file useless.

To change disks, remove the current disk and insert the new one. Then hold down CTRL (Control) and press the C key. This will cause CP/M to reset the disk drive for the new disk. If CTRL-C is not pressed, the new disk will not respond properly because CP/M still expects the old disk to be there. It will issue the following message:

Bdos err on d: RO

This means that the disk doesn't match what is expected, so it won't write to it. Typing CTRL-C will remedy the situation.

1.18 PROTECTING DISK FILES

All files may be individually assigned a read/write or read/only status. A file can be protected by using the STAT command and specifying read/only. If a program tries to open the file to write data to it, the error message:

Bdos err on d: RO

will be displayed. To return to the command prompt, type CTRL-C.

Note that although CP/M may see in the directory that a file is labeled read/only, that distinction is not noticed directly by the hardware. For example, if a power surge occurs, the disk drive or disk controller circuit may produce a brief disk head load command that would cause the head to touch the disk. In some cases, this can cause data to be distorted on the disk in a random fashion. Once changed, the disk may cease to be readable. No amount of doctoring would be able to retrieve the lost data.

The importance of making back-up copies of files cannot be overemphasized. The best solution to the data volatility problem is to keep important data and files spread out over many disks and to make back-up copies often. After using disks for a while, you might begin to believe that they are very reliable. Statistically, you are eventually bound to lose something important. The best axiom is:

DON'T PUT ALL YOUR EGGS IN ONE BASKET.

1.19 OTHER DEVICES

The two essential devices on any CP/M system are the disk drive and the video display terminal. Most systems also have a printer and possibly a modem for telephone data communications. All devices have device names associated with them. The terminal or console is referred to as CON:, and the printer is called the LST:, or list device. Table 1.3 lists all device assignments defined in CP/M-86.

CON: The logical console device is bi-directional.
            This means that it can be assigned either as
            an input or an output device.

AXI: The logical auxiliary input device is an
            optional device in CP/M-86. If auxiliary
            devices don't exist, it does not need to
            be assigned.

AXO: The logical auxiliary output device is
            similar to the auxiliary input device, except
            that it can only be assigned as an output
            device.

LST: The logical list device is also optional in
            CP/M-86, but most systems have printers. It
            may only be assigned as an output device.

Table: 1.3:   Logical device names have been established in CP/M-86, for the convenience of the user. Files can be sent to or read from these devices with the use of PIP or a user written program.

These devices are called logical devices because they are independent of the physical hardware of the system. The BIOS contains customized subroutines that access the physical devices and read the data and control signals. The data is then transferred to CP/M-86 in a device independent fashion. In Table 1.3, the console device is listed as being used for both input and output, the list device is strictly for output, and the auxiliary devices have separate input and output device names. This may seem confusing at first, because the console device is an anomaly in the system. Since it can be used for both input and output, data can be sent to it or read from it. CP/M will understand what you are trying to do.

There can be many more physical devices than CP/M allows for in its logical device table. The STAT command can be used to reassign devices. For example, you may have a letter quality printer and a fast dot-matrix printer. To change printers, you could just issue a command to reassign the LST: device to the alternate printer.

TTY: This device is called a TTY or Teletype, and is now
            obsolete. However, CP/M still supports the name of
            the device, even though it may be used for entirely
            different purposes. Some implementations of CP/M even
            call the console device the TTY, simply because it
            saves the vendor from having to implement logical
            to physical device assignments.

CRT: The CRT or Cathode Ray Tube is another name for the physical console device.

BAT: Batch mode input (for the console).

UC1:   User console number 1.

PTR: Paper tape reader.

UR1:   User Reader 1.

UR2:   User Reader 2.

PTP: Paper tape punch.

UP1:   User Punch 1.

UP2:   User Punch 2.

LPT: Line Printer.

UL1:   User List device 1.

Table 1.4: Physical device names were assigned in CP/M long ago, but the names of obsolete devices (like TTY) still persist. The names are really arbitrary, the actual devices can be whatever the BIOS portion of CP/M defines them to be. For example, the PTR and PTP devices may actually be a dial-up modem.

Each logical device can be assigned to any of the physical devices listed. TTY: is short for teletype, which is now considered to be an obsolete device. Many systems use the TTY assignment to mean the standard console and printer references. Since the TTY assignment is the zero case (initialized when CP/M is loaded), it is convenient to use it, rather than forcing new device assignments. The mnemonic associated with each physical device does not imply that the device can serve no other purpose; for example, the TTY could be the video display, or the LPT could be a connection to another computer. The names used are for convenience and standardization.

2

Built-in Commands

2.1 INTRODUCTION

CP/M-86 has two kinds of commands: built-in and transient. The nature of each is obvious from the name.

Whenever you type in a series of characters after the command prompt (and then hit the RETURN key), CP/M first assumes that you have entered a built-in command. It checks its internal list of built-in commands and, if a match is found, executes the desired function.

If the command you entered is not a built-in command, CP/M will check the disk directory for a CMD file. Transient commands are discussed in the next chapter.

2.2 DIR (DIRECTORY)

One of the most frequently used commands is DIR, which displays a list of the files on the specified disk. This command can take the following forms:

DIR
DIR d:
DIR filespec

where DIR is the command name, and d: is a disk specifier. In the second form, "filespec" is a file name, with optional disk specifier and file type fields, as described in Chapter 1. Wildcard characters ? and * may be used in this command.

If you enter the DIR command without any options or command tail, DIR will assume that you want to list the directory for the currently logged disk.

A > DIR

will display all non-system files on disk A:.

To display the entire directory for disk B:, enter:

DIR B:

You can also get a list of certain files by using wildcard characters:

DIR B: *.CMD   will list all CMD files on the B: disk.

If no files are found on a disk, or if none of the wildcards matched anything, CP/M will respond with the NO FILE message.

```
A>DIR
A:ASM86     CMD  :  TOD        CMD  :  COPYDISK CMD  :  DDT86     CMD
A:FORMAT    CMD  :  ED         CMD  :  PIP      CMD  :  SUBMIT    CMD
A:HELP      CMD  :  HELP       HLP  :  STAT     CMD  :  GENCMD    CMD
A:MYPROG    ASM  :  TEXTFILE        :  TEST1         :  MYPROG    OLD
A>
```

2.3 DIRS (DIRECTORY OF SYSTEM FILES)

An alternate form of the DIR command exists, since CP/M-86 doesn't list files with the system attribute in the normal directory. The DIRS command works just like the DIR command, but only displays system files.

2.4 ERA (ERASE FILES)

ERA allows the user to erase unwanted files on a disk. It accepts filespecs with wildcard characters and is capable of erasing all files on a disk at once. The form is:

ERA filespec

A filespec *must* be present for the command to work. To erase a group of files, a wildcard could be used:

ERA *.CMD   will erase all CMD files on the default disk.

The extreme case of ERA is:

ERA *.*

which will erase all files on the default disk. In this case, CP/M will re-spond with the message:

All (Y/N)?

which is a request for a yes or no response, to make sure you want to delete all files on the disk. When a file is erased using ERA, the space allocated to the file on disk is automatically reclaimed for another file to use.
file that you did not want to erase, and you have not written any new information to the disk since it was erased, it is sometimes possible to restore the file by rebuilding the directory entry. A sample of such a program, called UNERASE, is given in Chapter 4.

```
A>DIR *.CMD
A:ASM86     CMD : TOD      CMD : COPYDISK CMD : DDT86    CMD
A:FORMAT    CMD : ED       CMD : PIP      CMD : SUBMIT   CMD
A:HELP      CMD : STAT     CMD : GENCMD   CMD
A>
```

2.5 TYPE (TYPE FILE)

Very often I find it necessary to display a file, whether it is a text file or a nontext file. The TYPE command attempts to list the contents of a file on the screen. The format is:

TYPE filespec

where "filespec" conforms to all the previously described drive speci-fier, file name, and file type options. Wildcard characters are not al-lowed.

Examples:

TYPE B:MYPROG.ASM

TYPE TEXTFILE

```
A>TYPE TEXTFILE
This is a sample file generated with the CP/M-86 "ED" editor
program.  The Type command can be used to display any file,
including non-text files, although their output may not be
human readable.  The Type command can be stopped to view the
text by entering a Control-S (hold down the Control or CTRL
key and press "S" at the same time).  To start listing again,
press any key.  A carriage return will cause the Type command
to terminate, and CTRL-C will restart CP/M-86.

A>
```

2.6 REN (RENAME)

Rename will change the file name and/or file type of any file on a disk. The format is:

REN d:newfile.ft2 = d:oldfile.ft1

where d:oldfile.ft1 is the old file specification, and d:newfile.ft2 is the new file specification. Note that the new name is to the left, and the old to the right. This seems to be the reverse of normal left-right conventions, but in CP/M and its utilities, it is standard to have the destination or receiving end on the left. The best way to visualize this is:

REN new = old

Also, remember that you can't change the disk specifier when renaming a file. If the file is on the A disk, you can't use the rename command to move it to the B disk. Rename only changes the name of a file in an existing directory entry; it doesn't move the file or create a new file. Wildcard characters are not allowed.

Examples:

REN TEST2 = TEST1
REN B:MYPROG.NEW = B:MYPROG.OLD

```
Before:

A>DIR
A:ASM86      CMD : TOD       CMD : COPYDISK CMD : DDT86    CMD
A:FORMAT     CMD : ED        CMD : PIP      CMD : SUBMIT   CMD
A:HELP       CMD : HELP      HLP : STAT     CMD : GENCMD   CMD
A:MYPROG     ASM : TEXTFILE      : TEST1        : MYPROG   OLD
A>

After:

A>DIR
A:ASM86      CMD : TOD       CMD : COPYDISK CMD : DDT86    CMD
A:FORMAT     CMD : ED        CMD : PIP      CMD : SUBMIT   CMD
A:HELP       CMD : HELP      HLP : STAT     CMD : GENCMD   CMD
A:MYPROG     ASM : TEXTFILE      : TEST2        : MYPROG   NEW
A>
```

2.7 USER (CHANGE THE USER NUMBER)

CP/M-80 versions above 2.0 and CP/M-86 have an extra field in their directory entries for a user number. This allows separate users of a system to each have their own directories on a common disk—a hard disk, for example. Since a hard disk can't be removed from the drive, all files on the disk are available at once. This would mean that all users would see all files when doing a directory list. The USER command allows each user (up to 16) to have what amounts to a separate directory area.

USER n

The "n" is the user number from 0 to 15. When in any user area other than zero, only files in that area will be accessible to you. The only exception to this is PIP, a utility program that is discussed in the next chapter. PIP is used to copy files, and it must be available to each user area at the outset.

3

Transient Commands and Utilities

3.1 INTRODUCTION

Transient commands are not part of CP/M-86, as are built-in commands. They reside on disk and are loaded as needed, just like any other program. They are referenced by CP/M as files with a file type of CMD. When a transient command is finished, control is returned to the console command processor (CCP). Most of the transient commands supplied by Digital Research can be called utilities, because they are tools for the programmer or user. The rest of this chapter describes all the transient commands supplied with CP/M-86.

The HELP command is one of the transient commands provided by Digital Research. It may be very useful in learning how to operate the various commands and utilities on CP/M.

Notation

Several forms of shorthand notation are used in this book to simplify the explanation of commands. Since many commands have optional operands and parameters, braces { } are used to indicate that the string of characters contained by the braces is optional. Brackets, when used, are required in the actual command. For example, the PIP command: PIP LST: = filespec{[T8]} indicates that the [T8] sequence is an optional parameter, but that the brackets are essential to the form of the parameter if used.

The second form of notation used has to do with control characters. Almost all ASCII keyboards have a CTRL or control key that acts like a shift key in most respects. When you see CTRL-C or Control-C or ∧C, the meaning is: hold down the control key (often labeled CTRL) and simultaneously press the C key. It is easiest to think of it as another shift key.

Often, it is necessary to indicate where other nonprintable characters are to be entered, such as carriage return or escape. Return is shown in commands as < Return > and escape is often abbreviated ESC. Also, file specifications or other character strings are often enclosed in left and right arrows < > to indicate the beginning and ending of the operand or parameter.

3.2 COPYDISK

COPYDISK is one of the most important utilities provided by Digital Research. No such utility was supplied with CP/M-80, so each manufacturer or vendor had to write a disk copy program to suit their hardware.

As discussed in Chapter 1, it is of great importance that all disks be backed up for safekeeping. COPYDISK makes this chore more bearable.

Disk Formatting

When floppy disks come from the manufacturer (fresh from the box, that is) they are unformatted. This means that they don't have any of the track and sector information that the disk controller circuitry reads when a particular track and sector is being sought. Before a disk can be used, it must be formatted for single-density or double-density operation, and if possible, for double-sided use. Usually, every microcomputer system comes with a formatting program, supplied by the vendor or manufacturer of the system. Before attempting to use COPY-DISK, make sure that the new disk you intend to copy to has been formatted.

When COPYDISK transfers information from the source disk to the destination disk, it does so by tracks and sectors, and transfers everything including the system tracks, the directory, and all blank space on the disk without regard for content. The output disk is an exact duplicate of the input disk. If you only wish to copy one or more files from disk to disk, you may be better off using the PIP program, also discussed in this section.

Invoking COPYDISK

To start COPYDISK, enter the command:

A > COPYDISK

The response will be:

```
A>COPYDISK

CP/M-86 Full Disk Copy Utility
     Version 2.0

Enter Source Disk Drive (A-D) ? A

Destination Disk Drive (A-D) ? B

Copying disk A: to disk B:
Is this what you want to do (Y/N) ? Y
Copy started
Reading track nn
Writing track nn
Verifying track nn
Copy completed.

Copy another disk (Y/N) ? N
Copy program exiting

A>
```

If you are copying from the A disk drive to the B disk drive, you would enter the options as above. It is also possible to copy a disk using only one drive. CP/M-86 treats the destination disk as the B: disk (in this case) and will issue messages telling you which disk to put in the A: drive. The following example demonstrates this feature:

```
A>COPYDISK

CP/M-86 Full Disk Copy Utility
     Version 2.0

Enter Source Disk Drive (A-D) ? A

Destination Disk Drive (A-D) ? B
Put Disk B into A; ENTER to continue
```

```
Copying disk A: to disk B:
Is this what you want to do (Y/N) ? Y
Copy started
Put Disk A into A; ENTER to continue
Reading track nn
Put Disk B into A; ENTER to continue
Writing track nn
Verifying track nn
Copy completed.

Copy another disk (Y/N) ? N
Copy program exiting
Put Disk A into A; ENTER to continue
A>
```

In both of the above cases, the messages Reading track nn, Writing track nn, and Verifying track nn are displayed for each track read, written, and verified.

3.3 HELP

The HELP command did not exist prior to CP/M-86. It provides a summary of all Digital Research supplied built-in and transient commands. Some manufacturers or vendors who add their own utility programs may add them to the help file as well.

This command has the format:

HELP {topic} {subtopic1 subtopic2 ...} {P}

where topic is one of the topics listed below, and subtopics are one or more subsections such as EXAMPLES. The {P} can be used to keep the HELP command from stopping every 23 lines. Normally it does this to allow for easy reading of the display a page at a time. After each 23 lines are displayed, HELP will display a prompt message and wait for Return or Enter before proceeding. The following is a sample session with HELP:

```
A>HELP

HELP UTILITY V1.0

At "HELP>" enter topic {,subtopic}...

EXAMPLE:  HELP> DIR EXAMPLES

Topics available:

ASM86        ASSIGN        COMMANDS
COPYDISK     DDT86         DIR
```

```
DIRS        ED          ERA
FUNCTION    FILENAME    GENCMD
HELP        PIP         REN
STAT        SUBMIT      TOD
TYPE        USER
```

HELP>DIR

DIR

FORMAT: DIR {filespec}

PURPOSE:

    Displays the names of non-
system (DIR) files in the directory
of an on-line diskette.

Additional topics available:

EXAMPLES

HELP>DIR EXAMPLES

DIR
  EXAMPLES

EXAMPLES:

```
A>DIR
A>DIR B:
A>DIR C:MYFILE.DAT
A>DIR *.CMD
A>DIR A*.A86
A>DIR PROG???.H86
A>DIR PROGRAM.*
```

HELP>
A>

As shown in the example, just entering HELP gives the user all options.
Entering a more extended command such as

HELP DIR EXAMPLES

would display directory command examples. This is a great timesaver
for the experienced user.

3.4 PIP (PERIPHERAL INTERCHANGE PROGRAM)

    The PIP command should be called the COPY command since that
is what it really does. PIP can be used to transfer individual files (or

groups of files) from one disk to another, can create a duplicate of a file on the same disk, and can transfer files from disk to a character-oriented device (such as the console or printer) or vice versa. It can also be used to concatenate (combine) two or more files to create a third file. The PIP command can be used as a filter to insert or delete characters as it copies the file from source to destination.

Copying Single Files

The simplest use of PIP is to copy a single file from a source device to a destination device. As with the rename command, the source is specified on the right side of the equal sign and the destination is on the left. This is the standard used in most programming languages. The equal sign actually means "assigned the value of" when used in this manner.

The possible forms of the PIP command are:

Transfer direction: new ← old

PIP d: {[Gn]} = source-filespec{[options]}
PIP dest-filespec{[Gn]} = d:{[options]}
PIP dest-filespec{[Gn]} = source-filespec{[options]}

The first form will copy a file from the default disk to the d: disk (where d: is any valid disk drive specifier). The source (right side of equal sign) contains the source file specification and options (in brackets) if needed. The destination side (left of the equal sign) always specifies one unique file, and if just the disk (d:) is given, the file specification of the original file is used. The Gn option can be used to write the file to user number n on the specified destination disk. See the section on PIP options for more details about the options parameter.

The second form of the command is very similar to the first, but the destination file specification (including the drive code if needed) is fully qualified. This will look for the file dest-filespec on drive d: and copy it to the default disk (or to the disk specified on the left side). The name will remain dest-filespec.

The third form includes both the original file specification and the new name of the file. This allows the file name or file type (source-filespec) to be changed (renamed to dest-filespec) in the copy process.

Error Conditions

The most common error encountered in a file copy operation is lack of disk space on the destination disk. This is easily cured by first checking the disk (with the STAT command) before attempting to write a new file to it. Make sure that enough space exists to create a copy of the file.

When PIP makes a copy, it creates a destination file with the same file name as your destination file, but with a file type of $$$. The new file is written and closed, and then if the close operation is completed, it will rename the file to your specified file type. Even if a file exists on disk with the name of your destination file, PIP will create another temporary file, and then rename it and delete the existing file. This means that if a file exists on the destination disk that has the same file name and file type as your new destination file, a second copy will be written before the old copy is erased. You must make sure that an equivalent amount of space is available or you will get a BDOS write error.

PIP will cause all file attributes such as SYS and R/O to be retained on the new copy of a file.

Examples

PIP A: = B:MYPROG.ASM
PIP A:MYPROG.ASM = B:

These two examples will create a file on the A: disk named MYPROG.ASM and will copy the contents of the file MYPROG.ASM on the B: disk to the file on the A: disk.

PIP A:MYPROG.BAK = B:MYPROG.ASM
PIP A:NEWDATA = B:OLDDATA

These examples copy files from the B: disk to the A: disk and rename the files in the process.

PIP B:MYPROG.ASM = A:MYPROG.ASM[G2]

This example shows how to copy a file from the user number 2 area on the A: disk to the user 0 area on the B: disk.

Copying Multiple Files

Wild card characters are allowed in PIP, making it easy to copy a number of files from one disk to another. The form is:

PIP d:{[Gn]} = d:source-filespec{[options]}

It is important to note that the left hand or receiving end of the copy must specify only the destination disk drive. Since potentially more than one file will be copied, a file specification cannot be included. Both asterisk and question mark wild cards are allowed.

Examples

PIP B: = A:*.*

This is the simplest form of the copy command. This command will cause PIP to copy all files from the A: disk to the B: disk. When PIP recognizes the command as being a multiple file copy, it will display COPYING on the screen, followed by each file specification that it is copying.

PIP B: = A:*.CMD

This command will copy all files with the file type of CMD. It operates identically to the above example.

PIP B:[G2] = A:MYPROG.*

PIP B:[G2] = A:MYPROG.???

Both of these commands will copy all files with a file name of MYPROG to the user 2 area of the B: disk.

Combining Files

PIP will allow multiple files to be concatenated or combined as well as copied. The form of the concatenation command is:

PIP dest-file {[Gn]} = source-file1{[option]},
    source-file2{[option]},...

Each source file is optional, and any number can be specified, up to the limit of 255 characters (one line buffer full). Options can be included for each source file.

Examples

B:MYPROG.ASM = MYMAIN.ASM
    ,MYSUBR1.ASM,MYSUBR2.ASM

This example causes three files (on the default disk) called MYMAIN.ASM, MYSUBR1.ASM, and MYSUBR2.ASM to be concatenated and copied to MYPROG.ASM on the B: disk.

Transferring Files to and from Character-Oriented Devices

CP/M-86 supports character-oriented devices such as the logical console, printer, and auxiliary input/output. The console can be either an input or output device, but the printer is strictly output. These devices are labeled:

CON: logical console
LST: logical list device
AXO: logical auxiliary output device
AXI: logical auxiliary input device

In addition, PIP supports some special devices:

NUL: A dummy source device that generates 40 hexadecimal zeroes (nulls).
EOF: A dummy source device that generates a single (∧Z) CTRL-Z (used by CP/M as an end-of-file marker).
PRN: A printer (output) device that automatically generates tab expansions to every eighth column, numbers lines, and outputs a page eject or form feed on every 60th print line. This device is equivalent to: LST: with options of [T8NP60]

The form of this PIP command is:

PIP dest-filespec{[Gn]} = source-filespec{[options]}

where dest-filespec can be: AXO: CON: PRN: LST:
and source-filespec can be: AXI:{[options]} CON:{[options]} NUL: EOF:

Examples

PIP CON: = MYPROG.ASM[T8]

This command is functionally equivalent to TYPE MYPROG.ASM. It lists the file on the logical console device and expands tabs on every eighth column.

PIP TESTFILE = CON:

This command will accept characters from the logical console and store them in a file called TESTFILE. A CTRL-Z (∧Z) will terminate input and cause the file to be stored on the default disk.

PIP LST: = CON:

This command will take console input and direct it to the list device. As with the above example, CTRL-Z will abort the command.

PIP AXO: = MYPROG.ASM

This command will send the file MYPROG.ASM to the logical auxiliary output device. Often, a serial interface is attached as the auxiliary device, allowing the file to be sent down-line to another computer. Consult the user's manual for your system to see if this is possible.

PIP LST: = MYPROG.PRN[T8]

This command will cause the file MYPROG.PRN to be listed and will expand tabs on every eighth column. If the T8 option is left off, tabs will not be expanded and all text will appear to be smashed together. Some printers do expand tabs, so it is possible that they will be expanded for you. Experiment to determine the characteristics of your particular printer.

PIP PRN: = MYPROG.PRN

This command is identical to:

PIP LST: = MYPROG.PRN[T8NP60]

It causes tabs to be expanded on every eighth column, numbers lines, and issues a form feed (page eject) on every 60th line of text.

Other Capabilities

If just the PIP command name is entered without any command tail, PIP will enter a multiple command mode, allowing several commands to be issued in sequence without the annoyance of reloading the PIP program from disk each time.

If you type PIP, an asterisk (∗) will be displayed. At each asterisk, a command line may be entered. See the following example.

```
A > PIP
∗ LST: = MYPROG.ASM[T8]
∗ B: = A:MYPROG.ASM
∗ MYPROG.NEW = MYPROG.ASM
∗
A >
```

As each command line is entered, PIP will execute it, then return for another. The first line causes MYPROG.ASM to be listed on the printer with tab expansion. The second command tells PIP to copy MYPROG.ASM from the A: disk to the B: disk. The third line copies MYPROG.ASM to a new file called MYPROG.NEW. A return or CTRL-C will abort PIP and return control to the console command processor.

The Options Field

The options clause in each command allows files to be filtered or directives to be given to PIP about a file. All groups of options must be enclosed in brackets and can occur for each input file. The only option permitted on a destination file is the Gn command that specifies the user number the file is to be send to.

```
Option              Description

Dn      Delete any characters past column n.  This option
        is useful if  a source file contains lines too
        long to be displayed on an output device, such as
        a line printer.  If, for example, an assembler
        listing  contained comments beyond 80 columns
        and the output printer only handles 80 columns,
        the [D80] option could be specified.  Note that
        this command doesn't cause the text to "wrap around"
        to the next line,  it simply chops it off at the
        specified number of characters.

E       Echo transfer at logical console.  If this option
        is included, the source file will be displayed on
```

the console as the transfer is taking place.
This allows the copy operation to be monitored.
Note that only text files can be displayed with
this option.

F   Filter form–feed characters. Some output devices
consider a form–feed a special character, and
cause a page advance (or on a console, a clear
screen operation). If this is not desireable,
form–feeds can be filtered out of the source
file as the transfer is taking place. Also, if
form–feeds are set up for a certain number of
lines per page, they may be changed to another
page length by first deleting them, then
re–introducing them with the P command (see below).

Gn   Get source from or Go to user number n. When
this option is included after the source name,
the source file will be retrieved from the
directory for user number n. If used after the
destination file, the destination file is written
the directory of user number n. The number must
be in a range from 0 to 15.

H   Hex data transfer. If this option is used, PIP
checks all data from the source file for proper
Intel hexadecimal format. Error messages will be
displayed on the console for any discrepancies.

I   Ignore :00 records in the transfer of Intel
Hexadecimal format files. The I option automatically
implies (sets) the H option (see above).

L   Translate upper–case alphabetic characters in the
source file to lower–case characters in the
destination file. This option may be placed after
either the source or destination file names. Only the
destination file will be translated to lower–case.
The source file will remain the same.

N   Add line numbers to the destination file. If used,
this option causes PIP to number each line (if
lines end in Carriage Return), starting with the
number "1" and incrementing by 1. Each line number
will be placed at the start of the line, with a
colon after the number, and a tab after the colon.
If the T command is used, the tabs will be expanded
(see the T command).

O   Object file transfer for machine code (non–character)
files. Since an object file may contain an embedded
CTRL–Z end of file character as data or an 8086
instruction code, this option tells PIP to ignore
any end of file characters and transfer the entire file.

Pn   Set page length. This option can be used to insert
form–feeds after every "n" lines of text (that is,

n lines per page). A form—feed is also added as
the first character in the destination file.
If n = 1 or if n isn't specified, PIP assumes
that n = 60. This option can be used in conjunction
with the F option. If both are specified, [FP66]
for example, then PIP will ignore all form—feeds
in the source file and will insert new form—feeds
in the destination file, all at once.

Qs   Quit copying from the source device after string
"s" is found. When used with the S option (see
below), a portion of a source file (from one
string to another string) can be extracted and
transferred to the destination file. The string
argument must terminate with a CTRL—Z character.
For example: [Sstring1<CTRL—Z>Qstring2<CTRL—Z>]
would cause PIP to search the source file for
"string1", then copy from string1 to string2,
then quit.

R   Read system (SYS) files. If this option is used,
PIP will include system files in copy operations.
For example, if the following command were issued:
PIP B:=A:*.* only non—system files would be copied.
If PIP B:=A:*.*[R] was used, all files, including
system files would be copied.

Ss   Start copying from the source device at the string
"s". The string argument must be terminated with
a CTRL—Z. This option can be used to copy just
part of a file, starting with the specified string.
See the Q option for more details.

Tn   Expand tabs. For readability, tab characters
in source files are often expanded to columns
of eight characters when displayed or printed.
The n argument inserts enough spaces in place of each
tab to position the following character in a
column divisible by n.

U   Translate lower—case alphabetic characters in the
source file to upper—case characters in the
destination file.

V   Verify the copy operation. PIP compares the
destination file to the source file, to insure
that the data has been copied correctly. Both the
source and destination files must be on disk.

W   Write over files with the RO (Read Only) attribute.
If you tell PIP to write over a file that has been
set to RO, PIP will display a console message asking
if you really want to overwrite the file. If the W
option is included (following the source file name) PIP
doesn't bother to ask you if it is alright to overwrite
the destination file.

Z   Zero the parity bit. If used, this option sets
the top (most significant) bit of each character
in the source file to zero in the destination file.
This command is only useful for character or text
files. Do not attempt to use it on object files.
The file would be rendered useless.

Examples

PIP MYPROG.NEW = MYPROG. ASM[V]

This command specifies a verify option that forces PIP to check the destination file after it is written to verify that the source file was written correctly.

PIP LST: = MYPROG.ASM[T8UD80]

This command tells PIP to list the file and expand tabs on every eighth column, to translate all lowercase characters to uppercase, and to limit lines to 80 characters because the printer cannot accept lines longer than 80 characters.

3.5 ED (THE CP/M LINE EDITOR)

The editor provided with CP/M is only a line-oriented editor, not a screen editor or word processor. It is fairly clumsy to work with, especially if you are used to a screen editor. Trying to use it as a word processor is an exercise in futility, but if a screen editor is not available, it can be used to edit or create source programs.

Most editors treat the text file as a virtual work space, where some portion of the file (assuming that it is larger than the available memory space) is in memory. Figure 3.1 shows one way of viewing this situation.

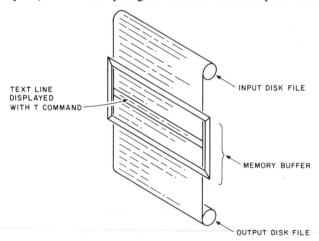

TEXT LINE
DISPLAYED
WITH T COMMAND

INPUT DISK FILE

MEMORY BUFFER

OUTPUT DISK FILE

Figure 3.1: The editor provides a window that can display a portion of the text in the memory.

The file is treated as a long scroll with a portion of it in view in a small window. This window is actually two windows in one—the large window represents the part of the file that is in memory, and the small window represents the part that is displayed on the screen.

Editors that use this scheme have commands to load new text into memory (to append) and to write text from the end of memory portion out the other end. If a file is small enough to fit in memory all at once, then the editor will automatically load it all into memory and, upon termination, will write the whole file out again to disk.

Starting ED

ED can be invoked by typing the command:

A > ED

at the command prompt. ED will be loaded from the default disk (assuming there is a copy on that disk). If it is not present, the standard CP/M error message will be given:

A > ED
ED?

If the default disk doesn't have a copy, but the A: disk does, you could invoke it with the command:

B > A:ED

If you don't specify a file to edit, you will get an error, and ED will terminate. If you specify one that doesn't exist on the default or specified disk, ED will respond with the message NEW FILE and will create the file for you.

ED also allows you to specify two files, one for the original text and a second for the destination. For example, the command line

ED OLDFILE.TXT B:NEWFILE.TXT

will cause ED to start editing a file called OLDFILE.TXT on the default disk, but when you save the file, the output will go to B:NEWFILE.TXT. A similar form of this command is:

ED MYFILE.TXT B:

where the original file is MYFILE.TXT on the default disk, but only the destination disk drive is specified. In this case, the file name and file type would be used for the destination file, but it would be created on the B: disk. If the destination file already exists, ED will respond with the message: Output File Exists, Erase It and will terminate.

NOTE: ED doesn't check for space on disk before it edits a file. Make sure there is enough room on the disk to write a new copy of the edited file before invoking ED. Once you are in ED, you will not be able to recover your latest edit session if you try to write to a disk that doesn't have enough extra space.

The Way ED Works

Whenever you use ED to modify a file, you are reading the file into memory (usually a piece at a time), modifying it, then writing a new copy to disk. The new copy always uses the file name of the original file, but the file type is "$$$". When the edit session is terminated and the file is completely written to disk and closed, the file is renamed to the name and type of the original file. The original is renamed to the file name with a type of BAK. With this scheme, the last version is always available to the programmer should something happen to the new copy or should he or she decide that the changes made were undesirable.

NOTE: If you do decide to go back to the back-up copy, follow this sequence of commands:

ERA MYPROG.TXT   (erase the new version that you don't want)
REN MYPROG.TXT = MYPROG.BAK   (rename the back-up copy to the desired name)
ED MYPROG.TXT   (proceed with ED)

NEVER DO THE FOLLOWING:

ED MYPROG.BAK

Issuing this command will cause the good back-up copy to be instantly destroyed, since ED always gets rid of the last back-up copy before proceeding.

The overall file handling of ED is shown in Figure 3.2. With the commands for read, write and append, you can retrieve from and store text on disk, and with the insert and type commands, you can input and display text on the console device.

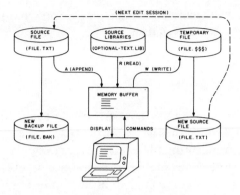

Figure 3.2: How the editor works with files.

Starting an Edit Session

When ED is ready for commands, it displays the asterisk (∗) prompt, preceeded by a colon (:). This means that the memory buffer for text is empty and that ED is waiting. The append command is then used to load some text lines into memory to be edited.

The Append Command

Append is abbreviated as A in ED. It is only necessary to use single characters for all commands. Most commands may be prefixed with a number that tells ED (depending on the command) how many lines or which line to operate on. If the number is replaced by a pound sign (#), then the number 65535 will be used.

The append command loads lines of text from the original disk file and puts them in the memory buffer. Often, files are short enough to be contained in memory all at once, so the command #A followed by a return may be used to load the entire file at once.

If the number is zero, ED appends lines from the input file until the buffer is about half full. The append command with no number preceeding it will load just one line into memory. The following examples are valid:

OA   loads enough lines to fill half the memory buffer
1A   loads one line into memory
A   loads one line into memory
#A   loads up to 65535 lines into memory
100A   loads 100 lines into memory
1000A loads 1000 lines into memory

If an append command is given and not enough lines are present to be loaded, ED will load as many as are available.

The Write Command

In larger files, it is necessary to load the first part, edit it, and then load the next part, proceeding through the file. After the first part has been edited, you have to write some of the file to disk before using the append command again. The write command is just the reverse of append. The number preceding it specifies the number of lines to be written to the output file. A #W commmand (or just W) would write the entire memory buffer to the output file. All writes start from the top of the buffer and go for as many lines as specified.

0W	writes lines until the buffer is half empty
1W	writes one line to the output file
W	writes all lines in the buffer to the output file
#W	writes all lines to the output file
100W	writes 100 lines to the output file
1000W	writes 1000 lines to the output file

NOTE: You may use the W command to write all lines to the output file and then use the H command to reedit those lines. It is the same as writing the file, then using the end command to terminate, and then editing the new file.

Ending a Session

After editing the file, you can terminate the ED session by using the E command. It has only one form, and no preceding numbers or symbols are allowed. When the command is entered, ED issues the equivalent of a write command to completely write all lines to the output file, and then closes the file. Next, it renames the original file to .BAK and renames the temporary file from .$$$ to the original file type. Now the original file or current file is the one just renamed, and the back-up file is the old original file.

Editing Commands

Once a portion of the file is in the memory buffer, you can manipulate it with some editing commands.

A file is treated as a long string of characters, grouped together as lines (each line ends with a carriage return and a line feed). Commands are issued according to the current location of a character pointer. The character pointer (CP) is kept track of by ED, and its purpose is to be an active reference point in the memory buffer for the user. The CP can be moved around—a character at a time, a line at a time, or from bottom to top of the buffer—by the use of editor commands.

Almost all commands are preceded by a number. The number may in some cases be negative, which causes it (usually) to execute the command backwards through the file. If the number is left off, ED assumes it is the number one. If you replace the number with a pound sign (#), ED uses the number 65535 as a maximum possible value. Note that -# is often a valid argument.

Moving the Character Pointer

The most obvious ED command is the one that immediately takes the CP to the top or bottom of the memory buffer. As shown in Table 3.1, the B command has two uses; in the form B, it moves the CP to the top of the buffer. -B moves the CP to the very last location in the buffer.

```
B, -B    Move the Character Pointer (CP) to the beginning
         (B) or end (-B) of the memory buffer.

nC, -nC  Move the CP n characters forward (nC) or n
         characters backward (-nC) in the memory buffer.

nD, -nD  Delete n characters before (nD) or after (-nD)
         the Character Pointer.

I        Start the Insert Mode. To leave the insert mode,
         type CTRL-Z (^Z) or Escape.

Istring^Z Insert a string of characters, but don't
          enter the insert mode.

nK, -nK  Kill (delete) n lines after the Character
         Pointer (nK) or before the CP (-nK).

nL, -nL  Move the CP n lines forward (nL) or n lines
         backward (-nL) through the buffer.

nT, -nT  Type n lines after the CP (nT) or before
         the CP (-nT).

0T       Type the current line.

n, -n    Move the CP n lines down (after) the CP (n),
         or n lines up (before) the CP (-n). The
         destination line is displayed.
```

nA	Append the next n unprocessed text lines from the source file to the end of the memory buffer.
OA	Append (same as nA) except read lines until the memory buffer is about one half full.
#A	Append until the memory buffer is full (or until end of file on the source file is found).
nW	Write the first n lines of the memory buffer to the temporary file (output file).
E	End the edit session. Save the new file and return to CP/M-86.

Table 3.1: Basic editing commands

The C or character command moves the CP forward or backward the number of characters specified by n. -nC moves it backward n characters. This command doesn't treat the carriage return and line feed (which are invisible on the screen) characters at the end of a line as special, so the n value must compensate for this.

The L or line command moves the CP forward or backward n lines at a time. If a negative number is given, the CP will be moved towards the top of the buffer. After a move, the CP is always set to point at the start of the current line. Thus the command -L will reposition the CP at the start of the previous line. The special case of OL moves the CP to the start of the current line.

The Number Command

The special case of the ED commands occurs when a numeric value is entered without a subsequent command. For example, if 100 were entered, followed by a return, ED would interpret it as "move forward 100 lines." If -100 were entered, ED would move toward the top of the buffer 100 lines. The number command is essentially the same as the L command.

Display Commands

Whenever the CP is moved around in memory, ED doesn't display any of the contents of the buffer. The type or T command allows the buffer to be displayed on the screen in various forms. A preceding positive number followed by T will type n lines to the screen for viewing. A negative number will display the n lines found just prior to the CP location. The following examples are legal:

T	type from the CP to the end of the current line
0T	inhibit the type command
1T	type from the CP to the end of the current line
10T	type from the CP to the end of the next 10 lines
-10T	type from the CP to the beginning of the preceding 10 lines

The CP is never changed by executing this command.

When ED is executing the type command, the display can be stopped for viewing by typing CTRL-S and can be started again by entering CTRL-Q. CTRL-C can be used to abort the type command.

Inserting and Deleting Characters

The insert or I command inserts characters into the buffer from the console keyboard. Two forms are allowed:

I

Istring∧Z or Istring<Return>

The first, followed by return, causes subsequent text string(s) to be entered at the current CP until CTRL-Z (∧Z) is typed. Any number of lines (to the buffer limit) can be entered this way. Once you have started entering lines this way, the only way to return to the command mode is through CTRL-Z or escape. The asterisk (*) will be displayed when you have returned to command mode. The second form is for entering just one line. It immediately returns to the command mode, rather than entering the insert mode.

The delete command deletes the number of characters specified by the numeric value preceding the D command. A positive number deletes characters from the CP to the number of characters specified. A negative number deletes n characters before the CP. The CP remains where it was before the delete command. The delete command, as with all character-oriented commands, treats return and line feed as characters.

The kill or K command deletes lines rather than characters. The numeric parameter specified before the command causes n lines to be deleted. A negative n deletes lines preceding the CP.

Replacing Characters and Lines

The substitute or S command allows you to easily search the memory buffer for character strings for either single or global replacement. The command takes the form:

nSold string∧Znew string<Return>

where n specifies the number of times the search and replace command should be executed. If n is left off, the command will be executed just once. The old and new strings are separated by a CTRL-Z character, and the line is, as always, ended with a carriage return.

The easiest way to substitute lines is to first delete the line with a kill command and then replace it with the insert command. For one line, the following will work:

KInew line<Return>

For multiple lines (four in this example):

4KI<Return>
this is line 1
this is line 2
this is line 3
this is line 4
∧Z (or ESC)

Combined ED Commands

ED commands can be combined on one line to save time and effort. Any number of commands can be strung together on a line with a carriage return at the end. Some require special treatment in this case, such as the search command, because the commands after the search must be logically separated from the search string. The only restrictions on combining commands are that the length of the input line should not exceed 128 characters, and, if the line contains a character string such as a search string, the length of the input line must not exceed 100 characters. The E (end) command or the Q (quit) command must not appear on the same line with other commands.

The I, S, J, X, and R commands have character strings after the command and must be treated specially. If another command follows any one of these, a CTRL-Z (or ESC) must be placed after the last command as a delimiter to tell ED that the command is finished.

Examples of combined commands follow:

20L20T<Return>   (move down 20 lines, and display the next 20 lines)

5Sold string∧Znew string∧ZB20T<Return>

(replace 5 strings, then return to the top of the file, and then display 20 lines)

More ED Commands

For the experienced user, there are some additional commands that can save time. The first is the page command. Since ED is not a full screen editor, it is often difficult to see all of a block of text at once. It is even more difficult to move around in the memory buffer without using combined commands like 23L23T to move down 23 lines and display the next 23 lines. The P or page command performs this function. The form is shown in Table 3.2. The preceding n value may be positive or negative. If no n is present, the 23 lines following the current CP location will be displayed on the screen, and the CP will be moved to point to the first character on the first of the 23 lines just displayed.

If OP is entered, ED will redisplay the current page without moving the CP. If a positive n is entered, ED will display n pages, leaving the CP pointing to the first character of the first line of the last page displayed. A negative n will move backward (toward the top of the buffer) n pages and will place the CP at the top of the last page displayed.

```
P, -P     Move the Character Pointer (CP) forward one page (P)
          (23 lines) or backward one page (-P) in the memory
          buffer.

n:        Reposition the CP at the start of line number n.

:n        Execute a particular command "through" line number n.
          For example, :nT would mean type all lines through
          line n.

Sstring^Znew-string^Z  Search the memory buffer for "string"
                       and replace with "new-string".

nFstring  Find the nth occurance of "string." If no number is
          specified, n will default to one.  Only positive
          numbers are allowed.

nN        Extended Find string command. Searches to end of file.

Jsearch-str1^Zins-str^Zdel-to-str^Z   Juxtapose strings.

nMcommands  Macro command.  Execute "commands" up to n times.

nXfilespec^Z  Xfer.  Transfer n lines to filespec file.

0X        Delete file X$$$$$$.LIB.

0Xfilespec^Z   Delete file "filespec."

Rfilespec      Read filespec into buffer at CP.

R              Read X$$$$$$.LIB into buffer at CP.

H              Head of file.  This command saves the current
               file, then reopens it for editing.
```

O	Original file. This command abandons all changes made to the file in the current edit session and returns to the original.
Q	Quit. Abandon the current file, and return to CP/M-86.
V	Turn line numbering on.
-V	Turn line numbering off.
0V	Display amount of free memory buffer space.
U, -U	Translate all lower-case alphabetics to upper-case (U). Turn off upper-case translation (-U).
nZ	Wait n seconds.

Table 3.2: Advanced ED commands

The n: (Line Number) Command

Sometimes it is necessary to go directly to a line number. The n: command moves the CP to the start of the specified line. Line numbers don't always remain the same (as in the BASIC for example). ED numbers lines from the top of the file, and if lines are inserted or deleted, the numbering sequence changes. ED line numbers are just a count of the number of lines in the buffer; the numbers are not stored with the output file, and they are not used for any other purpose.

The :n (Through Line Number) Command

Three ED commands allow the use of this line number reference preceding the actual command: T, L, and K. In each case, ED will execute the command for each line from the current line through the line number specified in :n. For example, to delete lines 3 through 10, issue the following command:

3::10K < Return >

This will move to line 3, then kill or delete each line through line 10.

Finding (But Not Replacing) Character Strings

The F or find command is similar to the S command, but it only finds the specified string. Only a positive number can be entered for n (see table 3.2) because ED can only search from the CP toward the end of the file. If no n is entered, ED will search for the next occurrence of the string. If a positive n is entered, ED will search for the nth occurrence of the string, skipping the intervening occurrences.

Another interesting feature of the F command is that if you enter the command in uppercase (F), the search string is translated to uppercase. If the command is in lowercase (f), the search string is not altered.

Searching Beyond the Memory Buffer

Often, when working with a file that is longer than the memory buffer, it is convenient to issue a search command that continues searching by scanning the remainder of the file that is still on disk. The N command searches through the memory buffer (similar to the F command), and if the string is not found, writes the current buffer contents to the output file, and then issues an 0A append command to load some more of the file into the buffer. This process continues until ED reaches the end of the file or until the string is found. If the end of the file is found, ED will print the message 'BREAK "#" AT N', where the pound sign means that the search function was abnormally terminated, and N means that the N command was the command in progress when the error occurred.

If ED reads through the entire file and doesn't find the string, you have to do one of two things to start editing again: stop ED and restart it from CP/M-86, or enter an H command to restore the file for re-editing.

The J or Juxtapose Command

The J command searches for a string, inserts a new string after the searched-for string, and then deletes all characters between the end of the new string and the beginning of a third string. The form is:

nJsearch string∧Zinsert string∧Zdelete to string<Return>

Since this is a confusing command, an example is helpful.

Original Text: This is a sample of text for the juxtapose Command.

Command: jis a∧Z text line ∧Zfor<Return>

Modified Text: This is a text line for the juxtapose Command.

As with the insert command and the find command, if the J command is entered in uppercase (J), all three text strings in the command will be treated as uppercase. If J is lowercase (j), then no translation to uppercase will take place.

The Macro Facility

The macro command allows a group of commands combined on a line to be executed repeatedly in sequence. With individual commands you can include a preceding number to repeat the command such as: 10Sold string∧Znew string<Return>, but each command is repeated by itself. The macro command can be used to write miniature programs to modify text or to create copies of a line quickly. For example, suppose a text file was being entered, and the typist noticed that the 10 lines all looked the same except for a few characters. Rather than typing in all the lines separately, he or she could use a macro and then replace only the parts that are different.

Text line: This is a sample line of text.

Macro Command: 10MiThis is a sample line of
text.∧L∧Z<Return>

Result:
This is a sample line of text.
This is a sample line of text.
This is a sample line of text.
This is a sample line of text.
This is a sample line of text.
This is a sample line of text.
This is a sample line of text.
This is a sample line of text.
This is a sample line of text.
This is a sample line of text.

The CTRL-L is a way of including a return in an insert string or search string. The CTRL-Z terminates the insert string command, and the final return terminates the macro command. If you leave out the CTRL-Z, the insert command will not terminate, and the nine lines after the first will start with "i", because ED will assume that the "i" is part of the string, not a command.

The execution of a macro always ends with a BREAK "#" AT message, regardless of its success or failure. To terminate a macro, enter CTRL-C from the console.

Moving Blocks of Text

The X or Xfer command allows a block of text to be written to a temporary LIB file on disk. The R command can then be used to read the block back in at the new CP location. The K command can be used to erase the original block. These three commands, used in proper sequence, allow text to be moved from one part of a file to another. Also, this technique is useful in repeating a large block of text.

For example, to move a block of 20 lines from line 10 in the memory buffer to line 100, you could use the following sequence:

10:      (move to line 10)
20X   (write the next 20 lines to the temporary file)
100:     (move to line 100)
R   (read the temporary file back in)
10:      (return to line 10)
20K   (delete the 20 lines of original text)

A file specification could be entered on both the X and R commands, but if none is included, ED will assume a file name of "X$$$$$$$" and a file type of .LIB. If a file by that name already exists on disk, the new information written with the X command is appended to the end of the file.

A special option exists for the X command: If OX is entered, a file can be deleted from disk while still within ED.

The Read Command

As discussed in the previous section on the Xfer command, the R or read command is used to retrieve the information stored in a library file. Any file with any file name and file type can be loaded at the location of the character pointer. If no file is specified, ED assumes X$$$$$$$.LIB. The R command actually inserts the library file in front of the CP location so that when the command is finished, the CP will point to the same character it did when the command was issued.

When combining commands, add a CTRL-Z after the R command to separate it from subsequent commands. For example, a read command followed by a "type 10 lines" command would look like:

Rfilename∧Z20T < Return >

Restarting ED

There are two ways to restart ED: reload the original file for editing or save the current changes and reedit the file. The first way essentially erases any changes made to the file since the beginning of the current session. The second way saves the entire file with the changes made and then reedits the file from the top down.

The Original Command

The first method is invoked by entering the original or O command. All changes made since beginnning editing will be lost. The file will be reopened and you will have to start entering all the changes again. This command responds with a prompt, asking if you really want to abort and start over. If you do, then type Y. If not, type N, and ED will continue with the current session.

This command is equivalent to using the Q or quit command and then restarting ED from the CP/M level.

The Head (of File) Command

The second method is invoked by using the head of file or H command. It saves the remainder of the file with any changes made and then reopens the newly saved file for another edit session. This has the same effect as entering an E or end command and then restarting ED from the CP/M level with the newly edited file.

Aborting ED

It is also possible to simply abort ED and lose the current edit session. The quit or Q command will respond by asking if you really want to terminate. If you do, respond with Y. If you proceed, ED will erase the temporary output file and close the source or input file. It will then return control to CP/M.

Using CTRL-C to Abort ED

Control-C can also be used to leave ED, but using it will not give ED a chance to save the new edit session or to close the source file properly. It won't, however, delete the temporary file. Sometimes this is useful if you run out of disk space and can't write out the entire edit file.

Error Messages

ED provides its own error messages, but you may encounter CP/M error messages if a file read or write is not successful. The form of ED error messages is:

BREAK "x" AT c

where "x" is one of the following symbols and c is the command abbreviation where the error was encountered.

ED Errors and Descriptions

#	Search failure. The string specified in an F, S, or N command could not be found.
?c	Unrecognized command abbreviation "c". The command is not available in ED. Alternately, this error can be caused by an E, H, Q, or O command that was included on the same line with other commands.
O	No .LIB file. The file specified by the R command cannot be found.
>	Buffer full. The memory buffer has been filled, or a string in an F, N, or S command was too long. In the first case, use the W command to write some of the buffer to the output file.
E	Command aborted. A keystroke from the console aborted the command while it was executing.
F	File error. Either the disk was full or the disk directory was full. It is possible that space could be made for the file by using the OX command to delete a file.

Recovering from Disk Full or Directory Full Errors

Often, a file is expanded during an edit session, and no space remains for the output file on disk. Two recovery procedures are available for this situation.

One, use the OX command to delete an unused file to create more space. For example, to make room, an unused file (hopefully an unimportant one) can be deleted from the current disk. The following command could be used;

OXOLDFILE.DAT

Two, use the library command to save the entire file to a different disk. For example, if the A: disk is the current disk, perhaps some space is available on the B: disk. The following command would save the entire buffer in a file called BUFFER.SAV for later retrieval.

B#XB:BUFFER.SAV

3.6 THE STAT (STATUS DISPLAY) COMMAND

The STAT command gives you access to a great variety of information about disk drives, files, and peripheral devices connected to the microcomputer system. You can also use it to change the attributes of files and to reassign logical devices to different physical devices.

NOTE: Some options that occur after a file specification in a command can either have no delimiters (as shown) or can have square brackets surrounding them, or can be preceded by a dollar sign $ character. No delimiters are needed for normal operation though.

The notation used by the STAT command can be somewhat confusing. First, the RW attribute of a file means that it is read/write. The RO attribute means read only. This means that the file can be read but not written to.

Displaying the Amount of Free Space on a Disk

The simplest form of the STAT command will display the remaining space on each disk that has been logged in. The form of the command is:

A > STAT

The response is:

A: RW, Free Space: 100K
B: RW, Free Space: 120K

This sample display tells you that two disks have been logged in since a warm start, and that the A: disk has 100K bytes of free space and is set to read/write status. The B: disk is also set to read/write and has 120K bytes of free space.

A similar form of the STAT command will accept a drive specifier as an operand. Suppose you wanted to know the free space on just the B: disk. The following command would work:

A > STAT B:

The response would be:

B: RW, Free Space 120K

Displaying the Amount of Space Used by a File

Just as with the above form of STAT, a file specification can be used as an operand. The amount of space of an individual file or group of files can be displayed. The form of the command is:

STAT d:filespec {SIZE}

where d:filespec is any valid file specification. The drive code is optional as usual. The size option after the file name is also optional and, if specified, will compute the virtual file size for both sequential and random files. In random files, the file size may not match the size listed by the regular STAT command. The size option will compute a more accurate file size by counting the number of filled and unfilled records in the file.

STAT will respond with a list of the files you have requested information on, including their size in records and in kilobytes, their attributes, and the number of file control blocks (FCBs) used by the file.

```
Drive A:                                User 0
Recs    Bytes     FCBs      Attributes      Name
 205    26K        2         Dir RW      A:ASM86    .CMD
 109    14K        1         Dir RW      A:DDT86    .CMD
  72     9K        1         Dir RW      A:ED       .CMD
  45     6K        1         Dir RW      A:GENCMD   .CMD
  52     7K        1         Dir RW      A:HELP     .CMD
 195    25K        2         Dir RW      A:HELP     .HLP
  59     8K        1         Sys RW      A:PIP      .CMD
  73    10K        1         Sys RW      A:STAT     .CMD
  21     3K        1         Dir RW      A:TOD      .CMD
-----------------------------------------------------------
Total:  108K       11
A: RW, Free Space:     48K
```

As shown above, the STAT command displays the particulars for all files specified in the filespec field of the command tail. The attributes field lists two items for each file. The first is the directory status. Files can be tagged as system files, which don't show up in a normal DIR command. The DIR attribute means that the file is a normal (non-system) file. The second attribute indicates the protect status of the file. RO means read/only, and RW means read/write. Files can be independently set to either status.

This form of the STAT command does a directory check (whenever a wild card character is included in the file specification) to make sure that no two files have allocated the same records on disk. If this has occurred, STAT will display the following error message:

Bad Directory on d:
Space Allocation Conflict:
User nn d:filename.typ

where d: is the disk, nn is the user number, and d:filename.typ is the file specification of the file containing doubly allocated space. The best solution to this problem is to erase the files listed and type CTRL-C. It may be possible to copy the file using PIP before erasing them.

How to Set a Drive to Read/Only Status

It is possible to set a whole disk drive to read/only status, as well as individual files. Once in read/only mode, a CTRL-C or system reset will return the drive to read/write status.

The form of the command is:

A > STAT d: = RO

where d: is the disk drive specifier. It is necessary to include the disk specifier in this version of the STAT command.

How to Set File Access Modes or Attributes

This form of the STAT command allows you to set the file attributes as specified above. The four options are: RO, RW, DIR, and SYS. As described earlier, RO stands for read/only, RW for read/write, DIR for directory, and SYS for system. A file can be set to either read/only or read/write, but not both at the same time. Similarly, a file can be set to either directory or system status, but not to both.

The format is:

A > STAT filespec RO RW SYS DIR

where filespec is any valid file specification with optional disk drive specifier.

Examples:

STAT MYPROG.CMD SYS   (this command sets MYPROG.CMD to system)

STAT *.CMD RO   (this command sets all CMD files to read/only)

How to Display Disk Status

Versions of CP/M beyond 2.2 allow for disk definition tables (in the BIOS) that tell the BDOS what format is used to record information on each disk drive. This information is available through the STAT command.

The form of the command is:

STAT DSK:
or STAT d:DSK:

```
     A: Drive Characteristics
1,248: 128 Byte Record Capacity
  156: Kilobyte Drive  Capacity
   64: 32 Byte Directory Entries
   64: Checked Directory Entries
  128: 128 Byte Records / Directory Entry
    8: 128 Byte Records / Block
   32: 128 Byte Records / Track
    1: Reserved Tracks
```

As shown above, the drive characteristics for each on-line disk are listed. The third line is probably the most useful, in that it tells you how much space the disk is formatted for in kilobytes. The next line tells you how many directory entries you can have on the disk.

How to Display User Numbers with Active Files

This STAT command tells you which user numbers are active (have allocated files) on a given disk. The form is:

STAT {d:}USR:

where d: is the optional drive specifier. The resulting display shows that user 0 is active and that files exist in user numbers 1, 2, and 15.

A: Active User: 0
A: Active Files: 0 1 2 15

How to Display STAT Commands and Device Names

The VAL command is somewhat like a HELP command for STAT. It displays all possible forms of the command and shows the possible device assignments for the four logical character I/O devices. The form is:

STAT VAL:

```
STAT 2.1

Read Only Disk: d:=RO
Set Attribute: d:filename.typ {ro} {rw} {sys} {dir}
Disk Status  : DSK: d:DSK:
User Status  : USR: d:USR:
Iobyte Assign:
CON: = TTY: CRT: BAT: UC1:
AXI: = TTY: PTR: UR1: UR2:
AXO: = TTY: PTP: UP1: UP2:
LST: = TTY: CRT: LPT: UL1:
```

How to Display Device Assignments

This command allows you to display the current logical to physical device assignments for the four CP/M-86 logical devices. As shown above, the STAT VAL: command can be used to display all possible assignments of the four devices.

Some versions of CP/M-86 (such as the IBM PC version supplied by IBM) do not use the standard logical to physical device assignments, but use an alternate form with a special ASSIGN command. Refer to your users manual for more details.

The form of this command is:

STAT DEV:

The resulting display is:

CON: is CRT:
AXI: is TTY:
AXO: is TTY:
LST: is LPT:

This means that the logical console is assigned to the physical CRT device, the auxiliary input is set to the TTY input, the auxiliary output is set to the TTY output, and the logical list device is assigned to the physical line printer port. Some of these devices (such as AXI and AXO) may not be used in your version of CP/M-86.

How to Alter Device Assignments

The form of the STAT command allows you to alter the assignments (as displayed with the previous STAT DEV: command). Any of the physical devices listed in the STAT VAL: command may be assigned to the four logical devices. For example:

STAT CON: = UC1:   (assigns the user console #1 to the logical console)

STAT LST: = LPT: (assigns the physical printer to the logical list device)

3.7 THE SUBMIT (BATCH PROCESSING) UTILITY

The SUBMIT facility is provided to automate a series of commands that must be entered repeatedly. The SUBMIT program accepts as input a text file created by ED or some other text editor or word processor, and executes the CP/M commands found on each text line of the file.

The form of the command is:

SUBMIT filename.SUB {parameters}

where the file specification can have any eight-character file name, but must be of type SUB. There can be up to nine parameters after the file specifer. They can be used to enter options into various commands within the submit file. The nine parameters are referenced in left to right order in the command tail and are referred to as $1 through $9 within the file. When SUBMIT sees a "$1" within the file, it will replace the first of up to nine parameters from the command tail. Each parameter in the command tail can be any sequence of ASCII characters, but each parameter must be separated from every other by at least one space (ASCII 20H).

The contents of MYFILE.SUB:

;This file assembles, loads and executes the file specified by $1.
ASM86 $1 $$$2
GENCMD $1
$1

The command line is:

SUBMIT MYFILE TESTFILE SZ

The resulting commands are:

ASM86 TESTFILE $SZ
GENCMD TESTFILE
TESTFILE

The parameters match up to the commands as follows:

SUBMIT MYFILE TESTFILE SZ   ←parameters passed to the SUB
                                                       file.
$1 $2   ←parameter tokens within the
                                                       SUB file.

Wherever the $1 token is found in the file, TESTFILE will be inserted in its place. Wherever $2 is found, SZ will be inserted. This procedure can be used for up to nine parameter tokens. Each token may be used more than once within the file, as demonstrated in the above example file.

In some cases, (as with the SZ example above, a dollar sign ($) is needed within the file. If a single dollar sign is used, the SUBMIT program would try to interpret it as a parameter token. To avoid this problem, two dollar signs ($$) are placed together to indicate that a real dollar sign is needed.

3.8 THE TOD (TIME OF DAY) COMMAND

The TOD command allows the user to set the date and time of day, and to view the date and time, either once or continuously. When CP/M-86 starts from a cold start, it initializes the date and time of day. The date is usually set to the date the latest version of CP/M-86 was released, and the time is almost always set to zero.

The date is represented as a month value (from 1 to 12), a day value (from 1 to 31) depending on the month, and a two-digit year value with a relative starting point of the year 1900.

The time is stored in 24-hour military format with hour values from 0 to 11 for the morning, and 12 to 23 for the afternoon. The minutes and seconds range from 0 to 59.

Entering the TOD command with no other options returns this (typical) display of the current date and time:

07/17/82   18:55:01

Setting the Time and Date

The second form of the command allows you to set the current date and time.

TOD month/day/year hour:minute:second

where the parameters fit the specifications given above. All parameters must appear as two-digit numbers. For example:

TOD 07/20/82 10:00:00

will set the date to July 20, 1982 and the time to 10 A.M. The TOD command then displays the message:

Press any key to set the time

to allow you to accurately set the time.

Displaying the Time and Date Continuously

The final form of the TOD command allows you to continuously display the time and date on the screen. The form is:

TOD P

The result is the same as with the first form (TOD) except that the display is updated on the screen as each second goes by. To stop the display, just press any key.

NOTE: It is not necessary to set the time and date for proper operation of CP/M-86. The TOD function is provided as a useful tool, but unlike some operating systems, you are not forced to use it.

4

Programmer's Tools

4.1 ASM-86 (The CP/M-86 Assembler)

Why do you need an assembler? The instruction set of any microprocessor is represented in mnemonics like: JMP LABEL or MOV AL,BL.
These labels mean "Jump or transfer control to the location known as
LABEL" and "Move the contents of the BL register to the AL register."
These are known as instruction mnemonics, but the microprocessor
doesn't understand them when they are written in English. For the
microprocessor to understand them, they must be placed in memory locations in binary. But binary is cumbersome for human beings. Each
byte is represented by eight binary digits or bits, each with a value of
one or zero. Thus, the JMP instruction looks like this: 11101001, followed by two more bytes that represent the binary address of the
LABEL.

The assembler reads in mnemonics and translates them into binary
codes. The binary codes are sent to the output file in hexadecimal (base
16) which is a convenient way of displaying binary on most computers.
The output file is called a hex file because it contains hexadecimal numbers. Additional information is included with the hex file that tells the
loader program (GENCMD) where to load the instructions into memory
for subsequent execution.

The assembler is basically a convenience utility that translates or
assembles your instructions into a form that the 8086 can readily exe-

cute. Unless you have very specific needs that only the assembler can handle, most programming can be done in high-level languages such as BASIC, Pascal, or PL/I.

A high-level language may be of two forms. The first is a compiler, which performs a job much like that of the assembler. It reads in your instructions and translates them into binary machine-readable instructions. The difference is that a high-level language doesn't use assembly mnemonics. It uses statements such as:

A = B + C

This might be translated into: load B, add C (to B), store result in A. Of course the instructions produced depend on the microprocessor used, but the effect is the same on all computers. A high-level language is simply a way of encoding requests in a more abstract (and human readable) way than the normal instructions of the computer.

The second form of high-level language is called an interpreter. As the name implies, it interprets high-level statements like the A = B + C given above, but instead of generating instructions for later execution, it reads the statement on the fly and performs the arithmetic as it goes. The result is stored in a reserved location called A, and the interpreter goes on to the next statement. None of the instructions are stored for later use. They are read and immediately forgotten. This form of high-level language is slower than a compiler because it runs the program as it goes. It must reinterpret each program line every time it encounters it. Most versions of BASIC are interpreters.

As stated before, the assembler is very like a compiler, except that it works with instructions that have a one-to-one correspondence with the binary instruction set of the computer.

ASM-86 accepts as input a source file containing 8086 assembler instructions and generates three output files: an 8086 machine language file in hexadecimal format, a symbol table file, and a listing file (see Figure 4.1). The 8086 machine language file (also known as the object file) may be in either Intel Hex or Digital Research Hex format (described in this section). ASM-86 is available in two forms. The first form is the most common; it is written in 8086 instructions and executes on the 8086. This form is often called a resident assembler.

The second form is an 8086 cross-assembler format designed to run on either an 8080-or Z80-based system with CP/M-80 (or a CP/M look-alike). It executes in the 8080 instruction set, but the object file produced by the cross-assembler will only run on an 8086. This allows software developed on an existing 8080 or Z80 system to be transferred to the 8086 microprocessor.

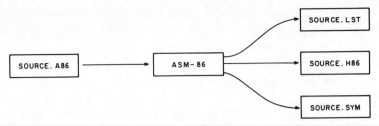

Figure 4.1: ASM-86 files (input and output diagram).

As shown in Figure 4.1, each of the input and output files have default file types associated with them. The input file normally has a file type of A86 although any other type may be used, if it is included with the file name when ASM-86 is invoked. The file type of H86 is used for the object code file, which is later read in by GENCMD to make a CMD file. The LST and SYM files are for documentation purposes and are not used again by GENCMD or any other program related to ASM-86.

Starting ASM-86

ASM-86 has many options that can be specified in the command line. The source file name in the command line must always be present for ASM-86 to operate. If it isn't, an error message will be displayed, and ASM-86 will terminate. The form of the command is:

ASM86 source-file {$ options}

The source file can be specified with or without the drive name or the file type. The following are all valid file specifications (for a source file on the A: disk called MYFILE.A86):

MYFILE
A:MYFILE
MYFILE.A86
A:MYFILE.A86

Note that if no file type is given, the default of A86 is used by ASM-86. If the drive name is not given, the default drive is used. Also, the file type, if specified, need not be A86. You are free to use any file type (i.e., .ASM, .TXT), but if it isn't specified, ASM-86 will assume it is A86.

The options must be preceded by a dollar sign $ character. The following options are available:

Parameter	Description	Valid Arguments
A	Source file device	A, B, C, ... P
H	Hex output file destination device	A ... P, X, Y, Z
P	Print file destination device	A ... P, X, Y, Z
S	Symbol table destination device	A ... P, X, Y, Z
F	Format of hex output file	I, D

Any options can be included in any order as long as they are separated by at least one space. A device name must follow each option, specifying its destination. For example, suppose you want to assemble a file, but sent its list file to the console device. You would enter:

ASM86 MYFILE $PX

The PX option tells the assembler to send the printer output to the X device, which is the console. To assemble a file and ignore the printer output, you could enter:

ASM86 MYFILE $PZ

which would send the printed output to the null file (NUL:). Specifying Y would send the output to the printer, which in the case of the P option is rendundant. Any device name from A through P will send the output to that disk drive.

More than one option can be included at one time. For example, to assemble a file called MYFILE, and to send the printed output to disk B: and the symbol table to the console, and to use the Hex-Intel format for the hex file, we could enter the following command:

ASM86 MYFILE $PB SX FI

If the format option is not specified, the assembler automatically produces the Digital Research format.

When the output is being sent to the console, CTRL-S may be used to stop the scrolling of the text for viewing purposes. The display may be restarted by typing any character.

Aborting ASM-86

ASM-86 may be manually aborted at any time. Striking any key on the console device will cause ASM-86 to display the message:

USER BREAK. OK(Y/N)?

If you enter Y, ASM-86 will terminate and return to the console command processor. If you enter N, ASM-86 will continue with the assembly.

An Example of ASM-86

Figure 4.2 is a short assembler example. Assembler source statements can be broken into three fields or columns: the label field, the mnemonic field, and the operand field. The label field is used to identify locations within the program that may be referred to in some other part of the program. If a label, such as TRANS, is used in a sequence of instructions, then it must be followed by a colon (:). If it refers to data, then no colon is needed.

```
;
;       ASM-86 Sample Program
;       by Mark Dahmke, 7-26-82
;       This program may be copied for any
;       use, without permission.
;
;
        CSEG                    ;Code Segment
;
START:  MOV     SI,OFFSET BUFFER ;Load the start address of the input buffer.
        MOV     BX,OFFSET TABLE  ;Load the base address of the translate table.
        MOV     CX,LENGTH BUFFER ;Load the length of the input buffer.
;
TRANS:  MOV     AL,[SI]         ;Load a byte from the buffer.
        XLAT                    ;Look in table for the translated
                                ;character.
        MOV     [SI],AL         ;Put the translated character back in
                                ;the buffer.
        INC     SI              ;Increment the pointer.
        DEC     CX              ;Decrement the counter.
        JNZ     TRANS           ;If CX does not equal zero, repeat.
        RET                     ;finished.
;
;
        DSEG                    ;Data Segment
;
        ORG     0100H           ;Since the first page (0000H-00FFH) of
                                ;the data segment is used as the
                                ;base page (as in CP/M-80), it must be
                                ;reserved in CP/M-86 also.  User data
                                ;should start at 0100H in the data segment.
;
BUFFER  DB      'This is the input buffer.'
;
;
; THIS TABLE CONTAINS THE COMPLETE ASCII CHARACTER SET.
;
TABLE   DB      0,1,2,3,4,5,6,7,8,9,10,11,12,13,14,15
        DB      16,17,18,19,20,21,22,23,24,25,26,27,28,29,30,31
```

```
        DB        ' !"#$%&''( )*+,-./'
        DB        '0123456789'
        DB        ':;<=>?@'
        DB        'ABCDEFGHIJKLMNOPQRSTUVWXYZ'
        DB        '[\]^',5FH,60H
        DB        'ABCDEFGHIJKLMNOPQRSTUVWXYZ'        ;TRANSLATE LOWER-CASE TO
DB      '{|}~',7FH                          ;UPPER-CASE.
;
;
        END
```

Figure 4.2 ASM source program example.

The CSEG instruction is not really an assembler instruction. It
doesn't get converted into a binary instruction. It is called an assembler
directive, and its purpose is to inform the assembler of some changing
condition. In this case, it tells the assembler that the following instructions are to go in the code segment when the hex output file is generated. After the return instruction, another directive can be found, but
this one tells the assembler to switch to the data segment of the program. In this way, the program can be easily separated into its respective components. The following is a complete list of ASM-86 directives:

```
CSEG          Code Segment.
DSEG          Data Segment.
SSEG          Stack Segment.
ESEG          Extra Segment.
ORG           Origin. This directive sets the offset counter in the
              current segment to the value after the ORG directive.
IF            Conditional Assembly directive. All statements between
              the IF and ENDIF directives are included conditionally,
              based upon the value of the expression after the IF
              directive.
ENDIF         This directive terminates a conditional assembly (IF)
              directive.
INCLUDE       This directive can be used to load in other source files
              during the assembly process, such as a library subroutine
              file.
END           This is always the last directive in a program. It tells
              the assembler to stop reading statements.
EQU           Equate. This directive is used to assign values and
              attributes to user-defined symbols.
DB            Define Byte. This directive defines initialized storage
              areas in byte format.
DW            Define Word. This directive defines initialized storage
              areas in the word format.
DD            Define Double Word. This directive defines initialized
              storage in the double word or 4 byte format.
RS            Reserve Storage. This directive allocates memory in bytes
              but doesn't initialize it. The byte attribute is not
              assigned to the symbol associated with the RS statement.
RB            Reserve Byte. Same as RS, but defines the storage in the
              byte format.
RW            Reserve Word. Same as RS, but defines the storage in the
              word format.
TITLE         The title string that follows the directive will be
              printed at the top of each page of the list file.
```

PAGESIZE	This directive defines the number of lines to a printer page.
PAGEWIDTH	This directive defines the number of characters per line of the list file.
EJECT	This directive causes ASM86 to insert a page eject where the statement occurs.
SIMFORM	This directive replaces form-feeds with a number of line-feeds to simulate form-feeds on the print out.
NOLIST	This directive stops the listing of the output file. It may be used to start and stop the listing of various parts of a program.
LIST	This directive reactivates the list option if disabled with the NOLIST directive.

The other segment directives are ESEG and SSEG. They allow the programmer to include the extra segment and stack segments respectively. The ORG directive allows the programmer to set the offset of the location counter for each segment. As shown in the example, an ORG statement may be placed in each segment of the program.

Conditional Assembly

Conditional assembly is a feature that most modern assemblers provide. To the uninitiated user, the idea of including conditional statements in the assembler may not seem obvious. Their main purpose is to allow one superset of a program to be written to include many alternate versions. For example, suppose a program was written by a vendor to intercept commands from a high-level language, such as Pascal, and send them to a graphics plotter. The high-level language interface remains the same for all plotters, but the plotter-level interface (that is, the command bytes sent to the plotter) change from one manufacturer's plotter to the next. The vendor wants to support all the plotters, but doesn't want to maintain separate programs for each version because they are mostly the same, except for the minor plotter differences. If a separate program were written for each plotter, any minor revision to the program would have to be added to every version, causing a logistics problem and more overhead. Also, the vendor might want to supply versions for Pascal, BASIC, and Fortran. The solution is to use conditional statements to say, in effect: If plotter x, use this sequence of instructions: if plotter y, use a different sequence. If BASIC, use one high-level interface; if Pascal, use a different one. The bulk of the program remains the same, but the details for each version are different. The top of the source file could then have one or two statements saying which version to assemble, and those few lines are the only ones changed for each assembly.

The ASM-86 assembler implements conditionals as follows:

IF <numeric expression>

```
<statement 1>
<statement 2>
...
ENDIF
```

where numeric expression may be any valid algebraic expression that the assembler will handle. If the expression is evaluated to be non-zero, then all the statements between the IF and the ENDIF directives will be included in the assembler program. If the expression evaluates to zero, then all the statements from IF to ENDIF are ignored.

The INCLUDE Directive

This directive allows the programmer to include another assembler source file in with the program. The form is:

INCLUDE filename

where filename is assumed to be of type A86, if no file type is included. If no drive name is included, the file is assumed to be on the same disk as the source file.

For example, if a library of standard symbol definitions were created, it could be included at the start of all programs. This would save much effort in re-keying standard definitions. Also, if a group of standard subroutines were always used, they could be included at the end of all source files.

Other Directives

The END directive is always the last source statement of an assembler program. Any source statements following the END directive will be ignored. If the END directive is not included, all statements will be read from the file until the end of file character (1AH or CTRL-Z) is found.

The EQU directive stands for equate. Its purpose is to assign values and attributes to symbols for use in a program. The following forms are allowed:

symbol EQU <numeric expression>
symbol EQU <address expression>
symbol EQU <register>
symbol EQU <instruction mnemonic>

The first form assigns a numeric value to the symbol. The second form assigns an address. Both of these forms may have values ranging from 0000H to 0FFFFH or in decimal from 0 to 65535.

The third form assigns a new name to an 8086 register. This can be used if a register is regularly used for some specific purpose in a program. Thus every reference of the symbol is simply replaced with the appropriate register name (as recognized by the assembler).

The fourth form can be used to redefine an instruction mnemonic. Similar in nature to the third form, the symbol can refer to an instruction mnemonic. If an instruction such as MVI AL,0 (load the AL register with zero) is frequently used, it could be renamed to ZEROAL to be more descriptive of the function performed. After the equate is read by the assembler, either MVI AL,0 or ZEROAL will tell the assembler to generate the equivalent MVI AL,0 instruction codes.

Several directives allow data bytes or words (16-bit values) to be stored in memory for use in a program. The first is DB which stands for define byte. The form is:

{symbol} DB <numeric expression>, {<numeric expression>,...}

or

{symbol} DB <string constant>,{<string constant>,...}

This directive can be used to store data bytes in memory one at a time or in groups. Numeric expressions are evaluated to 8-bit values, and strings are enclosed in quotes. For example:

MSG DB ' This is a sample string constant'

DATA DB 0,1,2,3,4,5,6,0FFH

DB 'This is a combination of the two.',0

The symbol is optional, but may be used to refer to the data in the program, as such:

MVI DX,OFFSET MSG

which would load the offset address (within the data segment) of the first byte in MSG.

The symbol, when used, has four attributes: the segment and offset attributes determine the symbol's memory address; the type attribute indicates that the symbol refers to data in single bytes; the length attribute tells the number of bytes or allocation units reserved.

The DW directive stands for define word and works exactly the way DB does, except that it allocates two bytes (one word) for each numeric expression in the operand field. Its type attribute is set to word.

The DD directive stands for define double and allocates memory in four-byte or two-word blocks. The numeric expression is always assumed to be an address, so the first two bytes of each block will be loaded with the offset address, and the second two will contain the segment address of the symbol.

The RS directive allocates memory, but doesn't initialize it. The numeric expression in the operand field gives the number of bytes to allocate. The RB directive works similarly, but gives the associated symbol the byte attribute. The RW directive allocates in words, with the number of words given in the operand field.

The TITLE directive can have a string constant in the operand field. The string is placed at the top of each page of the LST file. The string must not exceed 30 characters. For example:

TITLE 'This is a sample program.'

The PAGESIZE directive allows the programmer to set the number of lines per page of the LST file to whatever is convenient for the printer device. The default page size is 66.

The PAGEWIDTH directive defines the number of printed columns the printer can handle. The default is 120 characters per line unless the printed output is directed to the console. It is then set to 79.

EJECT allows the programmer to force a new printer page in the output file. This is mainly used to break out subroutines from the rest of a program for readability.

The SIMFORM directive replaces the form-feed character (used to advance the printer to the top of a page) with the appropriate number of line-feed characters to simulate a form-feed. This is useful since some printers can't recognize a form-feed character.

The NOLIST and LIST directives tell ASM-86 to start and stop listing the file. If a NOLIST is found, listing of the statements will be supressed until a LIST directive is found. The default start-up state is LIST.

ASM-86 Code Macro Facilities

ASM-86 doesn't support macros in the normal sense, but it does have a limited facility called code macros that allows the user to define his or her own pseudo-instructions. A macro is a block of instructions or bytes that are given a name and can be used like a regular instruction mnemonic. Every time the macro name is referenced in a program, the contents of the macro are reproduced in its place. Macros are not subroutines. A subroutine is called repeatedly, but is included in the program only once. A code macro can have two operands. Each operand is defined in terms of its type and size. The operand can then be referred to in the code macro itself. When the code macro is used in a program, the two operands are replaced by the operands specified in the actual operand field of the macro.

The form for the code macro definition is:

CodeMacro < name > { < formal name > : < specifier
letter > , { < modifier letter > : < range > }}

The formal name is a token or place holder. Every time the formal name is found in the body of the code macro, it is replaced by the symbol used when the macro is invoked in the program. The specifier letter identifies the type of formal name that is to be used.

The body of the macro can contain only the following directives: SEGFIX, NOSEGFIX, MODRM, RELB, RELW, DB, DW, DD, and DBIT. These directives are unique to code macros. DB, DW, and DD have different meanings within code macros. Here are some code macro examples:

```
CodeMacro ZEROAL
DB 0B0H,00H
EndM
```

For more information on ASM-86, consult the CP/M-86 Programmer's Guide.

4.2 GENCMD (Generate CMD File) Utility

This utility accepts as input the hex file output from ASM-86 and creates an executable CMD file as output. Hex file output from other languages can be fed into GENCMD also. The form of the command is:

```
GENCMD filespec {8080 CODE[An,Bn,Mn,Xn]
DATA[An,Bn,Mn,Xn] STACK[An,Bn,Mn,Xn] EXTRA[An,Bn,Mn,Xn]
X1[...] ... X4[...]}
```

The parameter list contains up to nine keywords, each with a list of values, as shown above. They are : 8080, CODE, DATA, STACK, EXTRA, X1, X2, X3, and X4.

The keyword 8080 tells GENCMD that the output file is to be generated as an 8080 memory model. In the 8080 model, the code segment and data segments overlap. The values listed after each keyword are enclosed in brackets. Each of the keyword and bracketed values must be separated from other keywords with at least one space. The values are listed here:

An   Load group at absolute location n.
Bn   Begin group at address n in the hexadecimal file.
Mn   The group requires a minimum of n * 16 bytes.
Xn   The group can address up to n * 16 bytes.

The An parameter tells GENCMD that the specified group (i.e., code, stack, data) should be loaded at an absolute location in memory. Don't use this unless you are sure that the requested memory will be available when the program is loaded.

The Bn parameter informs GENCMD of the beginning of address of the specified group in the input hex file. It is not necessary to include this parameter if you are using ASM-86, unless you have specified the option FI, which generates an Intel-Hex format file.

The Mn parameter is used if a data segment has an uninitialized data area at the end of the segment. Some 8080 programs don't define storage at the end of the program with explicit DB or DS statements. This parameter will correct the problem.

The Xn parameter is included because some programs (as with the Mn parameter) don't initialize their data areas. In the case of large memory buffers, some programs tend to allocate their data areas by looking at the top-of-memory bytes at data segment offsets 0006H and 007H (set by CP/M). The Xn parameter is a way of specifying that the program can use up to n * 16 bytes.

The following are some examples of GENCMD:

GENCMD MYPROG

This form assumes that the input hex file MYPROG.H86 is on the default disk drive and that the output CMD file is to be written back to the same disk.

GENCMD MYPROG 8080

This form is used when the original program was translated from CP/M-80. It sets the code data and extra segments to overlap (as in the 8080 environment). The stack segment is left in the console command processor.

GENCMD MYPROG STACK[M300]

This form tells GENCMD that the stack segment requires a minimum of 300 * 16 or 4800 bytes. Hexadecimal values may be entered by including an X prefix to the hexadecimal number, such as: XOFA3.

4.3 DDT-86 (The CP/M-86 Debugger Utility)

DDT-86 is an interactive test and debug facility for programmers. The name DDT has its origins in mainframe computers. When the concept of a debugger program was implemented, it seemed only natural to "debug" a program with DDT (the insecticide). Later, someone decided that DDT had to be an acronym for something, so they decided to call it Dynamic Debugging and Test program. Regardless of what it stands for, the term DDT has become synonomous with debugger.

DDT-86 is an almost exact look-alike to DDT on CP/M-80. A few new commands were added, and some changes were made to accommodate segment addressing, but it is otherwise functionally identical.

How to Start DDT-86

In CP/M-80, DDT-86 is stored on disk as DDT86.CMD. In CP/M-80, it was DDT.COM. To invoke DDT-86 on CP/M-86, enter the following command:

DDT86

or DDT86 filename

The first form simply loads DDT-86 into memory and displays the prompt character -, indicating that it is ready to accept commands. The second form will load DDT-86, but will also attempt to load the file specified in the command tail. If the file type is not specified, DDT assumes the file is of type CMD, and it will load it as CP/M-86 would load an object code file.

NOTE: One major difference between DDT on CP/M-80 and CP/M-86 is that DDT-86 will not load a hex file directly. GENCMD must be used to make a command file first. Even with DDT-86, the read command will load the H86 file, but won't convert it into object code as DDT-80 would.

The second form (as shown above) is equivalent to:

DDT86

-Efilename

The E command can be used to load the CMD file after DDT86 has been loaded. The E command will be discussed later.

Entering Commands on DDT-86

When DDT-86 is ready to accept commands, it displays a dash as a prompt (just as CP/M displays the right arrow > character). Any DDT command may be entered after the dash prompt. Alternately, the user can abort DDT by typing CTRL-C (hold down the control key and press C), but this can only be done if the CTRL-C is the first character on the command line. If you have already entered part of a command and wish to abort DDT, use backspace or CTRL-E to return to the beginning of the line. Then type CTRL-C.

A command line may have up to 64 characters and must end with a carriage return. The standard CP/M line editing functions work within DDT-86, because it uses the standard BDOS line input function (number 10. As shown in section 5.4, the line-editing characters include: CTRL-X: erase line and start over; CTRL-U: remove current line and go to new line; and CTRL-R: retype line. Also, CTRL-H or backspace can be used to remove errors.

Commands are one-character long in DDT-86. Table 4.1 lists all the DDT-86 commands. Each command can be followed by one or more arguments. Depending on the command, they may be hexadecimal values or file specifications. All numeric values used in DDT are assumed to be in hexadecimal (base 16).

As	Enter assembly language statements a
Ds,f	Display memory in hexadecimal (bytes) a starting at address s, through addre.
DWs,f	Display memory in hexadecimal (words) a
Efilespec	Load a program for execution or testing
Fs,f,b	Fill memory block with a byte constant. The starting address is s, the ending a f, and the byte constant is b.
FWs,f,w	Fill memory block with a word constant. The "w" is the word constant.

Gs,b1,b2	Begin execution (GO) at address s, with optional breakpoint addresses: b1 and b2.
Ha,b	Hexadecimal arithmetic. Result is: a+b, a-b.
Icommand-tail	Set up a file control block (FCB) and command tail.
Ls,f	List (disassemble) memory using 8086 mnemonics, from start address s to end address f.
Ms,f,d	Move a block of memory. Move the block from s to f to the destination d.
Rfilespec	Read a disk file into memory.
Ss	Modify (Set) bytes in memory, at address s.
SWs	Modify (Set) words in memory, at address s.
Tn	Trace program execution, for n statements.
TSn	Trace program execution and display segment registers, for n statements.
Un	Untraced program monitoring of n statements.
USn	Untraced program monitoring with display of segment registers, of n statements.
V	Display memory allocation of segments.
Wfilename,s,f	Write contents of memory block back to disk.
Xr	Examine and/or modify CPU registers.
Xf	Examine and/or modify CPU flags.

Table 4.1: DDT commands

The syntax of a DDT command is:

Carg1 arg2

Carg1,arg2

where C is the command and arg1 and arg2 are optional arguments. The first argument must follow the command with no intervening spaces. Subsequent arguments must be separated from each other by a space or a comma.

Terminating DDT-86

To terminate DDT and return to CP/M-86, just enter CTRL-C instead of a command. Note that CP/M-86 doesn't have the SAVE command that is used in CP/M-80 to save the results of a DDT session. The W command is used to write a file to disk before exiting DDT-86.

Segment Addressing in DDT-86

Since the 8086/8088 microprocessor uses segment addressing (see section 5.11), DDT-86 must be able to set the CS, DS, ES, and SS registers, as well as to specify the offset addresses within the segments.

With this segment and offset address scheme, up to one megabyte can be addressed. Whenever the offset (address within a segment) must be entered, simply use the four-digit hexadecimal address as you would within a program. When the segment must be specified, enter the most significant 16 bits (4 hexadecimal digits) of the segment address, followed by a colon, followed by the offset within the segment. For example:

04DF:0000

will generate the following 20-bit absolute address:

```
  04DF0 ← Segment address × 16
+ 0000  ← offset within the segment
  04DF0 ← 20-bit absolute address
```

The arithmetic performed here is as follows (each digit or letter represents 4 bits):

```
  ssss0 ← segment address × 16 (shifted left 4 bits)
+ dddd  ← offset within the segment
  aaaaa ← absolute 20-bit memory address
```

Here are some more examples:

0A00:04FF → 0A4FF

0000:1234 → 01234

F000:0A2B → F0A2B

0350:4821 → 07D21

When adding mentally, take the segment address (in hexadecimal), add a zero to the right end, and then add the offset to it.

Note: When a program is loaded from the command level or with an E or R command, the segment registers are automatically loaded with the segment addresses set up for the program code and data areas. Since DDT-86 already knows the assigned values for the segment registers, it is possible to give the name of the segment register rather than entering the four-digit address. For example, assume that the code segment is equal to 0158H and the data segment is 0400H. To refer (in a command) to offset 300H within the code segment, you could enter

CS:0300 instead of 0158:0300. All four segments may be entered directly in this way. Some commands (as you will see) default to a particular segment. For example, when displaying memory, DDT-86 assumes you want to dump data, so it looks at the data segment. If, however, you wished to display the code segment, you could enter CS:dddd where dddd is the offset address you were interested in.

Additional note: Whenever you are asked to enter a 20-bit address in a command, you should enter the ssss:dddd form. See the assemble command for further explanation.

The Assemble Command

The A or assemble command works like ASM-86 because it accepts mnemonics for the 8086 instruction set and converts them into opcodes. The only argument allowed is the address where assembly is to start. The address must be entered in the form described in the section on segment addressing. Any of the following are valid:

A0100	← puts instructions at CS:0100
A0120:0230	← puts instructions at 01430H
ACS:100	← puts instructions at CS:0100
ADS:1234	← puts instructions at DS:1234

When DDT-86 is started, the segment values for the command are set to zero. If you enter the assemble command, the segment address will be zero, unless you set it to something else.

A0100	If the segment address hasn't been specified yet, zero will be used.
A0120:0230	Including the segment address here will set the segment value to 0120 for subsequent assemble and list commands.
ACS:100	If CS hasn't been set, this command will act just like A0100 above. If CS has been set, then assembly will start at offset 100H from the current value of the code segment. That value will be saved for future assemble and list commands.
ADS:1234	Using DS in the command causes DDT to use the current data segment value as its starting point for all subsequent assemble commands. It can be reset to CS by entering ACS:0000.

Note: The segment value entered as an operand (left of the colon) is saved each time you enter an assemble or list command. If you don't specify a new segment address the next time you use the assemble command, the old value is used.

When you enter an assembly mnemonic, DDT converts it into machine instructions, increments the counter (as needed), and displays the next 20-bit address. You may enter any number of assembly mnemonics this way. The command can be terminated with a blank line or a period (and carriage return).

The Display Command

The D or display command prints out the contents of memory in hexadecimal and ASCII for viewing. Memory may be displayed in either byte or word (16-bit) format.

The forms of the command are:

D ← displays 12 lines (192 bytes) from the current display address.

Ds ← displays 12 lines from the start address (es) given.

Ds,f ← displays 12 lines from the start address (es) to the 16-bit offset given in f.

DW ← same as D except displays words instead of bytes.

DWs ← same as Ds except in word mode.

DWs,f ← same as Ds,f except in word mode.

The memory display for the first (byte mode) group of commands is shown in Listing 4.1. The display includes the 20-bit address (in the form of segment and offset), up to 16 memory locations, and up to 16 characters, each the ASCII representation of the respective 16 bytes.

```
-DOC85:00C0

0C85:00C0  00 00 00 00 00 00 00 00 00 00 00 00 00 00 00 00  ................
0C85:00D0  00 00 00 00 00 00 00 00 00 00 00 00 00 00 00 00  ................
0C85:00E0  00 00 00 00 00 00 00 00 00 00 00 00 00 00 00 00  ................
0C85:00F0  00 00 00 00 00 00 00 00 00 00 00 00 00 00 00 00  ................
0C85:0100  44 69 72 65 63 74 6F 72 79 20 43 6F 6D 6D 61 6E  Directory Comman
0C85:0110  64 0D 0A 24 20 3A 20 20 20 20 20 20 20 20 20 2E  d..$ :         .
0C85:0120  20 20 20 00 0D 0A 24 00 3F 3F 3F 3F 3F 3F 3F 3F     ...$.????????
0C85:0130  3F 3F 3F 00 00 00 00 00 00 00 00 00 00 00 00 00  ???.............
0C85:0140  00 00 00 00 00 00 00 00 00 00 00 00 00 00 00 00  ................
0C85:0150  5F 36 00 9A 0C 01 5F 36 00 00 00 00 00 00 00 00  _6...._6........
0C85:0160  00 00 00 00 00 00 00 00 00 00 00 00 00 00 00 00  ................
0C85:0170  00 00 00 00 00 00 00 00 00 00 00 00 00 00 00 00  ................
```

Listing 4.1 DDT "D" command.

The display word form of the command works the same way, except it formats the hexadecimal display into 16-bit (4-digit) words instead of bytes. The ASCII display is the same as the byte mode.

```
-DWOC85:00CO
OC85:00CO 0000 0000 0000 0000 0000 0000 0000 0000 ................
OC85:00DO 0000 0000 0000 0000 0000 0000 0000 0000 ................
OC85:00EO 0000 0000 0000 0000 0000 0000 0000 0000 ................
OC85:00FO 0000 0000 0000 0000 0000 0000 0000 0000 ................
OC85:0100 6944 6572 7463 726F 2079 6F43 6D6D 6E61 Directory Comman
OC85:0110 0D64 240A 3A20 2020 2020 2020 2020 2E20 d..$ :         .
OC85:0120 2020 0020 0A0D 0024 3F3F 3F3F 3F3F 3F3F    ...$.????????
OC85:0130 3F3F 003F 0000 0000 0000 0000 0000 0000 ???............
OC85:0140 0000 0000 0000 0000 0000 0000 0000 0000 ................
OC85:0150 365F 9A00 010C 365F 0000 0000 0000 0000 _6...._6........
OC85:0160 0000 0000 0000 0000 0000 0000 0000 0000 ................
OC85:0170 0000 0000 0000 0000 0000 0000 0000 0000 ................
```

Listing 4.2 DDT "DW" command.

The third form includes a 20-bit starting address and a 16-bit ending address. For example, the command:

D0100:3400,3500

uses the same segment address for both offsets. Memory will be displayed from 0100:3400 to 0100:3500 or in absolute addresses from 04400H to 04500H.

The Load File Command

The E or "load file for execution" command loads a file from disk into memory so that the G, T, or U commands can be used to execute it for test purposes. The form is:

E<filename>

where filename is the name of the file to be loaded. The default file (if not specified) is CMD. The segment register and the IP (instruction pointer or program counter) are loaded according to the contents of the header record of the CMD file.

Any blocks of memory allocated by other programs run under DDT control (loaded with previous E or R commands) are automatically released when the E command is used. When the load operation is complete, DDT-86 displays the start and end addresses of each segment that was loaded. The V command can be used to display these addresses at any time.

An error message is issued if DDT can't find the file specified.

The Fill Command

The F or fill command initializes or fills an area of memory with a byte or word constant. The forms of the command are:

Fs,f,b

FWs,f,w

where the F command fills bytes and the FW command fills words. The s argument is a 20-bit starting address (as discussed earlier) and the f argument is a 16-bit offset of the final byte or word of the block to be filled, within the segment specified in the s argument. The b argument of the first form is the byte constant (in hexadecimal) to be stored in each byte of the block. The word form of the command stores the w argument in each word, with the lower 8-bits first, then the upper 8-bits of the 16-bit word.

Every time DDT-86 writes a byte or word to memory with the fill command, the stored value is read back to verify it. If it can't get the correct value back, DDT issues an error message telling you that the memory block is faulty or nonexistant. If the s argument is greater than the f argument, an error message will be returned.

The Go Command

The G or go command has several forms. The first simply transfers control to a program. If no address is specified, DDT uses the last value it has for the start of the program which is derived from the code segment and IP (instruction pointer) (set when the E or R command was used to load a .CMD file).

The forms of this command are:

G
G,b1
G,b1,b2
Gs
Gs,b1
Gs,b1,b2

The first three forms assume that the address will be taken from the code segment and instruction pointer. The b1 and b2 values are 20-bit addresses of breakpoints. If you don't specify a segment address for any of the arguments, DDT uses the current contents of the CS register.

The second three forms of the command include the s argument, which is the 20-bit start address.

Breakpoints can be a useful tool in debugging a program. Rather than using the T or trace command to painstakingly step through each instruction, you can set a breakpoint address at which DDT will stop. The breakpoints aren't saved though; each time you enter the go command, you must reenter the breakpoints.

When control has been transferred to the program, it executes at normal speed until one of the two breakpoints is found. If this happens, DDT regains control, clears the breakpoints, and displays the 20-bit address of the breakpoint where execution stopped.

The stop address is displayed as follows:

*ssss:dddd

where ssss is the code segment value and dddd is the offset (corresponding to the IP) within the segment. Note that when execution stops at a breakpoint, the instruction at the breakpoint address has not been executed.

The Hexadecimal Math Command

The H or hex math command computes and displays the sum and difference of two 16-bit numbers. The form is:

Ha,b

where a and b are the two input arguments. The result is:

ssss dddd

where ssss is equal to a + b and dddd is equal to a − b.

The Input Command Tail Function

The I or input command tail function sets up the default FCB (file control block) and command tail buffer in DDT-86's base page. The information is copied into the base page of the current program (loaded with the E command). The form is:

I<command tail>

The command tail is a character string containing one or two file specifications. The first file specification is parsed (analysed) and placed in the default file control block at 005CH in the base page. The second (optional) file specification is parsed and placed in the second part of the default file control block at 006CH in the base page. The character string in <command tail> is also copied into the default command buffer at 0080H in the base page. The length of the command tail is stored at 0080H and a binary zero is placed at the end of the character string.

The base page address is displayed as the data segment value when a program is loaded using the E command.

The List Command

The L or list command is the opposite of the assemble command. It displays memory in the form of assembly language mnemonics. The forms are:

L
Ls
Ls,f

If no arguments are given (as in the first form), 12 lines of disassembled machine instructions are displayed, starting at the current address (see the assemble command for more details). The current address is saved from the last use of either the assemble command or the list command.

The second form lists 12 assembly instructions at the 20-bit address given in s. The third form lists instructions from the 20-bit address in s to the 16-bit ending address in f.

If the segment address is not given for either argument, the last segment address will be used. After each use of the L command, the "current address" is set to the next byte in memory after the last instruction displayed.

If you wish to terminate a lengthy display of instructions, type any key. To halt the display for viewing, use CTRL-S.

```
-L0C7A:0000

0C7A:0000 MOV    CL,09
0C7A:0002 MOV    DX,0100
0C7A:0005 CALL   00A1
0C7A:0008 MOV    AX,DS
0C7A:000A MOV    ES,AX
0C7A:000C MOV    SI,0127
0C7A:000F MOV    DI,005C
0C7A:0012 MOV    CX,0023
```

```
0C7A:0015 REP     MOVSB
0C7A:0017 MOV     BYTE [014A],04
0C7A:001C MOV     CL,11
0C7A:001E MOV     DX,005C
-L
```

The Move Command

The M or move command is used to move a block of data from one area of memory to another. The form is:

Ms,f,d

where s is a 20-bit starting address, f is a 16-bit ending offset, and d is the 20-bit address of the destination. If the segment is not specified in d, DDT will use the s segment address.

No checks are made to insure that the block doesn't overlap either the operating system or part of itself. For example, if the destination overlaps the source, part of the source will be overwritten and will not get copied.

The Read Command

The R or read command is identical to the E command except that it doesn't free up any previously allocated memory (allocated by another E or R command). The form

R<filename>

where filename may include both the name and file type of a file. Like the E command, the allocation addresses of the segments are displayed. The V command can be used to redisplay the segment start and end addresses. Up to seven files can be read in using the R command, because only eight memory allocations are allowed by the BDOS, (seven, plus DDT-86 itself). If the file doesn't exist or if there isn't sufficient memory to load the file (without overlapping another memory allocation area), DDT will issue an error message.

The Set Command

The S or set command allows the user to change the contents of memory (either bytes or 16-bit words). The forms are:

Ss
SWs

The first form is for bytes, the second for words. The s argument is a
20-bit address. If the segment address isn't given, DDT assumes that
you wish to modify the data segment. For example, if a program is
loaded with the E or R command and the data segment or DS register is
set to OC80H, the display will show:

S0100
OC80:0100 xx

where xx is the contents of that address. If the 16-bit or word form of
the command is used, the following would result:

SW0100
OC80:0100 xxxx

where xxxx is the 16-bit value at 0100 and 0101 (hexadecimal) in
memory.

When the address and contents line is displayed, you have three
choices: (1) hit return, which leaves the byte or word unchanged; (2) enter a new hexadecimal value and hit return; or (3) enter a period (or
other non-hexadecimal character) to terminate the S command. If the
memory location can't be changed, DDT will issue an error message indicating that the memory location is either faulty or nonexistant.

The Trace Command

The T or trace command allows the user to trace program execution for one to OFFFFH (65535) instructions. The forms are:

T
Tn
TS
TSn

The first form simply executes one instruction at the current code segment and instruction pointer (program counter) location. The second
form has the argument n, which is the number of instructions to
execute.

The third and fourth forms are the same as the first two, respectively, except that when each instruction is executed, all registers (in-

cluding the segment registers) will be displayed, instead of just the regular registers. If the S is added to the command, the register display will be the same as the X command.

If a large number of instructions are executed, it is possible to abort the command by typing any character. After the T command is executed, the address of the next instruction to be executed is placed in the list address used by the list command.

Note: Whenever a BDOS interrupt (INT 224) is executed, DDT simply traps it and returns as if only one instruction were executed. This has the effect of making the BDOS call appear as one instruction, rather than tracing all the way through the operating system.

The Untrace Command

The U or untrace command is identical to the trace command (although the name of the command would indicate otherwise) except that it can trace a large number of instructions without displaying the CPU registers for each instruction. The form is:

```
U
Un
US
USn
```

The n is the number of instructions to execute before returning control to DDT. This command can be aborted by typing any character on the console.

The Value Command

The V or value command displays segment memory allocations for the last program loaded with either the E or R commands. The form is:

```
V
```

If the E command was last used to load a file, the start and end addresses of each segment (i.e., code and data) loaded will be displayed. If the R command was used, the start and end addresses of the entire block of memory allocated to the program will be displayed.

If neither the E or R command has been used (and if no file was specified on the command line when DDT-86 was invoked), then the V command will respond with a question mark (?).

The Write Command

The W or write command can be used to write the contents of a contiguous block of memory to a file on disk. The forms are:

W < filename >
W < filename > ,s,f

where filename is any valid name with optional file type of the destination disk file. The s and f arguments are the optional 20-bit start and end addresses of the block to be written. As with all DDT commands, if the second segment address isn't specified, the segment address of the first argument (s) will be used.

The first form of the command uses the last allocated segment start and end addresses (from the R command) to determine what to write to the file. If the file wasn't read with an R command, DDT will display a question mark (?) indicating an error. The first form is useful when making patches to a file, assuming that the length hasn't been changed.

When the second form is used, the bottom four bits of the start and stop 20-bit addresses aren't used, so the data to be written must always reside on a 16-byte boundary.

Note: If a file with the name specified in the W command exists on disk, it will be deleted before DDT writes the new file.

The Examine CPU Registers Command

The X or examine command allows the user to examine the contents of all CPU registers and flags (the registers and flags for the program being debugged). Also, the values can be altered with this command. The forms are:

X
Xr
Xf

where r is an abbreviation for a register, and f is an abbreviation for a CPU flag.

The first form displays all registers and flags of the program being debugged and displays the mnemonic of the next instruction to be executed. The display format is:

```
     AX   BX   CX        SP   BP   SI   DI   CS   DS   SS
---- xxxx xxxx xxxx xxxx xxxx xxxx xxxx xxxx xxxx xxxx xxxx
ES   IP
xxxx xxxx <instruction mnemonic>
```

The first nine dashes are the nine CPU flags. If the flag is not set, a dash will appear. If set, the abbreviation of the flag will appear. Each register will have a value from 0000 to FFFF in hexadecimal. The CPU flags are abbreviated as follows:

O   Overflow
D   Direction
I   Interrupt Enable
T   Trap
S   Sign
Z   Zero
A   Auxiliary Carry
P   Parity
C   Carry

The second form of the X command allows the user to change register values in the CPU state of the program being tested. This means that after each instruction, the value of a register could be altered. This feature is very useful if, for example, a long loop (where CX is counting down to zero) could be quickly stepped through by changing the CX register to 0001H. It is also useful if the program being tested generated one bad value, but the rest of the program operates normally. The value could be changed in order to test the remainder of the program.

If the command

XCS

were entered, DDT would respond with:

CS 0C30

and wait for the new value. If return is typed, the value will be unchanged. If a new value is entered and return typed, the register will be updated. If a period is typed, the command will be aborted. If a return is entered, the next register (going from left to right on the display) will be displayed along with its hexadecimal value, and you will have the opportunity to modify it.

The third form allows the user to change the state of one of the CPU flags. DDT will respond as it would for a register, except the current value of a flag will be displayed. The new value must be entered as either zero (0) or one (1). Unlike the register command, the flag command only modifies one flag per Xf command.

Assembly Language Syntax for A and L commands

Most assembly language instructions used in DDT-86 conform to the standard 8086 assembly language. However, some minor differences do occur:

1. DDT-86 only uses hexadecimal values as operands.
2. Up to three prefixes (lock, repeat, segment override) may appear in one statement, but they all precede the mnemonic of the instruction. A prefix may be entered on a line by itself.
3. Some instructions must specify byte or word mode. The following byte and word string instructions are different from that of standard language format:

byte	word
LODSB	LODSW
STOSB	STOSW
SCASB	SCASW
MOVSB	MOVSW
CMPSB	CMPSW

4. The instruction mnemonics for near and far transfer of control instructions are as follows:

short	normal	far
JMPS	JMP	JMPF
	CALL	CALLF
	RET	RETF

5. If the operand of a CALLF or JMPF instruction is a 20-bit address, it must be entered as follows: ssss:aaaa
   where ssss is the segment address, and aaaa is the offset within the segment.
6. In the assembler, type information is kept on each symbol. Since DDT doesn't have access to this information, all byte and word distinctions in instructions are ambiguous. The operands must be preceded by the byte or word prefix to specify the type of the operand. These prefixes may be abbreviated as BY and WO.

```
INC    BYTE[DI]
ADD    BYTE [3000],34
OR     WORD [3400],0111
```

The prefix must be included or an error message will result.
7. All operands that directly address memory are enclosed in square brackets. This must be done to distinguish them from immediate values.

```
CMP AX,5        ;compare AX with the number 5
CMP AX,[5]      ;compare AX with the contents of location 5
                 in memory.
```

8. The forms of register indirect memory operands are:

```
[pointer register]
[index register]
[pointer register + index register]
```

where the pointer registers are BX and BP, and the index registers are SI and DI. Any of these forms can be preceded by a numeric offset.

```
MOV BX,[SI]
MOV BX,[BP]
ADD BX,[BP + SI]
MOV BX,100[BP + SI]
```

DDT-86 Debugging Session

The following listing is given to show how DDT can be used to disassemble, display memory, and trace the execution of a program. The program being debugged in this example is the same DIR command given in the listing in Appendix III. Refer to the listing in Appendix III to see what the source program mnemonics and symbols look like.

```
A>ddt86 b:my-dir.cmd

DDT86 1.1
        START         END
CS  0C7A:0000  0C7A:00AF
DS  0C85:0000  0C85:014F
-

-LO

0C7A:0000  MOV      CL,09
0C7A:0002  MOV      DX,0100
0C7A:0005  CALL     00A1
0C7A:0008  MOV      AX,DS
```

```
0C7A:000A MOV      ES,AX
0C7A:000C MOV      SI,0127
0C7A:000F MOV      DI,005C
0C7A:0012 MOV      CX,0023
0C7A:0015 REP      MOVSB
0C7A:0017 MOV      BYTE [014A],04
0C7A:001C MOV      CL,11
0C7A:001E MOV      DX,005C
-L

0C7A:0021 CALL     00A1
0C7A:0024 CMP      AL,FF
0C7A:0026 JZ       003C
0C7A:0028 CALL     0044
0C7A:002B MOV      CL,12
0C7A:002D MOV      DX,005C
0C7A:0030 CALL     00A1
0C7A:0033 CMP      AL,FF
0C7A:0035 JZ       003C
0C7A:0037 CALL     0044
0C7A:003A JMPS     002B
0C7A:003C CALL     00A4
-D0

0C85:0000 AF 00 00 7A 0C 00 4F 01 00 85 0C 00 00 00 00 00   ...z..O.........
0C85:0010 00 00 00 00 00 00 00 00 00 00 00 00 00 00 00 00   ................
0C85:0020 00 00 00 00 00 00 00 00 00 00 00 00 00 00 00 00   ................
0C85:0030 00 00 00 00 00 00 00 00 00 00 00 00 00 00 00 00   ................
0C85:0040 00 00 00 00 00 00 00 00 00 00 00 00 00 00 00 00   ................
0C85:0050 00 00 00 00 00 00 00 00 00 00 00 00 00 20 20 20   .............
0C85:0060 20 20 20 20 20 20 20 20 00 00 00 00 00 20 20 20        .....
0C85:0070 20 20 20 20 20 20 20 20 00 00 00 00 00 00 00 00        .......
0C85:0080 00 00 00 00 00 00 00 00 00 00 00 00 00 00 00 00   ................
0C85:0090 00 00 00 00 00 00 00 00 00 00 00 00 00 00 00 00   ................
0C85:00A0 00 00 00 00 00 00 00 00 00 00 00 00 00 00 00 00   ................
0C85:00B0 00 00 00 00 00 00 00 00 00 00 00 00 00 00 00 00   ................
-D

0C85:00C0 00 00 00 00 00 00 00 00 00 00 00 00 00 00 00 00   ................
0C85:00D0 00 00 00 00 00 00 00 00 00 00 00 00 00 00 00 00   ................
0C85:00E0 00 00 00 00 00 00 00 00 00 00 00 00 00 00 00 00   ................
0C85:00F0 00 00 00 00 00 00 00 00 00 00 00 00 00 00 00 00   ................
0C85:0100 44 69 72 65 63 74 6F 72 79 20 43 6F 6D 6D 61 6E   Directory Comman
0C85:0110 64 0D 0A 24 20 3A 20 20 20 20 20 20 20 20 20 2E   d..$ :         .
0C85:0120 20 20 20 00 0D 0A 24 00 3F 3F 3F 3F 3F 3F 3F 3F   ...$.????????
0C85:0130 3F 3F 3F 00 00 00 00 00 00 00 00 00 00 00 00 00   ???.............
0C85:0140 00 00 00 00 00 00 00 00 00 00 00 00 00 00 00 00   ................
0C85:0150 5F 36 00 9A 0C 01 5F 36 00 00 00 00 00 00 00 00   _6...._6........
0C85:0160 00 00 00 00 00 00 00 00 00 00 00 00 00 00 00 00   ................
0C85:0170 00 00 00 00 00 00 00 00 00 00 00 00 00 00 00 00   ................
-X

           AX   BX   CX   DX   SP   BP   SI   DI   CS   DS   SS   ES   IP
--I------ 0000 0000 0000 0000 092C 0000 0000 0000 0C7A 0C85 0051 0C85 0000
MOV    CL,09
-G0,0

*0C7A:0000
-T

           AX   BX   CX   DX   SP   BP   SI   DI   IP
--I------ 0000 0000 0000 0000 092C 0000 0000 0000 0000 MOV    CL,09
*0C7A:0002
-T
```

```
              AX    BX    CX    DX    SP    BP    SI    DI    IP
--I------- 0000  0000  0009  0000  092C  0000  0000  0000  0002 MOV    DX,0100
*0C7A:0005
-T


              AX    BX    CX    DX    SP    BP    SI    DI    IP
--I------- 0000  0000  0009  0100  092C  0000  0000  0000  0005 CALL   00A1
*0C7A:00A1
-T


              AX    BX    CX    DX    SP    BP    SI    DI    IP
--I------- 0000  0000  0009  0100  092A  0000  0000  0000  00A1 INT    E0Directory Command

*0C7A:00A3
-T


              AX    BX    CX    DX  - SP    BP    SI    DI    IP
--I------- 0000  0000  0113  010A  092A  0000  0000  0000  00A3 RET
*0C7A:0008
-T


              AX    BX    CX    DX    SP    BP    SI    DI    IP
--I------- 0000  0000  0113  010A  092C  0000  0000  0000  0008 MOV    AX,DS
*0C7A:000A
-T


              AX    BX    CX    DX    SP    BP    SI    DI    IP
--T  --- 0C85  0000  0113  010A  092C  0000  0000  0000  000A MOV    ES,AX
*0C7A:000C
-T


              AX    BX    CX    DX    SP    BP    SI  . DI  . IP
--I------- 0C85  0000  0113  010A  092C  0000  0000  0000  000C MOV    SI,0127
*0C7A:000F
-T


              AX    BX    CX    DX    SP    BP    SI    DI    IP

--I------- 0C85  0000  0113  010A  092C  0000  0127  0000  000F MOV    DI,005C
*0C7A:0012
-L


0C7A:0012 MOV    CX,0023
0C7A:0015 REP    MOVSB
0C7A:0017 MOV    BYTE [014A],04
0C7A:001C MOV    CL,11
0C7A:001E MOV    DX,005C
0C7A:0021 CALL   00A1
0C7A:0024 CMP    AL,FF
0C7A:0026 JZ     003C
0C7A:0028 CALL   0044
0C7A:002B MOV    CL,12
0C7A:002D MOV    DX,005C
0C7A:0030 CALL   00A1
-L


0C7A:0033 CMP    AL,FF
0C7A:0035 JZ     003C
0C7A:0037 CALL   0044
0C7A:003A JMPS   002B
0C7A:003C CALL   00A4
0C7A:003F MOV    CL,00
0C7A:0041 CALL   00A1
```

```
-G,3A
 : ASM86    .CMD : TOD     .CMD

*0C7A:003A
-X

              AX   BX   CX   DX   SP   BP   SI   DI   CS   DS   SS   ES   IP
--I------ 0003 0123 0044 0000 092C 0000 0123 0123 0C7A 0C85 0051 0051 003A
JMPS    002B
-T5

              AX   BX   CX   DX   SP   BP   SI   DI   IP
--I------ 0003 0123 0044 0000 092C 0000 0123 0123 003A JMPS    002B
--I------ 0003 0123 0044 0000 092C 0000 0123 0123 002B MOV     CL,12
--I------ 0003 0123 0012 0000 092C 0000 0123 0123 002D MOV     DX,005C
--I------ 0003 0123 0012 005C 092C 0000 0123 0123 0030 CALL    00A1
--I------ 0003 0123 0012 005C 092A 0000 0123 0123 00A1 INT     E0
*0C7A:00A3
-DCS:0

0C7A:0000 B1 09 BA 00 01 E8 99 00 8C D8 8E C0 BE 27 01 BF  .............'..
0C7A:0010 5C 00 B9 23 00 F3 A4 C6 06 4A 01 04 B1 11 BA 5C  \..#.....J.....\
0C7A:0020 00 E8 7D 00 3C FF 74 14 E8 19 00 B1 12 BA 5C 00  ..}.<.t.......\.
0C7A:0030 E8 6E 00 3C FF 74 05 E8 0A 00 EB EF E8 65 00 B1  .n.<.t.......e..
0C7A:0040 00 E8 5D 00 8C DB 8E C3 B1 05 D2 E0 BA 80 00 03  ..].............
0C7A:0050 D0 8B F2 46 BF 17 01 B9 08 00 F3 A4 B9 03 00 BF  ...F............
0C7A:0060 20 01 F3 A4 BE 17 01 BF 17 01 B9 0C 00 AC 24 7F   .............$.
0C7A:0070 88 05 47 E2 F8 BA 14 01 E8 12 00 A0 4A 01 FE 0E  ..G.........J...
0C7A:0080 4A 01 75 08 E8 1D 00 C6 06 4A 01 04 C3 8B DA 8A  J.u......J......
0C7A:0090 17 0A D2 74 0B 53 B1 02 E8 06 00 5B 43 E9 EF FF  ...t.S.....[C...
0C7A:00A0 C3 CD E0 C3 B1 09 BA 24 01 E8 F5 FF C3 00 00 00  .......$........
0C7A:00B0 AF 00 00 7A 0C 00 4F 01 00 85 0C 00 00 00 00 00  ...z..O.........
-
```

5

The BDOS and How to Use It

5.1 The Role of the BDOS in the System

BDOS stands for the basic disk operating system. The BDOS is the nucleus or heart of CP/M. All requests made of the operating system are made through it. The advantages of such a mechanism are obvious: if all commands are processed by one standard routine, then software written for one computer and version of CP/M will run identically on all other implementations of CP/M (on different computer systems, but the same microprocessor). In the early days of microcomputers, everyone developed their own operating systems and their own utility subroutines. Since they were all developed independently, no standards existed, so converting a program from one computer to another (even with the same microprocessor) was nearly impossible.

CP/M has evolved into a standard, largely because it is one of the most widely used operating systems, not because it is the best. When CP/M became available on the 8080 and Z80 microcomputers, many manufacturers of both software and hardware began making their products "CP/M compatible."

The issue of compatibility is directly tied to the BDOS and is somewhat tied to memory organization. All CP/M-80 programs have to be written to load at 0100H in memory. CP/M-86 programs load at offset 0000H from the code segment register, but their data segments (the portion of the program containing all variables, storage buffers, strings, etc.) must load at 0100H as in CP/M-80. The operating system assumes that this is the case and has problems if it isn't. Certain memory locations are used by CP/M-80 in low memory, from 0000H to 00FFH (and at data segment offset 0000H to 00FFH in CP/M-86), and must not be disturbed by a user program.

As shown below, CP/M-80 resides at the top of the available memory (64K bytes in this example), CP/M-86 resides at the bottom of memory. The philosophy behind placing CP/M-80 at the top of memory is based on the fact that 8080 programs cannot be easily relocated to any address in memory. Programs have been written to relocate specially designed files, but CP/M-80 doesn't have this capability built into it. Since relocatability is not practical, all programs must be written to load at 0100H. The problem comes when CP/M-80 is implemented for systems with less than 64K bytes. A utility program called MOVCPM was provided with the operating system to allow it to be moved up or down in memory as needed. In this way, programs written to load at 0100H could be run on all CP/M-80 systems, even if the operating system is located at a different address.

CP/M-86 was designed with relocatability in mind, so no complicated relocation programs were needed. Since all programs are based on

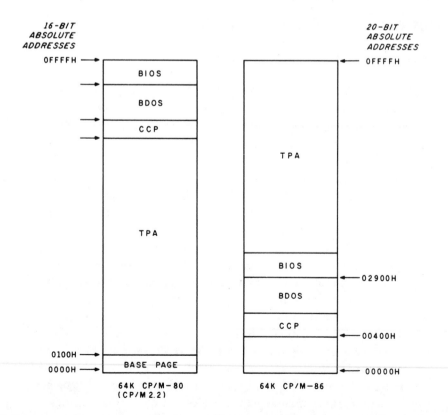

the use of the segment registers, you need only load a program at some arbitrary location in memory and set the segment registers to that starting location. Hence, CP/M-86 can reside anywhere in memory, and so can application programs. The issue of memory allocation (as it applies to the location of CP/M-86 and other programs) is not important. It should be noted that, if desired, CP/M-86 can be placed anywhere in memory, depending on the needs of the user.

Certain memory registers are used by the BDOS, and care must be taken when passing parameters to it. Also, after a BDOS call, some registers might be changed. The most important compatibility issue is that of exclusive use of the BDOS call for all I/O and other available services. If a program communicates directly with an input or output device, it may not work on another brand of computer. You must strictly

WHEN CP/M IS IN CONTROL.

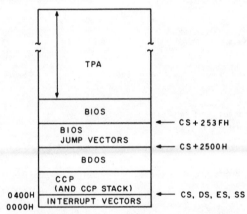

WHEN APPLICATION PROGRAM IS IN CONTROL
(USING THE "SMALL MODEL"
FOR SEGMENT MANAGEMENT)

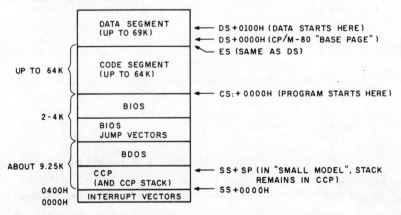

Figure 5.1: CP/M-86 memory map.

adhere to the BDOS conventions to insure the full compatibility or portability of software across all implementations of CP/M-86.

Figure 5.1 shows a CP/M-86 memory map. The BDOS is always resident in the system after CP/M has been loaded. The CCP or console command processor is also resident and is located next to the BDOS. In CP/M-80, the CCP is reloaded after each warm start to make sure it is intact. In CP/M-86, it is not reloaded except on a cold start.

5.2 8086 Architecture

Before continuing, it will be necessary to discuss the internal organization of the 8086 and 8088 microprocessors. Figure 5.2 shows the registers available to the programmer.

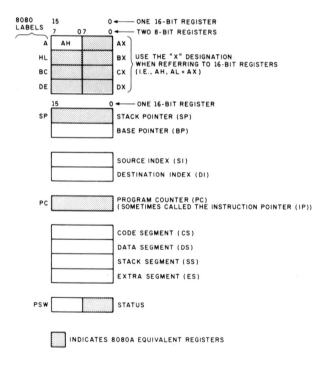

Figure 5.2:   8086 registers.

The AX, BX, CX, and DX registers are all 16 bits wide. Each of these are actually two 8-bit registers called AH, AL, BH, BL and so on, where the H and L are short for "high" and "low" respectively. When referring to registers, AX refers to the 16-bit "A" register, while AL would refer to the 8-bit "lower half" of the A register.

Since memory is addressable up to one megabyte on the 8086, some way must be provided to access all of it, since a 16-bit register can only address 65535 bytes. On the 8086, the four segment registers, CS or code segment, DS or data segment, SS or stack segment, and ES or extra segment extend the addressing range as follows: the 16-bit value of each segment register is shifted left four bits (multiplied by 16) to make it into a 20-bit address that can access one megabyte. The CS or code segment register is used to address one megabyte, but it is also used to make programs totally relocatable. The value of the program counter (PC or IP) is added to it to get the displacement into the current code segment. In this manner, the CS register can be set to the start of a 64K-byte block anywhere in memory (on any 16-byte boundry that is), and a program can reside at the start of the segment. As far as the program is concerned, it always appears to be at the bottom of a 64K-byte block of memory.

The data segment is used in a similar fashion and allows up to 64K bytes of data to be accessed at one time. A total of 256K bytes of memory can be accessed at one time when the CS, DS, ES, and SS registers are used. If the program needs additional space, the segment registers can be changed dynamically to address other 64K-byte segments. The following diagram shows examples of the instruction sequences that allow segment registers to be changed.

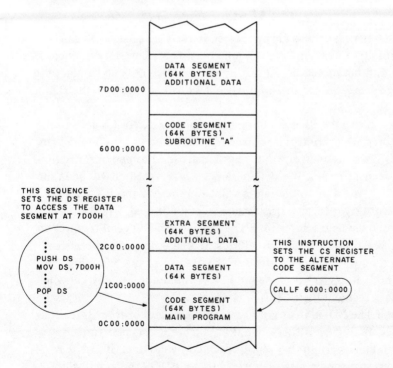

5.3 BDOS Function Calls

The BDOS is always called through 8086 software interrupt 224. Interrupt 224 has been reserved by Intel Corporation for CP/M-86 and MP/M-86. In CP/M-80, the BDOS is entered by issuing a call to location 0005H. Certain 8086 CPU registers are used by the BDOS to determine the nature of the request. Table 5.1 shows these conventions.

```
BDOS Entry Registers

CL:  Single byte function number (required)
DL:  Single byte parameter (as needed)
DX:  Word or two byte parameter (as needed)
DS:  Base address of data segment (required)

BDOS Return Registers

AL:          Byte value (usually the error code)
AX and BX:   Word or two byte value (as needed)
ES and BX:   Double-word value returned with
             offset address in BX
             and segment address in ES.
```

Table 5.1: Register conventions used by the BDOS. Upon entry, the BDOS function code must be in the CL register. The DS register normally does not need special attention, as long as it addresses the segment containing the File Control Block usually addressed by DX.

The function code is always passed in the CL register and can range from 0 to FFH or 255, although only 49 are currently defined. If the BDOS function requires a single-byte parameter, it can be placed in the DL register. A word or 16-bit parameter can be placed in the DX register.

On entry to the BDOS, all segment registers except ES are saved and restored when control is returned to the transient program. When the BDOS returns control, some registers are used to pass information back to your program. If a byte parameter is returned, it will be in the AL register. Word or 16-bit values will be in the AX and BX registers. A double-word (two 16-bit words) value will be returned with the offset in BX and the segment address in ES. Whenever a BDOS call requires an offset address in DX (the FCB address for example), the DS register must contain the segment address of the data segment containing the FCB. This is necessary because the BDOS could not possibly know in which data segment the FCB is located.

Note: The BDOS does not necessarily save and restore all registers (e.g., AX, BX), even if they are not used by the particular function called. To make certain that registers contain valid data, it is wise to save and restore any registers in use before a BDOS function call.

Func	Description	Entry parameters (CL = function #)	Results
0	System Reset	DL = abort code	
1	Console Input		AL = ASCII character
2	Console Output	DL = ASCII character	
3	Reader Input		AL = ASCII character
4	Punch Output	DL = ASCII character	
5	List Output	DL = ASCII character	
6	Direct Console I/O	DL = (OFFH, input) (OFEH, status) or ASCII character	AL = ASCII character or status
7	Get I/O Byte		AL = I/O byte value
8	Set I/O Byte	DL = I/O byte value	
9	Print String	DX = String offset address	
10	Read Console Buffer	DX = Buffer offset address	characters in buffer
11	Get Console Status		AL = console status
12	Return Version Number		BX = version number
13	Reset Disk System		
14	Select Disk	DL = selected disk	
15	Open File	DX = FCB offset address	AL = return code
16	Close File	DX = FCB offset address	AL = return code
17	Search for First	DX = FCB offset address	AL = directory code
18	Search for Next		AL = directory code
19	Delete File	DX = FCB offset address	AL = return code
20	Read Sequential	DX = FCB offset address	AL = return code
21	Write Sequential	DX = FCB offset address	AL = return code
22	Make File	DX = FCB offset address	AL = return code
23	Rename File	DX = FCB(old name, new name)	AL = return code
24	Return Login Vector		BX = login vector
25	Return Current Disk		AL = current disk
26	Set DMA Address	DX = DMA offset address	
27	Get Addr(Alloc)		ES,BX = alloc addr
28	Write Protect Disk		
29	Get Addr(R/O Vector)		BX = R/O vector value
30	Set File Attributes	DX = FCB offset address	AL = return code
31	Get Addr(Disk Parms)		ES,BX = DPB addr
32	Set/Get User Code	DL = (OFFH, get) or usercode	AL = current code
33	Read Random	DX = FCB offset address	AL = return code
34	Write Random	DX = FCB offset address	AL = return code
35	Compute File Size	DX = FCB offset address	r0, r1, r2 set
36	Set Random Record	DX = FCB offset address	r0, r1, r2 set
37	Reset Drive	DX = drive vector	AL = 00H
40	Write Random with Zero Fill	DX = FCB offset address	AL = return code
50	Direct BIOS Call	DX = BIOS Descriptor	AX, BX as set by BIOS
51	Set DMA Base	DX = Base Address	
52	Get DMA Base		ES,BX = DMA address
53	Get Max Mem	DX = Offset of MCB	AL = return code
54	Get Abs Mem	DX = Offset of MCB	AL = return code
55	Alloc Mem	DX = Offset of MCB	AL = return code
56	Alloc Abs Mem	DX = Offset of MCB	AL = return code
57	Free Mem		
58	Free All Mem		
59	Program Load	DX = FCB offset address	AX = return code or BX = base page addr

Table 5.2: CP/M-86 BDOS function calls include entry and return parameters.

It is often convenient to break up the BDOS function calls into logical groups. The simplest of the functions are the non-disk-related calls. Other groups include the disk function calls and the memory management functions.

5.4 Non-disk BDOS Calls

Many BDOS functions are provided to handle simple requests such as console-input, console-output, and print-string. Functions 0 through 12 perform these requests. As shown in Table 5.2, each call may have entry parameters and may return results. The following sections lists each BDOS call.

System Reset The system reset function returns control to the CCP or console command processor. An abort code may be placed in DL. A zero code indicates that the active program terminated, while a 01H code indicates that the program has terminated but that the program is to remain in memory.

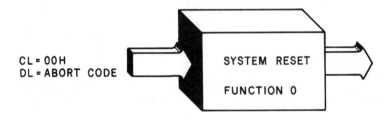

CL = 00H
DL = ABORT CODE

SYSTEM RESET

FUNCTION 0

Console Input The console input function reads a character from the logical console device and places it in the AL register. All printable ASCII characters, including carriage return, line feed, and backspace are echoed to the console, while tabs are expanded in columns of eight characters. The BDOS will wait for a character to be received before returning to the calling program, so it is wise to check the console status before reading a character if you cannot afford to have the system lock out, while waiting for a keystroke.

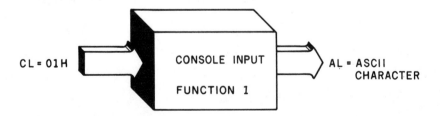

CL = 01H

CONSOLE INPUT

FUNCTION 1

AL = ASCII
CHARACTER

Console Output This function sends the character in the DL register to the logical console device. Tab characters are expanded in columns of eight characters, and a check is made for Control-S for start-stop scrolling on the screen. If Control-S is pressed while console output is active, output will be halted until another Control-S is pressed.

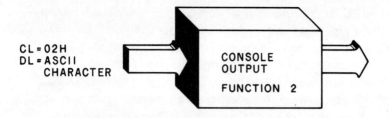

CL = 02H
DL = ASCII
   CHARACTER

CONSOLE
OUTPUT

FUNCTION 2

Reader Input Similar to the console input function, reader input reads a character from the logical reader device and returns it in the AL register. Unlike console input, characters such as tab are not treated specially. Control is returned to the calling program when a character is available.

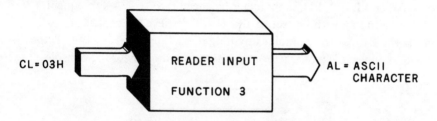

CL = 03H

READER INPUT

FUNCTION 3

AL = ASCII
   CHARACTER

Punch Output This function sends the character in DL to the logical punch device.

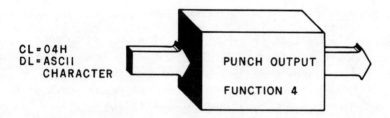

CL = 04H
DL = ASCII
   CHARACTER

PUNCH OUTPUT

FUNCTION 4

List Output This function sends the character in the DL register to the logical list device.

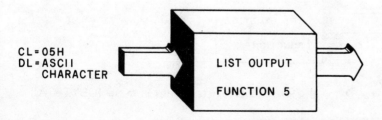

CL = 05H
DL = ASCII
   CHARACTER

LIST OUTPUT

FUNCTION 5

Direct Console I/O Sometimes it is necessary to receive unedited console input for a program that handles its own input editing. This function will either send or receive a character from the logical console device, but such control characters as control-S and control-P are passed on to the program, instead of being intercepted by the BDOS. This function is especially useful in converting programs from previous versions of CP/M where some of the console I/O was done directly through the BIOS. Direct use of the BIOS should always be avoided for compatibility reasons.

If the DL register contains an 0FFH value, the BDOS will return a character from the console. If no character is available, it will wait for one. If the DL register contains an 0FEH value, the status of the console will be returned. If AL is equal to zero, a character hasn't yet been received. If AL if 0FFH, a character has been received. A subsequent call to function 6 with DL set to 0FFH will retrieve the character.

If the DL register contains anything other than 0FFH or 0FEH, the BDOS assumes it is a character and will send it directly to the console.

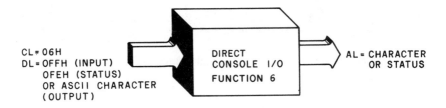

Get I/O Byte The I/O byte is provided in CP/M as a way of assigning physical devices to logical devices. The I/O byte contains the current assignments of the logical devices. The I/O byte contains the current assignments of the logical devices designated as: console, reader, punch, and list. The IOBYTE must be properly implemented in the BIOS for this function to work. See Chapter 6.

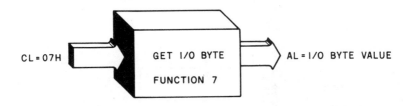

Set I/O Byte The value of the DL register is stored in the IOBYTE. All logical devices may be reassigned using this function. See Chapter 6 for details.

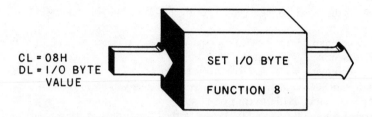

CL = 08H
DL = I/O BYTE
    VALUE

Print String   This function sends the string of ASCII characters in memory at the location pointed to by DX to the logical console device. A dollar sign $ character terminates this string. This function expands tabs, checks for control-S start/stop scrolling, and checks for printer echo (control-P).

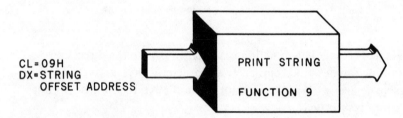

CL = 09H
DX = STRING
    OFFSET ADDRESS

Read Console Buffer   This function takes much of the work out of reading in and editing a string of characters for subsequent processing. The read buffer reads in characters one at a time, until the buffer is full, or until a return or line feed is detected. The address of the buffer is placed in DX and takes the following form:

CL = 0AH
DX = BUFFER
    OFFSET ADDRESS

The mx byte tells the BDOS the maximum buffer size, while the nc byte is returned by the BDOS and indicates the actual number of characters in the buffer (upon completion). The mx byte must be loaded before calling this function and may range from 1 to 255. If mx is set to zero, the BDOS will treat it as a one.

The following line-editing characters are supported:

^E	Moves the cursor to the beginning of the following line without erasing the buffer.
^H	This command is identical to backspace.
^I	This command is identical to tab.
^M	This command is identical to carriage return.
^R	Retype the current buffer contents (redisplay what you have typed in).
^U	Reset the input buffer to empty.
^X	Reset the input buffer and backspace to the start of the line, erasing all characters.
^S	Stop display scrolling. Pressing any key will start scrolling again.
^C	Abort the current program or restart CP/M (must be the first character entered on the line).
Return	Enter the command line or terminate text entry.
Backspace	Erase the last character entered on the line.
Tab	Move the cursor to the next tab stop (every 8th column).

Get Console Status   This function is similar in part to the direct console I/O function described earlier. If a character is present at the logical console device, a 01H value is returned in the AL register. If it is not ready, a zero is returned.

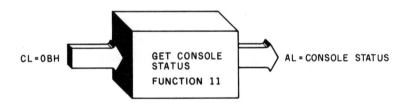

CL = 0BH   GET CONSOLE STATUS FUNCTION 11   AL = CONSOLE STATUS

Return Version Number   Some programs require a certain version of CP/M to operate. To allow the programmer to easily determine which version is present, this function returns two bytes in the BH and BL (collectively, BX) registers. The BH register is set to one if MP/M is running and to zero if CP/M is running. The BL register contains the hexadecimal number 20H indicating version 2, with subsequent versions given as: 21H, 22H... 2FH. The initial release of CP/M-86 returns a 22H to be compatible with CP/M-80.

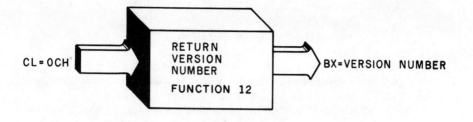

5.5 Disk-Related BDOS Functions

The most complicated BDOS functions are the disk interface routines. All file operations require a pointer or address that references a file control block (FCB). The file control block is a 36-byte data area that is used by CP/M and by the user to keep track of the location and attributes of a disk file. File control blocks are normally stored on disk in the disk directory, but are loaded individually into memory when a program requests to open a file.

File Control Block (FCB):

	dr	f1	...	f7	f8	t1	t2	t3	ex	s1	s2	rc	d0	...	dn	cr	r0	r1	r2
decimal	00	01	...	07	08	09	10	11	12	13	14	15	16	...	31	32	33	34	35
hex	00	01	...	07	08	09	0A	0B	0C	0D	0E	0F	10	...	1F	20	21	22	23
default fcb	-5C	5D	...	5F	60	61	62	63	64	65	66	67	68	...	7B	7C	7D	7E	7F

where: dr Drive code (0 – 16)
              0 → use default drive for file
              1 → select disk drive A
              2 → select disk drive B
              . . .
              16 → select disk drive P

f1 – f8 File name field (uppercase ASCII with bit 7 = 0)

t1 – t3 File type field (uppercase ASCII)
              Bit 7 of each character (denoted as t1′, t2′, and t3′ are used as follows:
              t1′ → 1 = read only file
              t2′ → 1 = SYS file, 0 = DIR file
              t3′ → 1 = file has been archived (not used by CP/M)

ex Contains current extent number.
              ex is normally set to zero by the user when a file is opened, but can range from 0 to 31 when in use.

s1	Reserved for internal use.
s2	Reserved for internal use.
rc	Record count in current extent; ranges from 0 to 128.
d0 – dn	File allocation blocks (used by CP/M only).
cr	current record to read or write in a sequential file operation, normally set to zero by user when the file is opened.
r0 – r2	Optional random record number in the range 0 – 65535, with overflow to r2. r0 and r1 form a 16-bit word value with r0 as the low byte and r1 as the high byte.

Figure 5.3: The File Control Block.

In most modern operating systems, files are not necessarily stored sequentially on disk. The individual records of a file are stored separately on disk wherever there happens to be empty space. Figure 5.4 shows a typical disk file storage map.

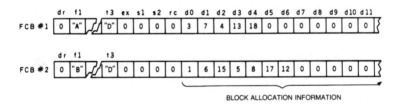

BLOCK ALLOCATION INFORMATION

PHYSICAL BLOCK #	CONTENTS	PHYSICAL BLOCK #	
0		12	BASIS
1	THIS SEQUENCE	13	THE AID
2		14	
3	THIS IS THE TIME	15	"ALLOCATION BLOCKS"
4	TO COME TO	16	
5	SHOWS HOW CP/M–86	17	ON A BLOCK BY BLOCK
6	OF LOGICAL 1K BYTE	18	OF THEIR COUNTRY.
7	FOR ALL GOOD MEN	19	
8	ALLOCATES DISK SPACE	20	

Figure 5.4: Disk allocation map and sample FCBs.

This organization makes it easier to manage a disk, although it becomes less obvious to the user. Older microcomputer operating systems used a sequential allocation system that required the user to "pack" the disk periodically to squeeze out all the blank spaces left by deleted files. CP/M-86 automatically reclaims the space left by deleted files and reuses it when new files are created. The result is a mosaic of records from different files. From the point of view of the user, the allocation method will always be transparent and in no way affects daily operation.

As shown in Figure 5.3, the first 33 bytes of the FCB are always required and are actually recorded in the disk directory. The last three bytes are used for random file access when the file is open and the FCB is in memory. The default FCB (set up by CP/M for an application program) is located at offset 005CH from the DS register.

5.6 Disk-Related BDOS Errors

Three errors are possible when working with disk files. Almost all error conditions are caused by some physical hardware errors inherent in disk drives. When one occurs, the BDOS will list one of the following messages on the logical console device:

```
BDOS ERR ON x: BAD SECTOR
BDOS ERR ON x: SELECT
BDOS ERR ON x: R/O
```

The x: indicates the disk drive (A: through P:) on which the error was detected. When an error condition arises, the BDOS will suspend operations and wait for a keyboard response. The allowed responses are discussed along with each of the errors below.

Bad Sector   This error is issued when an actual read or write sector command generates an error at the hardware level. This usually means that a flaw exists on the disk. Depending on the microcomputer system and the way CP/M-86 has been implemented, it may also mean that a disk was not inserted in the drive or that a disk was inserted that is not compatible with the disk format specified by the manufacturer of the microcomputer system.

Response: The user may respond in two ways. A Control-C will terminate the current program and return to the console command processor in CP/M. A return will cause the error to be ignored by the

BDOS. The latter response may cause unpredictable results. The BDOS may return a file record that contains garbage data, or it may simply repeat the bad sector error. If in doubt, terminate the program. It is better to stop the program than to risk losing valuable data, or, worse yet, to make a disk unreadable by accidentally writing on it in the wrong place.

Select   This error only occurs when a disk (A: through P:) is not supported by the implementation of CP/M-86 that you are using. If, for example, disks A: and B: are available, and the user makes a reference to disk C:, the error message would result. This error can also occur if a program has a logic error and begins executing instructions in incorrect sequence. The FCB may be changed inadvertently, and a subsequent select disk command would request a nonexistent disk drive.

Response: Since the selected disk drive is not available, there is no possible way to ignore the error. CP/M-86 causes the active program to terminate when any key is struck. A warm-start is not performed after this error.

R/O   This message means read/only and occurs when a disk drive has been marked by CP/M as a read/only disk. This can happen for two reasons. Disk drives can be made read/only by using the STAT command or by BDOS function call 28 (write-protect disk). The other reason is if a disk is inserted in a drive without first performing a warm-start (enter Control-C on the console) to reset the disk system. This annoyance is due to a feature of the BDOS that checks the directory entries of the disk currently in a drive to make sure it is the logged disk. If the disk has been changed without logging it (by warm-starting), the disk is marked read/only to protect it.

Response: If any character is struck on the console, the program will abort and control will return to the console command processor. Before proceeding, you must issue a warm-start to reset the disk system. This is not done automatically after the abort action.

5.7 BDOS Functions 13 through 40

The following BDOS functions are directly related to the disk system and file management and, with a few exceptions, are compatible with CP/M-80 disk functions.

Reset Disk System This function is used to reset the entire disk system. All disk drives are reset to a read/write condition (see functions 28 and 29), and disk drive A is selected as the currently logged drive. Function 37 (reset drive) can be used to reset just one drive. This function is similar to the warm-start issued by the CCP when a Control-C is entered on the console.

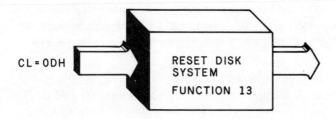

CL = ODH   RESET DISK SYSTEM

FUNCTION 13

Select Disk The disk drive specified in the DL register is named as the default disk drive. If the specified drive is reset (i.e., it is not marked read/only), it is also logged in as the currently active drive. This condition will remain until a cold-start, a warm-start, a drive reset (function 37), or disk system reset (function 13) is performed. All file references that do not refer to a disk drive will automatically refer to the default or selected disk.

The DL register may range from 0 (drive A) to 15 (drive P). On subsequent read or write operations, if the drive code byte of an FCB contains a 00H, the default drive will automatically be used. If the drive code contains a 01H, drive A will be referenced; 02H refers to drive B and so on to 10H for drive P. This is one major inconsistency of the BDOS functions. A code of 00H refers to the default drive in some functions and to drive A in others.

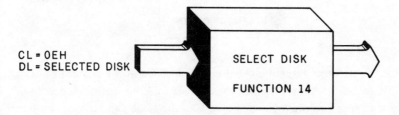

CL = OEH
DL = SELECTED DISK   SELECT DISK

FUNCTION 14

Open File This function causes the BDOS to activate the FCB (pointed to by DX) that specifies a file in the currently active user number. Byte 0, the drive code byte of the FCB, is used to select the disk drive. If it is 00H, the default drive is specified. The program is responsible for setting up the first 13 bytes of the FCB, which include the drive code, the file name and file type, and the extent value. Normally the extent byte is initialized to zero before the open file function is called. Also, the current record (cr) byte should be initialized to zero to read the first record of the file after it is opened. To be safe, it is wise to zero out the remainder of the FCB before attempting to open a file.

The open file function does support the use of a question mark (3FH) in any position of the file name or file type as a wild card character. If present, a question mark will cause the BDOS to accept any character in that position as valid when it searches the disk directory for the file.

If the file is found, the entire directory entry is copied into the remaining bytes of the FCB set up by the user. This means that the FCB with the file name that was used to open the file will be filled in by the BDOS to include all information about the file from the disk directory. Only the first (or specified) extent will be loaded. Subsequent extents (16K blocks of the file) will be loaded as needed by the BDOS. This means that only the first 16K bytes of the file can be directly accessed through the current FCB.

NOTE: Before using an FCB to read or write a file, an open-file or make-file operation must be performed. If this is not done, the FCB will reflect the allocation map of the actual file on disk, and other files on disk could be overwritten.

The open-file function returns a directory code from $\bar{0}$ through 3 if the open operation was successful and returns 0FFH (255 in decimal) if the file could not be found.

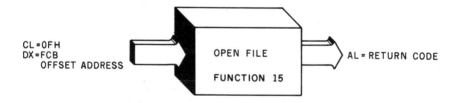

```
CL=0FH
DX=FCB                    OPEN FILE          AL = RETURN CODE
   OFFSET ADDRESS
                         FUNCTION 15
```

Close File   This function will close the file specified in the current FCB (in the DX register). Assuming that the current FCB has been opened properly with a call to open file or make file, the close function stores the FCB (possibly modified) in the disk directory on the specified drive. The return code is the same as open file (0 through 3 if successful; 0FFH if not).

If a file has been opened and only read from, there is no need to issue a close-file command since nothing has been changed in either the file or the directory. For compatibility with MP/M-86, it is recommended that all files be closed formally even if only read operations have taken place. MP/M does not deactivate FCBs the way CP/M does. If any information has been written to the file, it is essential that it be closed to update the directory.

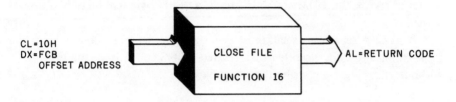

CL=10H
DX=FCB
   OFFSET ADDRESS

CLOSE FILE

FUNCTION 16

AL=RETURN CODE

Search for First   This function scans the directory for an entry that matches the FCB referenced by DX. If a file is found, a return code of 0 through 3 is returned and the FCB for the matched file can be found in the buffer used for disk operations at the current DMA address. The FCB is located at 32 times (AL × 32) the value in the AL register (shift the value of the AL register left 5 bits). If the directory entry is not found, the AL register will contain 0FFH.

This function accepts the question mark wild card character (3FH in ASCII) in the drive code, file name, file type, or extent fields. If a question mark is placed in the drive code field, the default disk drive is searched, and the search function will return any matching directory entry from any user number whether allocated or empty. This allows the programmer to read all directory entries regardless of their contents. If the drive code field does not contain a question mark, the standard search function is performed—matching only those directory entries that match the current user number and drive code. If the drive code byte is zero, then the s2 byte of the FCB will automatically be set to zero.

CL=11H
DX=FCB
   OFFSET ADDRESS

SEARCH FOR
FIRST
FUNCTION 17

AL=DIRECTORY CODE

Search Next   The search-next function is the same as the search-for-first function but the directory scan continues after the last matched directory entry. This allows the program to search for second occurrence of a directory entry. With the use of a wild card character (3FH), this function simplifies the process of locating all files with the same file name or file type.

As with the search-for-first function, a code of 0 through 3 is returned if a match is found, and the directory entry can be found in the buffer at (AL × 32). If no match is found, a 0FFH byte will be returned.

NOTE: A search-next call must occur after either a search-for-first or a search-next call. No other disk-related BDOS calls can be made without upsetting the continuity of the search.

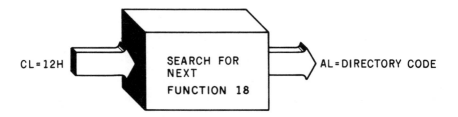

```
CL = 12H          SEARCH FOR        AL = DIRECTORY CODE
                  NEXT
                  FUNCTION 18
```

Delete File   The delete-file function is similar to the open-file function but removes a file (or files) that matches the FCB referenced by DX. The file name and file type may contain wild card characters (3FH). All files that match the FCB will be deleted in one operation. If the file name and file type fields contain all question marks, all files will be deleted in one call of delete file. The drive code byte of the FCB may not contain a wild card character. If successful, the function returns a zero in AL and, if not, returns a 0FFH.

```
CL = 13H
DX = FCB              DELETE FILE       AL = RETURN CODE
   OFFSET ADDRESS
                     FUNCTION 19
```

Read Sequential   This function will read a record from the file referenced by DX, assuming that the file has been opened through the use of open file or make file (see functions 15 and 22). Upon execution, the next 128-byte record is copied from disk to memory at the current DMA address. The cr or current record field of the FCB is used to locate the desired record in the file. Record number cr is read from the current extent of the file, and the cr field is incremented to reference the next current record. If the cr field overflows (exceeds 128), then the next extent of the file is opened (the BDOS reads the directory and finds the next directory entry of the file), and the cr count is reset to zero. Since there are 128 possible records in an extent and 128 bytes per record, 16,384 bytes or 16K is the maximum length of an extent. The BDOS automatically manages longer files by setting up multiple directory entries with different extent numbers, one for each 16K byte segment of a file. A file can have up to 31 extents.

A value of 00H is returned in AL if the read was successful, and a 01H will be returned if no data is found at the next record position in the file. If this condition occurs, it is usually an indication that the end of the file has been reached. The error condition can also arise if an attempt is made to read a record that was not initialized, or if the file was written using the random file write function. (See function 34).

CL = 14H
DX = FCB
    OFFSET ADDRESS

READ SEQUENTIAL FUNCTION 20

AL = RETURN CODE

Write Sequential   This function is similar to read sequential. Assuming that the FCB addressed by DX has been opened with open file or make file (function 15 or 22), write sequential copies the 128-byte record at the DMA address to disk at the location cr or current record in the file. If cr goes over 128, a new extent will automatically be created, and cr will be reset to zero. A write operation can overwrite records in an existing file; cr must be set to zero after opening a file if you intend to stat writing records from the first record in the file.

Write sequential returns AL = 00H if the operation was successful. If unsuccessful, there are two possible return codes: 01H, if no directory space was available for creating a new extent—this occurs if the cr value exceeded 128, and a new extent was needed; a value of 02H is returned if no more unallocated records were available on disk. This means that the disk is full.

CL = 15H
DX = FCB
    OFFSET ADDRESS

WRITE SEQUENTIAL FUNCTION 21

AL = RETURN CODE

Make File   This function is quite similar to open file, but the FCB addressed by DX must contain the name of a file that does not yet exist on the selected disk. If the file does not yet exist, the BDOS will create a new directory entry and initialize it to look like an empty file (no records allocated). If there is a chance that the file specified in the FCB exists on disk, a preceeding delete file operation will make sure that the make file function will be successful. A return code of 0FFH indicates that the operation was not successful—meaning that no directory space was available. A return code of 0 through 3 indicates that the operation was successful.

Because the make file operation activates the FCB, a subsequent open file command is not necessary.

```
CL = 16H
DX = FCB
    OFFSET ADDRESS          MAKE FILE          AL = RETURN CODE

                            FUNCTION 22
```

Rename File   This function allows the programmer to rename a file on the selected disk. The FCB addressed by DX has a different format for this function (see below). The first 16 bytes of the FCB identify the file to be renamed, and the second 16 bytes specify the new file name and file type. The dr or drive code at byte 0 of the FCB specifies the disk drive used in the function call. A drive code of zero specifies the default disk. The drive code in the second 16 bytes will be ignored. The file name and file type must be unambiguous (no question mark wild cards), and the new file specification in the second half of the FCB must not exist on disk already. If the first file specification (the one to be renamed) is not found on disk, a return code of 0FFH will be in the AL register. A return code of 0 through 3 indicates that the operation was successful.

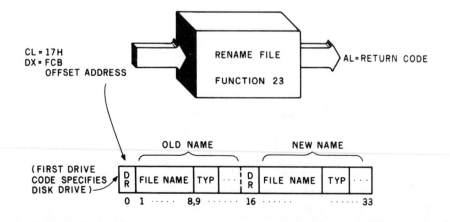

```
CL = 17H
DX = FCB
    OFFSET ADDRESS          RENAME FILE          AL = RETURN CODE

                            FUNCTION 23
```

OLD NAME   NEW NAME

(FIRST DRIVE
CODE SPECIFIES   DR | FILE NAME | TYP | ··· | DR | FILE NAME | TYP | ···
DISK DRIVE)
                 0   1 ····· 8,9 ······ 16 ······   ····· 33

Return Login Vector   This function returns a 16-bit value in the BX register where the least significant bit corresponds to the first disk drive (A:), and the most significant bit corresponds to the last possible disk drive (P:). If the bit is zero, the drive is off-line and has not been selected. A one value indicates that the drive has at some time (since cold-start, warm-start, disk reset, or drive reset) been activated or selected.

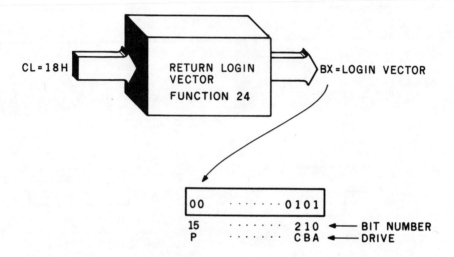

Return Current Disk   The return-current-disk function returns in the AL register the value of the currently selected disk (selected by a call to function 14, select disk). The value in AL ranges from 0 to 15 corresponding to disk drives A: through P:.

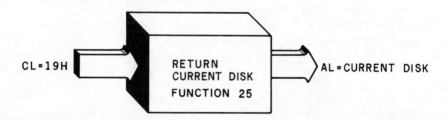

Set DMA Address   Function 26 sets the DMA (direct memory access) address for all disk operations. Some microcomputers use actual DMA circuitry to perform transfers to and from disk. Most systems use parallel port input and output instructions and perform the transfer byte by byte under software control. The transfer software acts the same as the DMA hardware (although slower) and uses the DMA address set by this function as the transfer address in memory.

In CP/M-80, the DMA address was specified in the DE registers, just as DX is used in CP/M-86, but since the 8080 had only 64K bytes, no other address information was needed. In the 8086/8088, the offset to the DMA address must be specified in DX, but the data segment must also be set. Thus, it is often necessary to use function 51 to set the DMA base address so that the DMA address in the DX register of this function will point to the actual DMA area. This function does not produce a return code.

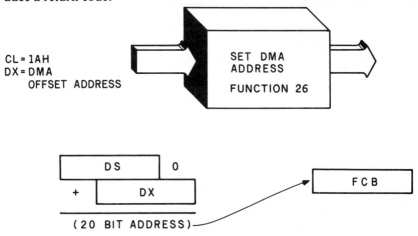

CL = 1AH
DX = DMA
    OFFSET ADDRESS

SET DMA ADDRESS

FUNCTION 26

Get Allocation Vector Address Each disk drive has an allocation vector which contains information about the allocated blocks on the disk. The allocation vector is not used except by programs that need to determine the amount of space available on a disk. The STAT program is a good example of this. This function returns the segment base and allocation vector address in the ES and BX registers respectively. Note that the contents of the allocation vector may not be valid if the disk has been marked read/only. It is wise to first check the read/only vector (function 29) before getting the allocation vector.

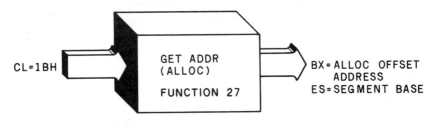

CL = 1BH

GET ADDR (ALLOC)

FUNCTION 27

BX = ALLOC OFFSET
    ADDRESS
ES = SEGMENT BASE

Write Protect Disk   Each disk as a whole can be write protected against accidental write operations. The protection status of the disk is temporary and will be reset on cold-start, warm-start, disk system reset, or drive reset. If an attempt is made to write to a protected disk, the message:

BDOS ERR x: R/O

will be displayed (see BDOS error section).

Get Read/Only Vector   This function returns a 16-bit vector similar to that returned by function 27 (get allocation vector). The least significant bit corresponds to the A: drive, and the most significant bit refers to the P: drive. Each bit, if turned on, indicates that the specified disk drive has been marked as read/only. The read/only status is set for a particular drive if a call is made to function 28 (write protect disk,) or if a disk has been removed from the drive and a different one put in its place. The BDOS automatically checks a disk to see if it is the same,

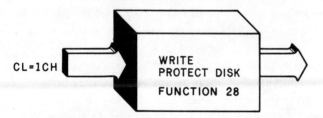

and if detecting a different disk, will mark it as read/only until a cold-start, warm-start, drive reset, or disk system reset occurs. The read/only vector is returned in the BX register.

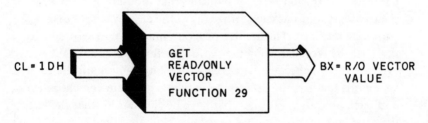

Set File Attributes   Function 30 sets the file attribute bits present in the FCB. The currently allowed attributes are: R/O, system, and archive. They are referred to as t1', t2' and t3' respectively. The top (most significant) bits of the three file type bytes are used to implement the attributes, as well as the top bits of the file name (f1' through f8').

When called, this function will search the disk specified in the FCB drive code field and will update all directory entries that match the file specification. This function does not allow for question mark wild card characters. The file name and file type must be unique.

Attributes f1' through f8' are not presently used or defined by Digital Research, but f5' through f8' are reserved for future system expansion. F1' through f4' may be used for application programs for special purposes, because they are not involved in the matching process during file open-and-close functions.

Note that the STAT program can be used to set or change file attributes directly. See Chapter 3 for a complete discussion.

Current attribute assignments:

t1'   This bit can be used to set the read/only attribute for the file specified. If set, no write commands will be processed for the file. This bit will remain set until deliberately reset under program control.

t2'   The system identifies the file as one related to the operating system or to a frequently used utility program. Any file may be marked with this attribute; it is merely provided so that files always present on a disk are not displayed in the directory when it is listed with the DIR command.

t3'   The archive attribute is provided for purposes of standards and compatibility of software, but is not actually implemented in CP/M-86. If this bit is set, it indicates that the file has been written to archival or backup storage (as in the case of a hard disk with tape backup). The archive program must be user written and must set the bit itself using the set file attributes function. Whenever the file is subsequently updated, the bit is automatically reset. Using this feature, the user-written archive program can check for and back up only those files that have been changed since the last time the update program has been run. Note that the file is archived, but is not removed from the specified disk.

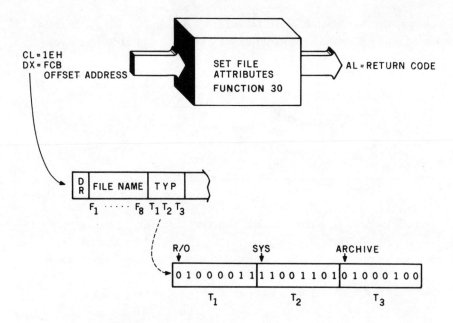

Get Address of Disk Parms   This function returns the address and segment base of the disk parameter block of the currently selected disk. The offset address is returned in BX and the segment base is returned in the ES register. Using this function, you can gain access to the disk parameter block to locate information about the physical characteristics (space, number of sectors per track, etc.) of a disk drive. See Chapter 6 (Disk Parameter Block) for further information.

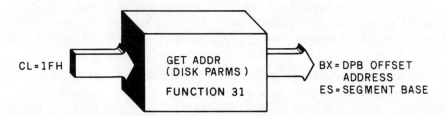

Set/Get User Code   This function allows a program to change or determine the value of the user code. The DL register may be loaded with either 0FFH or a number from 0 to 15. If 0FFH, the BDOS will treat the function call as a query operation and will return the current user

code in the AL register. If DL ranges from 0 to 15, the BDOS will assume that you wish to change the user code to the value in DL.

CL = 20H
DL = 0FFH (GET)
  OR USER CODE
  (SET)

SET/GET
USER CODE

FUNCTION 32

AL = CURRENT CODE
  (GET) OR
  NO VALUE (SET)

Read Random   The read random function performs a read operation,
but allows any record in a file to be read directly at random. As with
the read sequential function, the record is read from disk and copied
into the buffer at the current DMA address. A 24-bit (3 byte) field in
the FCB (bytes r0, r1, r2) is used to address the desired record (see
below).

Note that the least significant byte (r0) is first, and the most significant byte (r2) is last. Only the first two bytes are significant in terms of
addressing a record, since the last (r2) byte is only used to indicate an
overflow condition where there was an attempt to read a record beyond
the end of the file. The first two bytes (r0 and r1) are treated as a 16-bit
or double-byte value that contains the record to read.

To begin using the read random function, it is necessary to open
the file and access the base extent (extent 0) so that the BDOS is properly initialized. After this has been done, you may place the number of
any desired record into r0 and r1 and issue a read random command.
On return, the AL register will contain zero if the operation was successful. If not, an error code (see Table 5.3) will be returned. Note that
unlike the read sequential function, the record number is not automatically advanced by the BDOS after the read is performed. Calling the
function again will cause the BDOS to read the same record again.

On each random read, the extent and current record values are updated by the BDOS. It is possible to read or write the file sequentially
from the current random access position. If you read or write a file sequentially, and then return to the random mode, the r0 and r1 bytes will
still contain the old random record number, and a random read will still
read the same old record again. It is also possible to use the random
mode to stimulate sequential operation by manually incrementing the r0
and r1 bytes after each read or write operation.

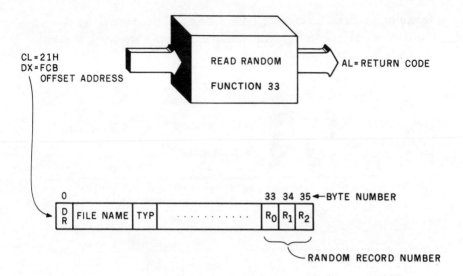

Write Random   This function is similar in many ways to the read random function except for the obvious difference that it is writing data to disk. The record to be written is copied from the current DMA address and written to disk in the requested record location in the specified file. If the record is to be written to a record or extent that does not yet exist, the BDOS will allocate the record or extent before proceeding. The r0 and r1 bytes (see read random) are not incremented as a result of the write operation, but the current record (cr) and extent values of the FCB are updated to correspond to the requested record. As with read random, it is possible to simulate sequential operation by manually incrementing the r0 and r1 bytes after each write random operation. Also, since the write (and read) random functions do not increment the random record number, a new extent is not automatically activated when

```
Return
Code              Description
-----             -----------
 0        Operation Successful.
 1        Read an unwritten record - This error indicates that
          a record not previously written was being read.
 2        not used
 3        Cannot close current extent - This error occurs that
          an attempt was made to change extents.  It is caused
          by either an overwritten FCB or a read random operation
          on a file that hasn't been opened.
 4        Seek to an unwritten extent - The extent requested
          has not been created. This error is similar to error 1.
 5        not used
 6        Random record number out of range - This error code is
          returned whenever byte r2 of the FCB is non-zero.
```

Table 5.3:   Read-random error codes.

the end of an extent is reached. Table 5.4 lists all the error codes returned in the AL register by write random. If zero is returned, the function was successful.

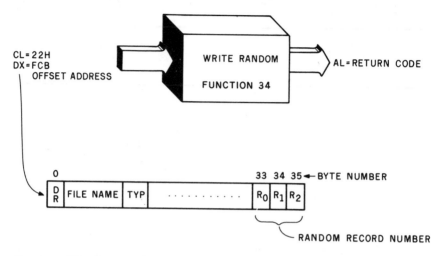

Compute File Size   This function will compute the size of a file. The DX register must contain the FCB offset address as with other file operations. The random read/write bytes (r0, r1, and r2) are used by this function to return the file size. The file specified in the FCB must not contain question mark wild card characters. The value returned in the r0, r1, and r2 bytes will be the size of the file in records. If the r2 byte is non-zero, the maximum file size of 65536 records was found. If the r2 byte is zero, then the r0 and r1 bytes contain the 16-bit size of the file (see below).

```
Return
Code            Description
-----           -----------
 0      Operation Successful.
 1      not used
 2      No available data block - returned when the write random
        command attempts to allocate a new data block, but non exist.
 3      Cannot close current extent - This error occurs that
        an attempt was made to change extents.  It is caused
        by either an overwritten FCB or a write random operation
        on a file that hasn't been opened.
 4      not used
 5      No available directory space - occurs when the write command
        attempts to create a new extent, but no directory space exists.
 6      Random record number out of range - This error code is
        returned whenever byte r2 of the FCB is non-zero.
```

Table 5.4:   Write-random error codes

This function has two useful purposes: it can find the size of a file for display or calculation purposes, and it can find the logical end of a file for append operations. The random record value returned in r0 and r1 will be the last record of the file. Subsequent write operations can then take place without worrying about overwriting any good information.

It is possible that the file size returned may not be the correct file size because random write operations could create a situation in which the first and last records of a file have been written (and allocated) but none of the intervening records have been written. Thus the physical size of the file will be reported on, but the virtual size (amount actually used) will not be known. There is no convenient way to learn the virtual size of a file, except by reading all records to see if an error code is returned.

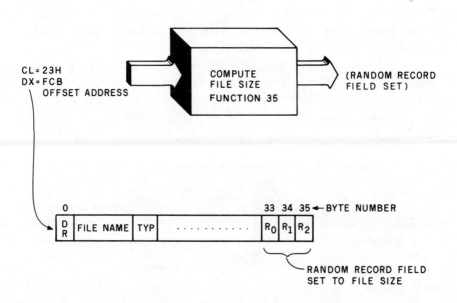

Set Random Record This function as a conversion, causing the BDOS to compute the random record number from the current cr or current record count and the current extent value. This can be useful if you are reading or writing a file sequentially and wish to switch to random operations.

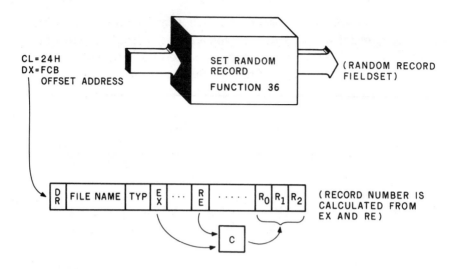

Reset Drive   This function restores the drives specified in the DX register to the reset state. The reset state is the state a drive is in after a cold-start or warm-start; it is not logged-in and is in read/write mode.

The DX register on entry must contain a 16-bit vector that lists the drives to be reset. The least significant bit corresponds to the A: drive, and the top bit refers to the P: drive. If any of these bits are set to 1 (one), the corresponding drive is reset by the BDOS. A zero value is returned in AL on completion to maintain compatibility with MP/M.

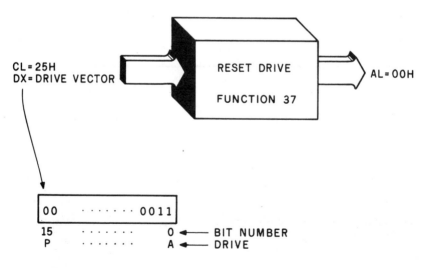

Write Random with Zero Fill   This function is very similar to the write random function, except that it fills all unallocated records with zeros. In a write random operation, unallocated records contain garbage data. Error codes identical to those returned by write random are returned in AL by this function. A zero is returned if the write was successful.

CL = 28H
DX = FCB
  OFFSET ADDRESS

WRITE RANDOM
WITH ZERO
FILL
FUNCTION 40

AL = RETURN CODE

5.8 CALLING THE BIOS DIRECTLY FROM THE BDOS

In previous versions of CP/M, many programmers went directly to the basic input/output system (BIOS) to perform some functions such as console input or output. The problem with this strategy is that any change to the location of the BIOS means that the program must be rewritten. In CP/M-86, there is no convenient method of even locating the BIOS, so it would be difficult to write programs that call BIOS functions directly. Needless to say, using the BIOS in any version of CP/M makes a program much less portable.

CP/M-86 has a special function call designed to alleviate this problem while still allowing adventuresome programmers to call the BIOS directly.

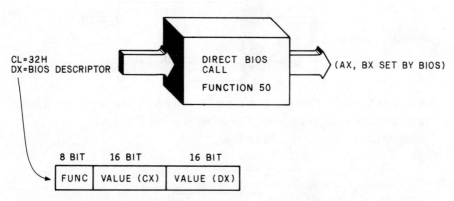

CL=32H
DX=BIOS DESCRIPTOR

DIRECT BIOS
CALL

FUNCTION 50

(AX, BX SET BY BIOS)

8 BIT	16 BIT	16 BIT
FUNC	VALUE (CX)	VALUE (DX)

Direct BIOS Call Function 50 performs a BIOS call and allows values to be passed to the BIOS subroutine. The DX register must contain a pointer to a five-byte memory area containing a one-byte function number (see list of BIOS functions in Chapter 6), a two-byte value for the CX register, and a two-byte value for the DX register. When the function is executed, the CX and DX registers are set to the values in the memory area. The AX and BX registers are returned as set by the BIOS call.

5.9 THE DMA BASE SEGMENT ADDRESS

In the 8080A, Z80, and 8085, addressing was 16-bit absolute, so only the 16-bit DMA address needed to be set. The 8086 uses base + offset addressing so when the DMA address is set, the segment base must also be set. Function 26 sets the DMA offset (the address within the segment). CP/M-86 has a second function (number 51) that sets the DMA base segment address. The parameter passed in DX for this function is the top 16 bits of the actual 20-bit segment address. This value is loaded into the DS register when the DMA buffer is actually accessed by the BDOS.

When a program is loaded into memory for execution, the DMA base is set to the value of the DS register (the start of the program's data segment), and the DMA offset address is set to 0080H, which corresponds to the CP/M-80 default DMA address.

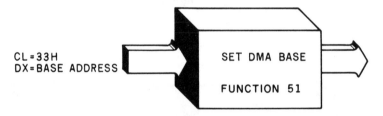

Get DMA Base   This function retrieves the DMA base segment address and the DMA offset address. The offset is in the BX register, and the segment address is in the ES register.

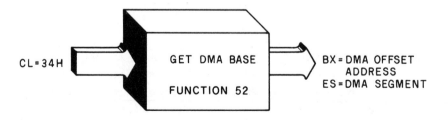

5.10 MEMORY MANAGEMENT

As discussed earlier, the 8086 microprocessor has a total of four segment registers; code segment, data segment, stack segment, and extra segment. The code segment or CS register is used to locate the base of the program, as we have seen. The data segment or DS register operates in a similar way for the data area of a program. Thus data and program can be separated and each can be up to 64K bytes long. The stack segment or SS register is used every time a PUSH or POP instruction is executed and for subroutine CALLs and returns. The program's stack pointer is added to the SS just as the program counter is added to the CS register. The fourth register is the extra segment, which is used as an auxiliary to the data segment.

As stated in Chapter 1, in using the segment scheme, it appears that programs cannot be larger than 64K bytes and that no more than 64K bytes of data may be addressed. The programmer has complete control of the segment registers and can set up as many data or code areas as desired. Several machine instructions are provided to make this easy.

5.11 MEMORY MODELS

Since the program and data areas can be separately addressed in the 8086, the user has several options on how to organize a program in memory. Several memory models are provided in CP/M-86. They are the Small model, the Compact model and the 8080 model. Normally, CP/M-86 selects the memory model to be used for a given program, but the user does have some control. See Chapter 4, the 8086 assembler, for more information.

Figure 5.5 shows the three memory models. The initial values of the segment registers are loaded when CP/M-86 (or an application program) loads a program into memory. The header record of each CMD file tells the operating system what model to use.

The 8080 model is used to support programs written for CP/M-80. In this case, it is assumed that the program in question was translated from 8080 assembler language to the 8086, with few structural changes. Since the 8080 has no segment registers, all program, data, and stack areas were mixed within one 64K-byte address space. This is easily simulated by putting the start address of each segment at the same place in memory. In this model, assuming that no other changes have been made, the stack is left within CP/M-86 (in the CCP) so the user does not need to be concerned with it. If the stack is to be placed elsewhere, the user should load the stack segment as well as the stack pointer to insure that all of CP/M remains intact.

The small model takes memory management one step further and allows separation of the program and data areas for those 8080 translated programs that lend themselves to easy modification or for those that have separated data and program areas. The code segment is set up to address one 64K block, and the data segment and extra segment registers address a second block of 64K. The stack segment and stack pointer remain within the CCP as with the 8080 model. Note that the data segment in both the 8080 and small models is set up for a 0100H byte offset to allow for the CP/M-80 base page. Since all CP/M-80 programs begin at 0100H in memory, the base page may have special jump vectors or interrupt routines, and still contains the default DMA address and default FCB blocks. This saves much recoding of CP/M-80 programs.

The Compact model allows for each segment to be separately defined. This mode gives the programmer full flexibility to use the resources of the segment-addressed memory environment.

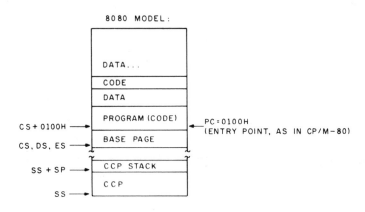

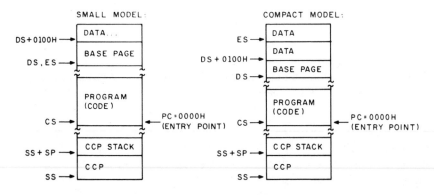

Figure 5.5: Memory models.

5.12 THE BASE PAGE

CP/M-86 automatically establishes a base page for programs, similar to the base page (0000H–00FFH) maintained by CP/M-80. The base page in CP/M-86 is always the first 256 bytes of the data segment 64K byte region. The contents of the base page correspond to CP/M-80, as shown in Figure 5.6. Each group of bytes occurs in the standard least significant or low order byte first, to match with the 8080 and 8086 addressing convention of low byte, then high byte. In the small and compact models, the first three bytes are the 20-bit address of the last code group location. The top four bits are zero, since the address is only 20 bits long. In the 8080 model, the first two bytes alone (LC0 and LC1) represent a 16-bit address, and the high order byte (LC2) is always zero.

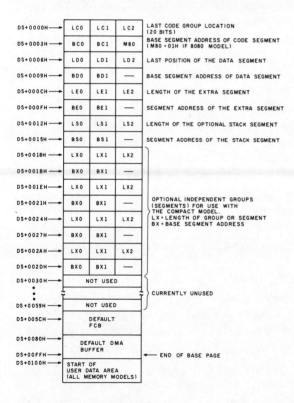

Figure 5.6: Base page contents.

BC0 and BC1 represent the base segment address of the code group. The M80 byte is set to one if the 8080 model is in use. The LD bytes represent the last position available in the data segment. Note that the first two bytes are in the same place as the top of the Transient Program Area in CP/M-80. This makes it easy to convert programs. The

BD bytes give the base segment address of the data segment. The LE bytes represent the length (20 bits) of the extra segment, and the BE bytes give the base segment address of the extra segment. LS and BS represent the length and base segment addresses of the stack segment. The remaining LX and BX bytes are optional addresses for four additional segments that can be defined by the programmer.

The initial values of all the above base page values are set by the contents of the CMD file header record.

5.13 PROGRAM LOADING AND MEMORY ALLOCATION

As in CP/M-80, the console command processor accepts two file names (placed after the command) and loads them into the default FCBs at 005CH and 006CH relative to the data segment (DS). Also, the DMA base and DMA address are initialized to the base of the data segment and 0080H respectively.

After the desired program has been loaded into memory, the console command processor transfers control to it by issuing an 8086 far call instruction. Normally, the stack is left in the CCP unless the program reloads it deliberately. The CCP stack has 96 bytes available for the user. If this is insufficient, it is up to the user to reload the stack segment and stack pointer registers.

Upon completion of a program, two methods are available to terminate it: a far return instruction causes the CCP to regain control as if it had called a subroutine (which, in fact, it did). This option *requires* that the CCP stack be used during execution. If the stack has been damaged since the CCP gave control to the program, the far return instruction may not return control to the CCP. The safest way to regain control is to execute a BDOS function 0 (system reset) command. If desired (for debugging purposes), the BDOS can be ordered to leave the program in memory after it has terminated. See function 0 in this chapter for more details. It is also possible to manually terminate a program by typing CTRL-C on the console during line-edit input. This has the same effect as if BDOS function zero were called.

NOTE: Upon termination, no disk reset occurs as in CP/M-80. The BDOS and CCP modules are not reloaded from disk. It is up to the user to reset the disk system if necessary.

5.14 BDOS MEMORY MANAGEMENT FUNCTIONS

Memory allocation in CP/M-86 can be referred to in two different ways: physical memory organization and logical memory organization.

Physical organization is used to describe the static allocation map which defines the available memory regions, that is coded into the BIOS by the user. Since some computer systems may have two or more noncontiguous or independent memory blocks, this software mechanism informs the operating systems (the BDOS) as to the number (up to eight), location, and size of the regions.

Once the physical memory organization is known, the BDOS can map programs (or segments) into the physical memory when a program is loaded. Up to eight regions may be dynamically allocated by CP/M-86. When a program is loaded by console command, the allocation is taken care of by the BDOS. If a program is loaded explicitly by calling BDOS function 59 (Program Load), the BDOS finds space and allocates memory for the new program that is "owned" by the calling program. In the current version of CP/M-86, multiple programs can remain in memory as long as they issue a system reset with the DL register set to one. Programs loaded in this fashion can take control only through interrupts. These programs can be deleted or stopped by typing CTRL-C on the console. Each entry of a CTRL-C causes the last program created to be deleted. Programs are deleted in the opposite order in which they are created.

Using the program load function, programs can themselves load other programs and allocate data areas. Each program owns the programs it creates. This can create a hierarchy of ownership, in which each program owns the next one in memory. Even if each program appears to be independent, the cancelling of any program that owns others will cause all the owned programs to be cancelled as well.

A program may also release a portion of a memory region, but the released portion must be at the beginning or the end of the region. A block of memory in the middle of a region cannot be reused until the program has terminated and the entire region released.

The memory control block or MCB is used by BDOS functions 53 through 59 to describe memory operations. As shown here, the MCB consists of three parts: the M-Base, M-Length, and M-Ext. The M-Base is a 16-bit memory base (segment) address, giving just the top 16 bits of a 20-bit address. M-Length is the length of a memory region given in 16 bits (of a 20-bit address). The M-Ext value is defined by the function call and is sometimes used to return an error code. An error condition is usually indicated by returning 0FFH, as is standard for most BDOS calls.

	16 BITS	16 BITS	8 BITS
MCB (MEMORY CONTROL BLOCK) →	M - BASE	M - LENGTH	M-EXT

Get Max Mem   This function returns the location of the largest available memory region less than or equal to M-Length paragraphs. If one is found, the M-Base field of the MCB is set to the base address of the area, and M-Length is set to the length of the area. The AL register gives the return code (zero is successful, 0FFH is not). The M-Ext byte returns zero if no additional memory is available and a one if some memory is available for allocation.

Get Abs Max   This function will find the largest possible region at the absolute segment address (M-Base), up to a maximum length of M-Length. If successful, M-Length is set to the actual length available. The AL register returns the value 0FFH if the call was unsuccessful, and zero if successful.

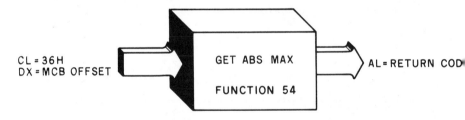

Alloc Mem   This function will allocate a memory area defined by the MCB. The user must specify the M-Length required, and the BDOS will return the M-Base segment address of the allocated region. Register AL will contain zero if the request was successful, and 0FFH if the amount of memory requested could not be allocated.

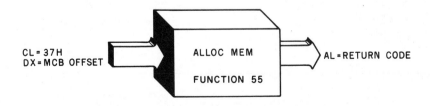

Alloc Abs Mem   The allocate absolute memory function requests a memory region according to the MCB. Both the M-Base and M-Length are specified by the user. Register AL returns zero if successful, and 0FFH if not.

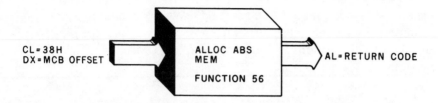

```
CL=38H
DX=MCB OFFSET          ALLOC ABS        AL=RETURN CODE
                       MEM

                       FUNCTION 56
```

Free Mem   The free memory function releases a memory area allocatd to the calling program. The M-Ext byte determines the nature of this function call: if M-Ext is equal to 0FFH, then all memory allocated by the calling program is released. If M-Ext is zero, then the memory region of length given in M-Length at the location in M-Base is released.

Note that when releasing memory, you should never attempt to release the middle section of a region. Always release memory that is at the beginning or end of the originally allocated block.

```
CL=39H
DX=MCB OFFSET          FREE MEM         (MCB)

                       FUNCTION 57
```

Free All Mem   This function releases all allocated memory regions. It is normally used only by the console command processor upon system re-initialization.

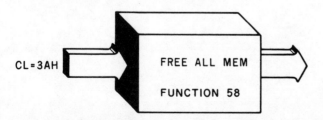

```
CL=3AH                 FREE ALL MEM

                       FUNCTION 58
```

Program Load   This function will load a CMD file. The DX register must contain the FCB offset of a unique file specification of the desired command file. Before issuing this function, the FCB must be successfully opened with function 15 (open file). On return, the AX register contains a return code of 0FFFFH if the load was not successful. If successful, both the AX and BX registers contain the 16-bit segment address of the base page. The base page, in turn, contains information on the addresses and lengths of all the segments.

Note that when you load a program with this function, the base page is established, but the DMA base and DMA offset addresses are not loaded with default values. It is therefore necessary that the program call BDOS functions 51 and 26 to set up the DMA address for the new program.

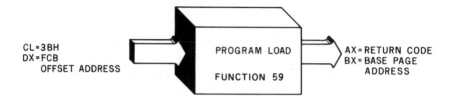

CL=3BH
DX=FCB
  OFFSET ADDRESS

PROGRAM LOAD

FUNCTION 59

AX=RETURN CODE
BX=BASE PAGE
  ADDRESS

Note: The IBM Personal Computer version of CP/M-86 (version 1) may have an error in the program load function. It is possible that when you load a file from other than the default disk drive, the file header may not be interpreted properly when allocating memory for the various segments. Consequently, some programs may not run. To alleviate this problem, make sure the program loads from the default disk. Do not specify a disk drive.

6

The BIOS (Basic Input/Output System)

6.1 THE PURPOSE OF THE BIOS

CP/M-86 is designed to operate in almost any 8086/8088 microcomputer system. This is accomplished by having one portion of the operating system be accessible to the manufacturer or vendor (even the user). This portion is called the basic input/output system or BIOS (usually pronounced "by-ahs" or "by-ohs" for short).

The BDOS calls on the BIOS to gain access to the physical hardware of the microcomputer being used. This provides for a very machine-independent environment for the BDOS. Imagine the BIOS as a slave that the BDOS can order around. The BDOS knows what it wants to do (with the disk controller or console serial port, for example), but doesn't know exactly how to talk to the hardware. It does have a rapport with the BIOS, though, and can ask it to communicate with the hardware and return the results.

Under almost all circumstances, the customized BIOS will be installed in your version of CP/M-86 before you receive it. If you buy it from Digital Research directly though, it probably will not contain a BIOS that will work with your microcomputer, unless you own an Intel SBC 86/12 microcomputer with an Intel 204 disk controller.

Note: Since the implementation of a custom BIOS is fairly complicated and time consuming, it is wise to buy a prewritten, installed BIOS for your 8086 or 8088 computer. It is easier, however, to modify the

BIOS if one already exists. For example, suppose you wish to add another serial port or a printer port. If you have had some experience with assembler language (even 8080 or Z80), it is possible to make minor changes to improve a BIOS. This is covered at length in Chapter 7.

The inner workings of the BIOS and full instructions on how to generate one starting from the ground up are covered in great detail in the CP/M-86 Operating System-Systems Guide. Rather than duplicate that material, this chapter explains in more general terms what the various parts of the BIOS do.

6.2 THE ORGANIZATION OF THE BIOS

The BIOS is part of CP/M and resides in memory at all times. Figure 6.1 shows the typical layout of memory for CP/M-86.

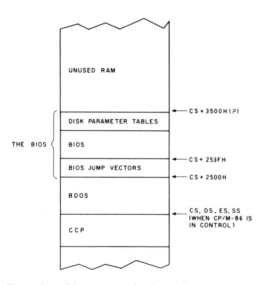

Figure 6.1: Memory organization of CP/M.

The BIOS is made up of several subsections. The first 63 bytes contain 21 jump vectors (each three bytes long); see Figure 6.2. Each of the jump vectors has an assigned purpose, such as restart CP/M or get a console character. As stated earlier, the BDOS calls on the BIOS to gain access to the physical hardware of the microcomputer being used.

As shown in Figure 6.1, the BIOS resides in memory at offsest 2500H from the base of CP/M-86. This offset is constant, but the upper limit of the BIOS may change, depending on the size and special requirements of the hardware of some microcomputer systems. For example, some disk controllers are interrupt driven, some are set up to use DMA (direct memory addressing), and some use I/O ports to com-

municate with the CPU. The complexity of the BIOS depends on the
nature of the hardware.

```
Offset from                          BIOS
Start of BIOS   Instruction       Function #    Description

    0000H       JMP  INIT             0          Cold Start
    0003H       JMP  WBOOT            1          Warm Start
    0006H       JMP  CONST            2          Console Status Check
    0009H       JMP  CONIN            3          Console Character Input
    000CH       JMP  CONOUT           4          Console Character Output
    000FH       JMP  LIST             5          List - Character Output
    0012H       JMP  PUNCH            6          Punch - Character Output
    0015H       JMP  READER           7          Reader - Character Input
    0018H       JMP  HOME             8          Move Current Disk to Track 0
    001BH       JMP  SELDSK           9          Select a Disk Drive
    001EH       JMP  SETTRK          10          Set Track Number
    0021H       JMP  SETSEC          11          Set Sector Number
    0024H       JMP  SETDMA          12          Set DMA Offset Address
    0027H       JMP  READ            13          Read Selected Sector
    002AH       JMP  WRITE           14          Write Selected Sector
    002DH       JMP  LISTST          15          Return List device Status
    0030H       JMP  SECTRAN         16          Sector Translation
    0033H       JMP  SETDMAB         17          Set DMA Segment Address
    0036H       JMP  GETSEGB         18          Get MEM Region Table Offset
    0039H       JMP  GETIOB          19          Get IOBYTE
    003CH       JMP  SETIOB          20          Set IOBYTE
```

Figure 6.2: Jump vectors.

6.3 THE SYSTEM INITIALIZATION SECTION

The first two jump vectors (shown in Figure 6.2) are for system re-
initialization. The first one is called directly by the CP/M-86 loader
program and performs any needed hardware initialization when CP/M-
86 is loaded from cold start. The second is called the warm-start vector,
because it is called whenever a program terminates (through BDOS
function zero). After the warm-start operation is completed, control is
immediately transferred to the console command processor.

6.4 SIMPLE CHARACTER-ORIENTED INPUT/OUTPUT DEVICES

The next six jump vectors transfer control to various character I/O
routines. For example, CONST, CONIN, and CONOUT pass characters
to and from the logical console device. The next one (LIST) sends a
character to the logical list device. Function number 15 (LISTST) returns the status of the list device. The reason why the list status routine
is not located next to the list output routine is simple: when the first
version of CP/M-80 was written, no list status routine existed. It was
added later, but to avoid rearranging all the jump vectors, it was added
as function 15. In CP/M-86, other jump vectors were added after it.
The logical reader and punch devices are actually obsolete names. They
were intended for a paper tape reader and punch, but are now used as
auxiliary input and output devices.

In all of the above subroutines, a character being sent out to a device must be placed in the CL register, and any character or status information being returned will appear in the AL register.

Logical-to-Physical Device Mapping

The IOBYTE is implemented in the BIOS. Its purpose is to route logical device requests to the selected physical device. The IOBYTE is a single byte that is defined within the BIOS. In CP/M-80, it was at absolute address 0003H in memory, but in CP/M-86, it has not been assigned a permanent address. The BIOS function calls GETIOB, and SETIOB allows it to be written and read by all programs, including the STAT utility, which normally sets its value.

Figure 6.3 shows the assigned bits in the IOBYTE. Each logical device may be assigned to one of four physical devices. It is up to the programmer or system implementor to set up the IOBYTE and to check it in each logical device handler subroutine (i.e., CONIN, CONOUT).

Note: The IOBYTE is not required by CP/M-86. If it is not implemented, logical devices will have a one-to-one correspondence with physical devices, and when GETIOB is called, dummy values will be returned to the BDOS. In this case, the STAT device assignment commands will have no affect on the available devices. In fact, it is recommended that when installing a BIOS for CP/M, the IOBYTE be

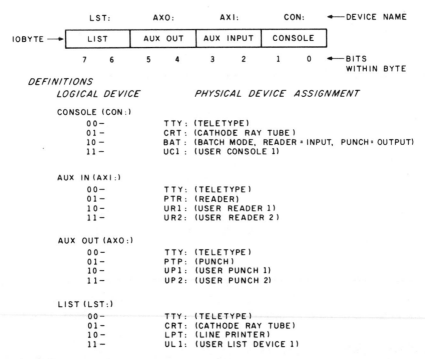

Figure 6.3: IOBYTE and assignments.

left out to simplify the BIOS unitl it is thoroughly debugged. It can always be put in later.

6.5 DISK INPUT/OUTPUT AND DISK DEFINITIONS

BIOS functions 8 through 14 and function 16 are used for disk controller communications. For example, the HOME function causes the currently selected disk to return to track zero. The SELDSK function activates the disk (passed in the CL register) and makes it the current disk (this is how the default disk is activated).

The READ and WRITE functions transfer a single record (128 bytes) from the current DMA buffer (set with SETDMA) to or from the currently selected disk (SELDSK) at the current track and sector (SETTRK and SETSEC). The BDOS refers to the disk directory on disk to know where to read or write information when needed.

Disk Definition Tables

Version 2.0 of CP/M-80 and CP/M-86 (as well as MP/M-80 and MP/M-86) are all table-driven (unlike CP/M 1.4). This means that all the disk definitions and allocation information is kept in the BIOS rather than in the BDOS. This allows for more flexibility in interfacing disk drives to the system. In CP/M 1.4, it was assumed that all disks attached to the system were identical—eight-inch single density or 5.25 inch. Now, many systems have one or more floppy disks and an additional hard disk for mass storage. A few even have RAM disks (large-capacity random access memory circuits that simulate disk drives). If the disk definition tables are kept out of the reach of the programmer, it becomes difficult to implement these other non-floppy disk devices. With the release of CP/M-80 version 2.2, Digital Research opened up these tables to the user.

Since the actual implementation of the tables is performed by an experienced programmer, the user rarely has the need to modify them. Also, the CP/M-86 Systems Guide covers the implementation techniques quite thoroughly, so this section explains them by showing how the various control blocks interact and how the BDOS extracts information from them.

Each defined disk drive has a 16-byte table, called the disk parameter header, associated with it. It contains information about the disk drive and has several bytes of "scratch pad" area for the BDOS to work with. Figure 6.4 shows the internal layout of the disk parameter header (DPH). Each of the eight fields in the DPH are one word (2 bytes) long. All DPHs in the BIOS are organized into a table, starting at address DPBASE, with 16 bytes per entry, up to the nth disk drive. The

BDOS learns the address of the DPH for a given disk when it is returned by the SELDSK function. The SELDSK subroutine must return the address for the BDOS to work properly.

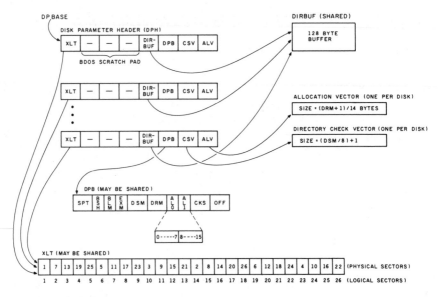

Figure 6.4: The internal layout of the disk parameter header (DPH).

The disk parameter header contains the following fields:

XLT Offset address of the logical-to-physical sector translation vector. If no translation is to take place, the value is zero. All disks that use the same sector translation order can refer to the same vector.

DIRBUF Offset address of a 128-byte scratch pad area for directory operations within the BDOS. All DPH entries use the same DIRBUF.

DPB Offset address of the disk parameter block for this drive. All disks with identical characteristics (e.g., sectors per track) can refer to the same DPB.

CSV Offset address of a scratch pad area used by the BDOS for a software check for changed disks. Disks cannot share CSVs; there must be one for each drive.

ALV Offset address of a scratch pad area used by the BDOS to keep disk storage allocation information. A unique ALV must be provided for each disk drive.

The three empty entries in the DPH are 16-bit scratch pad area for the BDOS. Figure 6.4 shows the XLT or translate vector. Sector skewing is often difficult to understand, both in implementation and in purpose.

The reason it is done is that all disk drives have limited access speed because of the rotational delay of the disk. For example, if we request sector 1, store it in memory, and then request sector 2, we probably won't be in time to read it, because it has already passed the disk head on its way around. The speed of the microcomputer is also a limitation. The solution is to skew the sectors around the disk. This means that a logical sector is placed every sixth sector around the disk. All sectors are used, but not in sequential order. Figure 6.5 shows how this is done.

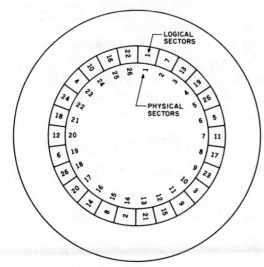

Figure 6.5: Sector skewing on a disk.

The XLT vector in Figure 6.4 has the same skew factor as the disk in Figure 6.5. Each sector maps onto the disk, but not in sequence. When sequential logical sectors are read, the disk will have rotated into position just in time for the next sector to be read, instead of having to wait a complete revolution.

The disk parameter block contains information about the size and layout of a particular disk.

SPT	Number of sectors per track.
BSH	Data allocation block shift factor.
BLM	Block mask.
EXM	Extent mask.
DSM	Total storage capacity of a disk drive.
DRM	Total number of directory entries that can be stored on a drive.
ALO,AL1	Allocation vector for reserved directory blocks.
CKS	Size of the directory check vector.
OFF	Number of reserved tracks at the beginning of the logical disk.

Most of these values are not important and are generated automatically by a program called GENDEF, used by systems programmers to implement the CP/M-86 BIOS (GENDEF is included on the distribution disk). However, some values, such as SPT and DSM are "human readable."

6.6. MEMORY MANAGEMENT FUNCTIONS

The remaining BIOS function (GETSEGB) is used by CP/M-86 to allocate memory. Since the 8086/8088 can address up to one megabyte, the simplistic 8080 approach will not work. The BIOS contains a memory region table (see Chapter 5, section 5.15) that defines the available physical memory areas. These areas do not have to be contiguous, which is one advantage over CP/M-80. The table contains only those areas available to transient programs. The table is shown in Figure 6.6a.

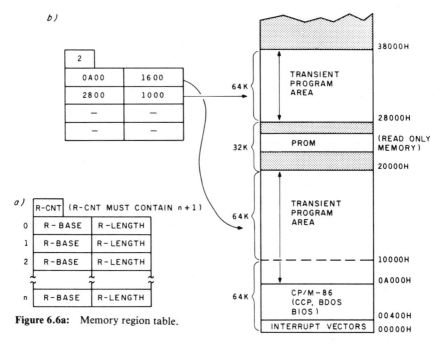

Figure 6.6a: Memory region table.

Figure 6.6b: Memory region table with actual regions.

R-Cnt is the number of memory region descriptors (equal to n + 1). R-Base and R-Length give the paragraph (segment-style address, containing the upper 16 bits of the 20-bit address) base and length of each physically contiguous area of memory. Figure 6.6b shows an example of the memory region table with actual regions.

7

How to Customize the BIOS (Excluding Disk I/O)

7.1 INTRODUCTION

Chapter 6 gave an overview of the BIOS and its relationship to the rest of CP/M-86. This chapter explains how to modify certain parts of the BIOS for special hardware devices. The most common changes made to the BIOS are in the character devices, not the disk interface. The disk interface software usually remains the same, unless you plan to add a hard disk, in which case the manufacturer of the hard disk will supply a new BIOS (if not, don't buy the hard disk).

If you purchase an IBM Personal Computer with CP/M-86, the device assignments are handled differently than in other implementations of CP/M. In fact, you are not given the BIOS, so it is impossible to make changes to it. However, the IBM BIOS supports all standard IBM external interfaces, and those vendors that are building interfaces for the IBM will explain in their manuals how to gain access (in the operating system) to their devices.

For most other manufacturers, the customized BIOS comes on the disk with CP/M-86. Changing it involves a few simple steps. One common change is to add the IOBYTE logical to physical device assignment feature. The IOBYTE is not essential to normal CP/M operation, but when added, does allow the four logical devices to be assigned to one of our physical devices each.

Listing 7.1 shows a sample BIOS without the IOBYTE feature. The

four logical devices, CONSOLE, LIST, AUXILIARY INPUT, and AUXIL-
IARY OUTPUT, are permanently assigned to four physical devices: console, list, reader and punch. At location B in the listing, all the low-level
interface subroutines are shown. Location A is where any device initialization routines, such as data rate and protocol settings for a serial
port, would go. Since device initialization routines are heavily hardware
specific, they are not included here.

The conout subroutine is a good example of a simple polling mode
routine. Polling is a fancy term for scanning or reading. It means that
the status of the device is monitored for a device-ready signal. When
the signal is present, the routine returns an all clear indication to the
calling program. The character is then sent. In this case, the status byte
is inputted from port CSTS to check the transmitter buffer empty signal coming from the serial port. If the signal is logic zero, the buffer
still has something in it—the serial port is not done sending the byte. If
the bit goes to logic one, the buffer is empty and ready for the next byte
to send. The JZ CONOUT instruction means: if the bit is zero, jump on
zero(JZ) to CONOUT. The loop repeats until the buffer is empty. Next,
the byte to send is loaded from the CL register to AL and is then output
to the CDATA port. The byte will then be sent to the serial port and on
to the console device.

7.2 ADDING THE IOBYTE FEATURE

The IOBYTE can be implemented with a minimum of trouble.
First, you must decide how you want to assign the physical devices attached to your microcomputer system. Figure 7.1 shows a typical device
assignment scheme. The four logical devices are shown on the left, with
their possible physical assignments next on the right. The available
physical devices are on the far right. Since the TTY: is a common default assignment, we will set up as a duplicate assignment for the physical console or CRT: device. This means that when ttyout is called,
control will actually transfer to the crtout subroutine. The routines are
not duplicated; they are the same. For the moment, ignore the last
physical device on the lower left (UL1:). The next section will discuss it
in detail.

Listing 7.2 shows how the BIOS can be modified to add the
IOBYTE. Rather than renaming all the actual subroutines (e.g., conout,
conin, reader, punch), it is easier to rename the jump vector entries to:
CST, CI, CO, LO, AXO, AXI, and LST. Their functions remain the
same, but they will now transfer control to new device handlers.

Further down in Listing 7.2 you will see the new logical device routines. Notice that, for example, CO first loads the IOBYTE and does a
series of tests to determine which I/O device it is assigned to. The

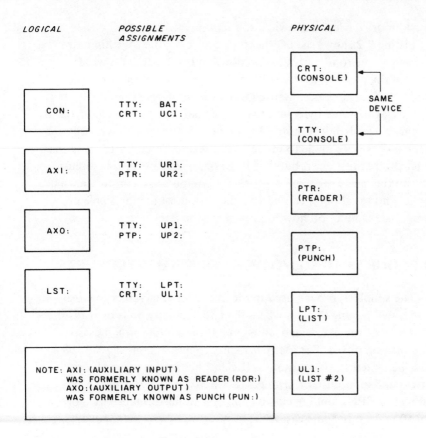

LOGICAL   POSSIBLE   PHYSICAL
               ASSIGNMENTS

Figure 7.1: Device assignments

IOBYTE test is strictly up to the individual BIOS routines. The BDOS does not do this for you.

Continuing with the example (CO:), the IOBYTE is loaded into the AL register and is "anded" with 00000011b or 03 hexadecimal. Referring to Figure 6.3, the two least significant bits (bits 0 and 1) contain the console device assignment. After the and instruction, these bits are isolated. If they are zero, control is transferred to ttyout. If the value is 01b, then control is transferred to conout; if 10b, then batout, and finally, if 11b then uc1out. Each of these four subroutines communicates with one physical device only. All the other logical devices have up to four physical devices, although some may be the same (such as TTY:).

7.3 ADDING ANOTHER PHYSICAL DEVICE

The physical device labeled UL1: (user list device #1) was not discussed in the previous section, because it was necessary to explain the IOBYTE logical to physical mapping technique first. After you have implemented the IOBYTE (or on a system that already supports it), you can add more devices and switch to them easily.

Listing 7.2 shows the LO (list out) device handler. Within it are several jumps, one to ul1out. Further down in the listing, you will find ul1out in the physical device section. For purposes of this example, all the I/O devices have been written using the same program logic. First, they check the status byte, and then they read or write the character. By comparing the listout routine with the new ul1out, you can readily see what changes were made to implement a second serial port. Of course, the hardware must exist, but that is beyond the scope of this discussion. Refer to the hardware manuals for your computer system to see what parallel and serial ports can be added. Also, most manuals give programming examples on how to implement the interface.

7.4 PROGRAMMING I/O DEVICES WITH INTERRUPTS

The simple approach used in the above sections refers to a technique called polling. This is where the CPU actually polls or reads the status byte of the device and waits (in a program loop)for the correct bit to turn on or off. For many personal computers (most 8080, Z80, and 6502 systems), this is quite sufficient, but in more complex personal systems and in multi-user or multi-tasking systems (multiple programs sharing the CPU), polling cuts overall system performance by more than 50 percent in some cases.

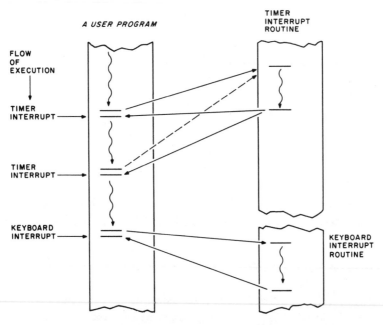

Figure 7.2: Interrupts—an example.

7.5 INTERRUPTS—HOW THEY WORK

Figure 7.2 shows a simple example of a system with two sources of interrupts. The first source is a 60Hz (cycle per second) clock timer or "tick" counter. Its only purpose is to interrupt the microprocessor every 1/60 second to increment a counter in memory. This allows the operating system to keep track of the time of day (see the transient command TOD in Chapter 3). The second interrupt in the example comes from the keyboard of the console.

As you can see in the figure, the user program executes normally until the CPU is signaled that an interrupt has taken place. It saves the instruction pointer and transfers control to a predesignated address of a subroutine that handles the interrupt. This routine is known (as would be expected) as the interrupt handler. The interrupt handler proceeds to save all registers and flags, then performs whatever function is expected of it (when it was written) to process the interrupt event. In the case of the timer, it would increment a byte that counts up to 60, then, on the 61st count, would increment the seconds counter, and so on through to the hours counter as needed. The handler would then restore all the registers and return to the interrupted user program as if nothing had happened. Indeed, the user program acts as if it was never interrupted, because its status hasn't changed. It will only appear to run slightly slower (although the slow down is not noticeable on the human scale).

The keyboard interrupt works in much the same way, but since the incoming keystroke is not used immediately, it must be stored somewhere, until the currently executing user program calls the BDOS and asks for a character from the console. Figure 7.3 shows how this might be handled: the console sends the character to the serial interface, which in turn interrupts the CPU. The CPU has a table of interrupt jump vectors in low memory, so control is passed directly to the keyboard interrupt routine (because the hardware knows where the interrupt came from). The interrupt routine saves the registers, reads the character, and stores it in a variable called KCHAR. It also sets a flag called KFLAG that is used by the BIOS CI routine to check for the character. After its function is accomplished, it restores the registers and returns control to the interrupted program.

The user program (which is unaware that the interrupt has taken place) calls the BDOS requesting a character from the console. The BDOS recognizes the request and calls the BIOS (specifically, the logical console input routine). The console input routine waits for the character by testing the flag KCHAR (instead of testing the serial interface status bit in the polling version). If a keystroke had not been entered prior to the call to the console in routine, KFLAG would still be zero. As soon as the interrupt routine sets KFLAG (even while conin is running) conin will see that it has gone to one and will read the character

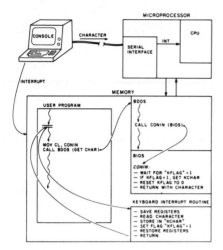

Figure 7.3: An example of a device interrupt.

stored at KCHAR. After reading the character, KFLAG must be reset to zero, so the next time conin is called, the old character won't be read a second time.

This software mechanism is called producer-consumer because the interrupt routine produces a character and the user program (through the BIOS) consumes the character.

Some systems take this scheme one step further. What if a large number of characters came to the serial interface before the user program could process them? The result would be an overflow. Only the last character would ever be seen, because the other would have been overwritten as they were placed in the single character buffer (KCHAR). To avoid this, a buffer or queue is often added to the interrupt handler and the BIOS. Figure 7.4 shows how a queue works.

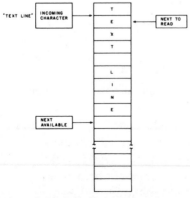

Figure 7.4: Queues.

The queue in Figure 7.4 is called a first-in first-out (FIFO) because the first character placed in the buffer is also the first one to be read out. The incoming character is placed in the next available location in the buffer. When the buffer fills, either the characters are ignored or a signal is sent to the sender to stop sending for a moment. The BIOS routine reads characters from the buffer at its own speed, using the pointer to the next character available location in the buffer. As each character is read, the pointer is advanced, until it runs up against the incoming next available pointer. At that time, the buffer is empty, and the console input routine must wait for more characters. This buffer is circular in the sense that when the pointers reach the end of the buffer, they are reset to the first character position. Thus, they go around repeatedly, reusing the same buffer, since very seldom will the entire buffer fill up.

7.6 HOW TO INSTALL A MODIFIED BIOS

Assuming that you have a working BIOS and a running CP/M-86 system, you can implement changes to the BIOS and create a new copy of the operating system.

First, use the ED text editor (or other similar text editor) to change your BIOS.A86 or CBIOS.A86 (depending on the vendor). It is wise to use PIP to make a copy of the BIOS source file, rather than changing the actual file. This allows you to go back to the original in case you have problems. Of course the original disk itself should be backed up for safekeeping.

Second, assemble the source file with ASM86 to produce a BIOS.H86 hex file. No special options are needed on the assembler. Concatenate this new BIOS hex file to the CPM.H86 file on your distribution disk (a copy of it, please).

```
PIP CPMX.H86 = CPM.H86,BIOS.H86
```

The CPMX.H86 hex file can then be converted into a .CMD file by entering:

```
GENCMD CPMX 8080 CODE[A40]
```

The base address must be forced to 400H in low memory. Then rename the file:

```
REN CPM.SYS = CPMX.CMD
```

This CPM.SYS file can be placed on your 8086 system disk. The steps (reviewed) are:

```
ED BIOS.A86
ASM86 BIOS
PIP CPMX.H86 = CPM.H86,BIOS.H86
GENCMD CPMX 8080 CODE[A40]
REN CPM.SYS = CPMX.CMD
```

This sequence should produce a working BIOS that can be loaded when you perform a system reset or cold start.

Listing 7.1:   Sample BIOS.

```
;=====================================================
;
;        SAMPLE BIOS
;
;  This is a sample BIOS adapted from the CBIOS
;  listing in Appendix F of the Digital Research
;  CP/M-86 Operating System - System Guide.
;
;  The purpose of this BIOS is not to show how
;  to implement an entire BIOS (including Disk
;  functions), but to show how to modify some
;  of the simple character I/O subroutines of
;  an existing BIOS.
;
;  Portions of this BIOS are not completely
;  listed, such as the interrupt handler logic
;  and some of the disk controller software.
;
;  Note:  Any portion of this listing may be
;  copied for use in any CP/M-86 BIOS or other
;  program.
;
;=====================================================
;
;
true     equ     -1                      ;(FFFFH)
false    equ     not true
cr       equ     0dh                     ;carriage return
lf       equ     0ah                     ;line feed
;
; I/O ports for serial devices
;
csts     equ     70h                     ;console status
                                         ;port
cdata    equ     71h                     ;console data
                                         ;port
;
lsts     equ     72h                     ;list device
                                         ;status port
ldata    equ     73h                     ;list device
```

```
                                            ;status port
;
rsts      equ     74h                       ;reader device
                                            ;status port
rdata     equ     75h                       ;reader device
                                            ;data port
;
psts      equ     76h                       ;punch device
                                            ;status port
pdata     equ     77h                       ;punch device
                                            ;data port
;
;
iobval    equ     0                         ;set up an
                                            ;initial iobyte
                                            ;value (see
                                            ;chapter 5)
;
bdos_int equ      224                       ;reserved bdos
                                            ;interrupt
;
bios_code equ     2500h                     ;offset of bios
ccp_offset equ    0000h
bdos_ofst  equ    0b06h                     ;bdos entry point
;
          cseg
;
          org     ccp_offset                ;this directive,
                                            ;followed by
;
ccp:                                        ;this label
                                            ;defines the start
                                            ;of the CCP to
                                            ;the bios.
          org     bios_code                 ;now start the bios.
;
          jmp     init                      ;cold start (come
                                            ;from bootstrap
                                            ;or loader)
          jmp     wstart                    ;warm start (come
                                            ;from bdos call 0)
          jmp     const                     ;console status
          jmp     conin                     ;console input
          jmp     conout                    ;console output
          jmp     listout                   ;list output
          jmp     punch                     ;punch output
          jmp     reader                    ;reader input
          jmp     home                      ;move to track 0
                                            ;on current disk
          jmp     seldsk                    ;select new disk
          jmp     settrk                    ;set track
          jmp     setsec                    ;set sector
          jmp     setdma                    ;set dma offset
                                            ;address
          jmp     read                      ;read a sector
          jmp     write                     ;write a sector
          jmp     listst                    ;return list
                                            ;device status
```

```
        jmp     sectran                 ;sector translate
        jmp     setdmab                 ;set segment
                                        ;address for
                                        ;DMA buffer
        jmp     getsegt                 ;return offset
                                        ;of memory region
                                        ;table
        jmp     getiobf                 ;return IOBYTE
        jmp     setiobf                 ;set IOBYTE
;
;
;=========================================
;
init:                                   ;print signon
                                        ;message and
                                        ;initialize
                                        ;hardware
;
        mov     ax,cs                   ;copy cs value
        mov     ss,ax                   ;to all other
        mov     ds,ax                   ;segment
        mov     es,ax                   ;registers
;
        mov     sp,offset stkbase       ;use a local stack
        cld                             ;set forward
                                        ;direction flag
;
;
; This section sets up interrupt vectors.
; Requirements may vary from system to system.
;
        push    ds                      ;save the DS register
        mov     iobyte,iobval           ;initialize iobyte
        mov     ax,0
        mov     ds,ax
        mov     es,ax                   ;set DS and ES to zero
;
        mov     int0_offset,offset int_trap     ;set
                                                ;interrupt 0
                                                ;to address
                                                ;trap routine.
                                                ;
        mov     int0_segment,cs                 ;set segment
                                                ;address
        mov     di,4
        mov     si,0
        mov     cx,510h                 ;copy trap vector to
                                        ;all 256 interrupts
        rep     mov ax,ax
;
        mov     bdos_offset,bdos_ofst   ;bdos offset to
                                        ;proper interrupt
        pop     ds                      ;restore ds
;
;
;----> "A" At this point, insert any additional
;          initialization logic required by the
;          physical hardware.
```

```
;
;
        mov     bx,offset signon        ;signon message
        call    pmsg                    ;print it
        mov     cl,0                    ;set default
                                        ;disk to A:
        jmp     ccp                     ;then jump to
                                        ;ccp cold start
                                        ;entry point
;
;
wstart:
        jmp     ccp+6                   ;direct entry into
                                        ;CCP warm start
                                        ;location.
;
;
int_trap:
        cli                             ;disable interrupts
        mov     ax,cs
        mov     ds,ax                   ;get address of
                                        ;data segment
        mov     bx,offset int_trp
        call    pmsg                    ;display message
        hlt                             ;force a hard stop
;
;
;=======================================
;
;
;----> "B" all character I/O routines go here.
;
;
;
const:                                  ;console status
                                        ;subroutine
        in      al,csts                 ;poll (read) the
                                        ;status port
        and     al,2
        jz      const_ret               ;return if
                                        ;data available
        or      al,255                  ;return OFFH if
                                        ;no data available
const_ret:
        ret
;
;
;
conin:                                  ;console character
                                        ;input routine
        call    const                   ;check status
        jz      conin                   ;if character
                                        ;isn't available,
                                        ;wait for it.
        in      al,cdata                ;if ready, read
                                        ;the character
        and     al,7fh                  ;remove parity
                                        ;bit if necessary
        ret
```

```
;
;
;
conout:                                 ;console character
                                        ;output routine
        in      al,csts                 ;check status port
        and     al,1                    ;see if transmit
                                        ;buffer is empty
        jz      conout                  ;if not, wait
        mov     al,cl                   ;get the character
        out     cdata,al                ;send it
        ret                             ;then return
;
;
;
listout:                                ;list device
                                        ;output routine
        call    listst                  ;check for status
                                        ;of device
        jz      listout                 ;if not ready, wait
        mov     al,cl                   ;if ready, get
                                        ;the character
        out     ldata,al                ;send character
        ret                             ;then return
;
;
;
listst:                                 ;list status
                                        ;subroutine
        in      al,lsts                 ;get the status bit
        and     al,80h                  ;transmitter
                                        ;buffer empty?
        jz      list_ret                ;return if ready
        or      al,255                  ;return if not
                                        ;ready
list_ret:
        ret
;
;
;
punch:                                  ;punch device
                                        ;output routine
        call    punchst                 ;check status
        jz      punch                   ;if not ready, wait
        mov     al,cl                   ;if ready, get it
        out     pdata,al                ;send character
        ret                             ;then return
;
;
;
punchst:                                ;punch status
                                        ;subroutine
        in      al,psts                 ;get the
                                        ;status bit
        and     al,80h                  ;transmitter
                                        ;buffer empty?
        jz      pun_ret                 ;return if ready
        or      al,255                  ;return if not ready
pun_ret:
        ret
;
rdrst:                                  ;reader status
                                        ;subroutine
        in      al,rsts                 ;poll (read)
                                        ;the status port
```

```
        and     al,2
        jz      rdr_ret                 ;return if
                                        ;data available
        or      al,255                  ;return 0FFH if
                                        ;no data available
rdr_ret:
        ret
;
;
;
reader:                                 ;reader character
                                        ;input subroutine
        call    rdrst                   ;check status
        jz      reader                  ;if character
                                        ;isn't available,
                                        ;wait for it.
        in      al,rdata                ;if ready, read
                                        ;the character
        and     al,7fh                  ;remove parity bit
                                        ;if necessary

        ret
;
;
getiobf:                                ;since the
                                        ;iobyte is not
                                        ;implemented in
                                        ;this version,
        mov     al,0                    ;return a zero
                                        ;(all TTY:)
        ret                             ;for simplicity.
;
setiobf:                                ;since the iobyte
                                        ;is not implemented
                                        ;in this version,
        ret                             ;do nothing.
;
;.
pmsg:                                   ;display message
                                        ;subroutine
        mov     al,[bx]                 ;get next byte
        test    al,al                   ;
        jz      return                  ;if zero, return
        mov     cl,al                   ;move to cl
        call    conout                  ;display on logical
                                        ;console device
        inc     bx
        jmps    pmsg                    ;repeat for next
                                        ;character
;
;
;========================================
;
;       Disk Input/Output Routines
;
;       These routines are not complete,
;       since they are only samples for
;       this bios.
;
seldsk:                                 ;sample select
                                        ;disk routine
ndisks  equ     2
        mov     disk,cl                 ;save disk number
        mov     bx,0
        cmp     cl,ndisks
```

```
           jnb       return
           mov       ch,0
           mov       bx,cx
           mov       cl,4
           shl       bx,cl
           mov       cx,offset dpbase
           add       bx,cx                    ;return DPH
                                              ;address in bx
return: ret
;
;
;
home:                                         ;move current disk
                                              ;to track 0
           mov       trk,0
           rs        10                       ;remainder of



                                              ;subroutine
           ret
;
;
settrk:                                       ;set track address
           mov       trk,cx
           ret
;
setsec:                                       ;set sector address
           mov       sect,cx
           ret
;
sectran:                                      ;translate sector
                                              ;cx using table
                                              ;at [dx]
           mov       bx,cx
           add       bx,dx                    ;add sector to
                                              ;trans table
           mov       bl,[bx]                  ;get logical sector
           ret
;
;
setdma:                                       ;set dma offset
           mov       dma_adr,cx
           ret
;
;
setdmab:                                      ;set dma segment
                                              ;address
           mov       dma_seg,cx
           ret
;
getsegt:                                      ;return MRT
                                              ;(memory region table)
           mov       bx,offset seg_table      ;address
           ret
;
;
;
read:                                         ;read sector
           rs        50                       ;remainder of routine
           ret
;
;
write:                                        ;write sector
           rs        50                       ;remainder of routine
           ret
```

```
;
;
;
;==========================================
;
; Data areas
;
;
data_offset equ    offset $
;
;
        dseg
;
;
        org    data_offset            ;data follows
                                       ;code directly
;
iobyte  db     0                       ;IOBYTE
disk    db     0                       ;disk number
trk     dw     0                       ;track number
sect    dw     0                       ;sector number
dma_adr dw     0                       ;dma offset address
                                       ;(from DS)
dma_seg dw     0                       ;dma segment address
;
signon  db     cr,lf
        db     'System Generated 07/31/82'
        db     cr,lf,0
;
;
int_trp db     cr,lf
        db     'Interrupt trap halt'
        db     cr,lf,0
;
;
;System Memory Segment Table (Sample)
;
segtable db    1                       ;set up 1 segment
        dw     tpa_seg
        dw     tpa_len
;
;
;
;Disk parameter tables
;
;
dpbase  equ    $                       ;base of DPH table
;
dpe0    dw     xlt0,0000h              ;translate table
        dw     0,0                     ;scratch pad
        dw     difbuf,dpb0             ;dir buffer,
                                       ;disk param block
        dw     csv0,alv0               ;check and allocation
                                       ;vectors
dbe1    dw     xlt0,0000h              ;translate table
        dw     0,0                     ;scratch pad
        dw     dirbuf,dpb1             ;dir buffer,
                                       ;disk param block
        dw     csv1,alv1               ;check and allocation
                                       ;vectors
```

```
;
dpb0      equ      offset $                  ;disk parameter block #0
          dw       26                        ;26 sectors per track
          db       3                         ;block shift
          db       7                         ;block mask
          db       0                         ;extent mask
          dw       242                       ;disk size - 1
          dw       63                        ;directory (max entries)
          db       192                       ;alloc0
          db       0                         ;alloc1
          dw       16                        ;check size
          dw       2                         ;offset


xlt0      equ      offset $                  ;sector translate table
          db       1,7,13,19
          db       25,5,11,17
          db       23,3,9,15
          db       21,2,8,14
          db       20,26,6,12
          db       18,24,4,10
          db       16,22
;
als0      equ      31                        ;allocation vector
css0      equ      16
;
; DISKDEF 1,0
;
dpb1      equ      dpb0                       ;both disks the same
                                             ;use same DPB
;
als1      equ      als0                       ;same allocation vector
css1      equ      css0                       ;same checksum vector
;
;
;         ENDEF
;
;
; Scratch pad memory
;
;
begdat    equ      offset $                  ;start of scratch area
dirbuf    rs       128                       ;directory buffer area
alv0      rs       als0                      ;alloc vector
csv0      rs       css0                      ;check vector
alv1      rs       als1                      ;alloc vector
csv1      rs       css1                      ;check vector
enddat    equ      offset $
datsiz    equ      offset $-begdat           ;size of scratch area
          db       0                         ;marks end of module
;
;
;
;
loc_stk rw         32                        ;local stack for
                                             ;initialization
stkbase equ        offset $
;
last_off equ       offset $
tpa_seg equ        (last_off+0400h+15) / 16
tap_len equ        0800h - tpa_seg
;
          db       0                         ;fill last address
                                             ;for gencmd
;
;
; data section
;
;
          dseg     0                         ;bottom of memory
          org      0                         ;set up interrupt
                                             ;vectors
;
int0_offset    rw        1
```

Listing 7.2: Modified BIOS.

```
    int0_segment    rw      1
;
;
        rw      2 * (bdos_int - 1)
;
bdos_offset     rw      1
bdos_segment    rw      1
;
;
;
        end
        .
        .   (BIOS source listing)
        .
        .
;
; I/O ports for serial devices
;
csts    equ     70h                     ;CRT: console status port
cdata   equ     71h                     ;CRT: console data port
;
lsts    equ     72h                     ;LPT: list device status port
ldata   equ     73h                     ;LPT: list device data port
;
rsts    equ     74h                     ;PTR: reader device status port
rdata   equ     75h                     ;PTR: reader device data port
;
psts    equ     76h                     ;PTP: punch device status port
pdata   equ     77h                     ;PTP: punch device data port
;
l1sts   equ     80h                     ;UL1: list device #2 status port
l1data  equ     81h                     ;UL1: list device #2 data port
;
;
iobval  equ     10010101b               ;set up an initial iobyte
                                        ;value (see below):
;
;
; The IOBYTE will be initialized to iobval (10010101b) as follows:
;
;                       logical         physical
;       bits    value   device          assignment
;       ----    -----   ------          ----------
;
;       0,1     01      CON:            CRT: (Console)
;       2,3     01      AXI:            PTR: (Reader)
;       4,5     01      AXO:            PTP: (Punch)
;       6,7     10      LST:            LPT: (Line Printer)
;
;
;
;
;
        .
        .
        . (BIOS source listing, continued)
        .
;
        org     bios_code               ;now start the bios.
;
        jmp     init                    ;cold start (come here from
                                        ;bootstrap or loader)
        jmp     wstart                  ;warm start (come here from
                                        ;bdos call 0
```

```
;   use logical device names in jump table
            jmp     CST                     ;console status routine
            jmp     CI                      ;console input routine
            jmp     CO                      ;console output routine
            jmp     LO                      ;list output routine
            jmp     AXO                     ;auxiliary output routine
            jmp     AXI                     ;auxiliary input routine
;
            jmp     home                    ;move to track 0 on current disk
            jmp     seldsk                  ;select new disk
            jmp     settrk                  ;set track
            jmp     setsec                  ;set sector
            jmp     setdma                  ;set dma offset address
            jmp     read                    ;read a sector
            jmp     write                   ;write a sector
            jmp     LST                     ;return list device status
            jmp     sectran                 ;sector translate routine
            jmp     setdmab                 ;set segment address for DMA buffer
            jmp     getsegt                 ;return offset of memory region table
            jmp     getiobf                 ;return IOBYTE
            jmp     setiobf                 ;set IOBYTE
;
;



;========================================
;
            .
            .
            .  (BIOS source listing)
            .
;
;========================================
;
;
;----> "B" all character I/O routines go here.
;
;----- :::: LOGICAL DEVICE SERVICE ROUTINES :::: -----
;
;
; CO is the logical console output routine
;
CO:         mov     al,iobyte               ;get iobyte to check for
                                            ;physical device assignment
            and     al,00000011b            ;isolate the two console
                                            ;assignment bits
            jz      ttyout                  ;if zero (00b), use TTY:
            cmp     al,00000001b
            jz      conout                  ;if one (01b), use CRT:
            cmp     al,00000010b
            jz      batout                  ;if two (10b), use BAT:
            jmp     uclout                  ;if here, it must be three (11b)
                                            ;so use UC1:
;
;
; CI is the logical console input routine
;




CI:         mov     al,iobyte               ;get iobyte to check for
                                            ;physical device assignment
            and     al,00000011b            ;isolate the two console
                                            ;assignment bits
            jz      ttyin                   ;if zero (00b) use TTY:
            cmp     al,00000001b
            jz      conin                   ;if one (01b) use CRT:
            cmp     al,00000010b
            jz      batin                   ;if two (10b) use BAT:
            jmp     uclin                   ;if here, it must be three (11b)
                                            ;so use UC1:
```

```
;
;
; CST is the logical console status routine
;
CST:    mov     al,iobyte               ;get iobyte to check for
                                        ;physical device assignment
        and     al,00000011b            ;isolate the two console
                                        ;assignment bits
        jz      ttyst                   ;if zero (00b) use TTY:
        cmp     al,00000001b
        jz      const                   ;if one (01b) use CRT:
        cmp     al,00000010b
        jz      batst                   ;if two (10b) use BAT:
        jmp     uclst                   ;if three (11b) use UC1:
;
;
; LO is the logical list output routine
;
LO:     mov     al,iobyte               ;get iobyte to check for
                                        ;physical device assignment
        and     al,11000000b            ;isolate the two list device
                                        ;assignment bits
        jz      ttyout                  ;if zero (00b), use TTY:
        cmp     al,01000000b
        jz      conout                  ;if one (01b), use CRT:
        cmp     al,10000000b
        jz      listout                 ;if two (10b), use LPT:
        jmp     ullout                  ;if here, it must be three (11b)
                                        ;so use UL1:
;
;
;
; LST is the logical list device status routine
;
LST:    mov     al,iobyte               ;get iobyte to check for
                                        ;physical device assignment
        and     al,11000000b            ;isolate the two list device
                                        ;assignment bits
        jz      ttyst                   ;if zero (00b), use TTY:
        cmp     al,01000000b
        jz      const                   ;if one (01b), use CRT:
        cmp     al,10000000b
        jz      listst                  ;if two (10b), use LPT:
        jmp     ullst                   ;if here, it must be three (11b)
                                        ;so use UL1:
;
;
; AXI is the logical auxiliary input routine
;

AXI:    mov     al,iobyte               ;get iobyte to check for
                                        ;physical device assignment
        and     al,00001100b            ;isolate the two axi: device
                                        ;assignment bits
        jz      ttyin                   ;if zero (00b), use TTY:
        cmp     al,00000100b
        jz      reader                  ;if one (01b), use PTR:
        cmp     al,00001000b
        jz      urlin                   ;if two (10b), use UR1:
        jmp     ur2in                   ;if here, it must be three (11b)
                                        ;so use UR2:
;
;
; AXO is the logical auxiliary output device
;
AXO:    mov     al,iobyte               ;get iobyte to check for
                                        ;physical device assignment
        and     al,00110000b            ;isolate the two axo: device
                                        ;assignment bits
        jz      ttyout                  ;if zero (00b), use TTY:
        cmp     al,00010000b
        jz      punch                   ;if one (01b), use PTP:
        cmp     al,00100000b
        jz      uplout                  ;if two (10b), use UP1:
        jmp     up2out                  ;if here, it must be three (11b)
                                        ;so use UP2:
```

```
;
;=======================================
;
;----- PHYSICAL DEVICE INTERFACE ROUTINES -----
;
ttyst:                          ;tty is same as console
const:                          ;console status routine
        in      al,csts         ;poll (read) the status port
        and     al,2
        jz      const_ret       ;return if data available
        or      al,255          ;return OFFH if no data available
const_ret:
        ret
;
;
;
ttyin:                          ;tty is same as console
conin:                          ;console character input routine
        call    const           ;check status
        jz      conin           ;if character isn't available,
                                ;wait for it.
        in      al,cdata        ;if ready, read the character
        and     al,7fh          ;remove parity bit if necessary
        ret
;
;
;
ttyout:                         ;tty is same as console
conout:                         ;console character output routine
        in      al,csts         ;check status port
        and     al,1            ;see if transmit buffer is empty
        jz      conout          ;if not, wait
        mov     al,cl           ;get the character to send
        out     cdata,al        ;send it


        ret                     ;then return
;
;
;
listout:                        ;list device output routine
        call    listst          ;check for status of device
        jz      listout         ;if not ready, wait
        mov     al,cl           ;if ready, get the character
        out     ldata,al        ;send character
        ret                     ;then return
;
;
;
listst:                         ;list status routine
        in      al,lsts         ;get the status bit
        and     al,80h          ;transmitter buffer empty?
        jz      list_ret        ;return if ready
        or      al,255          ;return if not ready
list_ret:
        ret
;
;
;
punch:                          ;punch device output routine
        call    punchst         ;check for status of device
        jz      punch           ;if not ready, wait
        mov     al,cl           ;if ready, get the character
        out     pdata,al        ;send character
        ret                     ;then return
```

```
;
;
;
punchst:                                ;punch status routine
        in      al,psts                 ;get the status bit
        and     al,80h                  ;transmitter buffer empty?
        jz      pun_ret                 ;return if ready
        or      al,255                  ;return if not ready
pun_ret:
        ret
;
rdrst:                                  ;reader status routine
        in      al,rsts                 ;poll (read) the status port
        and     al,2
        jz      rdr_ret                 ;return if data available
        or      al,255                  ;return OFFH if no data available
rdr_ret:
        ret
;
;
;
reader:                                 ;reader character input routine
        call    rdrst                   ;check status
        jz      reader                  ;if character isn't available,
                                        ;wait for it.
        in      al,rdata                ;if ready, read the character
        and     al,7fh                  ;remove parity bit if necessary
        ret
;
;
;


ullout:                                 ;list device #2 output routine
        call    ullst                   ;check for status of device
        jz      ullout                  ;if not ready, wait
        mov     al,cl                   ;if ready, get the character
        out     lldata,al               ;send character
        ret                             ;then return
;
;
;
ullst:                                  ;list device #2 status routine
        in      al,llsts                ;get the status bit
        and     al,80h                  ;transmitter buffer empty?
        jz      ull_ret                 ;return if ready
        or      al,255                  ;return if not ready
ull_ret:
        ret
;
; Dummy device assignments --- unused devices are routed to existing
;                                     devices.
;
batout  equ     conout
batin   equ     conin
batst   equ     const
;
uclout  equ     conout
uclin   equ     conin
uclst   equ     const
;
urlin   equ     reader
ur2in   equ     reader
;
uplout  equ     punch
up2out  equ     punch
;
;
;
;
;
getiobf:                                ;return the iobyte

        mov     al,iobyte
        ret
```

```
;
setiobf:
        mov     iobyte,cl               ;set iobyte
        ret
;
;
;
            .
            .
            . (BIOS source listing, continued)
            .
```

Appendix I

CP/M-86 Quick Reference Guide

File Specificaton (Filespec):

d:FILENAME.TYP

d:	disk drive specifier (optional)
FILENAME	file name field, 1 to 8 characters
TYP	file type field, 0 to 3 characters (optional)

Characters allowed in a filespec:

A-Z 0-9 – + ! " # $ % & ( ) / @

Characters not allowed in a filespec:

< > . , : ; = ? * [ ]

Examples: Valid Filespecs Invalid Filespecs

Valid Filespecs	Invalid Filespecs
MYFILE	MY.FILE.TXT
A:MYFILE	AB:TEXT
B:MYFILE	TEST,FILE
MYFILE.TXT	MYFILE?
N082382.DAT	CUSTOMER.DATA
MY-FILE.ASM	

Wild card character: * ?

* allows matching of the field with any entry.
? allows matching of the character with any entry.

Limitations: wild cards cannot be used in the drive specifier. Also, wild cards cannot be used in a destination or output filespec of a program.

Examples:

Filespec	Will match
FILE.TY?	FILE.TYP, FILE.TYM, FILE.TYX. . .
FILE.???	FILE.TYP, FILE, FILE.AAA. . .
T???.DAT	T.DAT, TTTT.DAT, TEST.DAT. . .
*.DAT	T.DAT, CUSTOMER.DAT, TEST.DAT. . .
.	all files
????????.???	all files (equivalent to *.*)
*.???	all files (equivalent to *.*)
????????.*	all files (equivalent to *.*)

Changing Default Disk Drives:

When CP/M-86 is loaded, the default disk is A. To change default drives, enter the desired drive as follows:

B: < return >

CP/M-86 will respond with:

B>

indicating the new default drive. To change back, enter:

A: < return >

Assigned File Types

CMD	8086 or 8088 machine language (object code) program.
BAS	CBASIC (or other) source program.
$$$	Temporary file.
A86	ASM-86 assembler source program.
H86	Assembled ASM-86 (or other compiler) program in hexadecimal format.
SUB	Submit file contains a sequence of CP/M (CCP level) commands to be executed in order by SUBMIT.

Logical Devices

CON:	Logical console device (bi-directional).
AXI:	Logical auxiliary input device (input only).
AXO:	Logical auxiliary output device (output only).
LST:	Logical list device (output only).

Physical Devices

TTY:	Teletype device (not obsolete, but still used to describe a teleprinter type device).
CRT:	The physical console device.
BAT:	Batch mode input (for console).
UC1:	User console #1.
PTR:	Paper tape reader (or auxiliary input device).
UR1:	User reader #1.
UR2:	User reader #2.
PTP:	Paper tape punch (or auxiliary output device).
UP1:	User punch #1.
UP2:	User punch #2.
LPT:	Line printer.
UL1:	User list device #1.

Control Character and Line-Editing Commands

Control characters are keyboard commands that are used for line editing or restarting the system. Control-C, CTRL-C and ∧C all mean the same thing: hold down the key labeled Control or CTRL and simultaneously press the C (or other) key. Use the control key like a shift key.

∧E	Moves the cursor to the beginning of the following line without erasing the buffer.
∧H	This command is identical to backspace.
∧I	This command is identical to tab.
∧M	This command is identical to carriage return.
∧R	Retype the current buffer contents (redisplay what you have typed in).
∧U	Reset the input buffer to empty.
∧X	Reset the input buffer and backspace to the start of the line, erasing all characters.
∧S	Stop display scrolling. Pressing any key will start scrolling again.
∧C	Abort the current program or restart CP/M (must be the first character entered on the line).
Return	Enter the command line or terminate text entry.
Backspace	Erase the last character entered on the line.
Tab	Move the cursor to the next tab stop (every 8th column).

BUILT-IN COMMANDS

Note: { } braces indicate optional parameters.

DIR (Display disk directory)
DIRS (Display system directory)

Forms:	DIR {d:}	(drive specifier)
	DIR {filespec}	(filespec with wild cards)
	DIRS {d:}	(display files with
	DIRS {filespec}	SYS attribute)

Examples: (same for both DIR and DIRS)

	DIR A:	display directory of A:
	DIR B:	display directory of B:
	DIR MY-FILE.*	display all files with file name 'MY-FILE'.
	DIR *.A86	display all files with file type 'A86'.

ERA (Erase files)

Form: ERA filespec

Examples:	ERA MYFILE.A86	erases one file.
	ERA *.A86	erases all files of type 'A86'.
	ERA MYFILE.?86	erases all files with type '?86' (e.g., MYFILE.H86, MYFILE.A86)
	ERA *.*	erases all files on the default disk (requests confirmation (before proceeding).
	ERA B:*.*	erases all files on the B: disk.

REN (Rename a file)

Form: REN {d:}newname{.typ} = oldname{.typ}

Examples: REN NEWFILE.A86 = OLDFILE.A86
            REN B:A.TXT = B:B.TXT
            REN B:A.TXT = B.TXT

TYPE (Display a File)

Form: TYPE
            {d:}filename{.typ}

Examples: TYPE MYFILE.A86
            TYPE B:MYFILE.A86

USER (Display and Set User Number)

Forms: USER   (display current user number)
            USER n   (set user number to n
                          where n is 0 to 15)

Examples: USER   (returns current user number)
            USER 5   (sets user number to 5)

TRANSIENT COMMANDS

TOD (Display and Set the Time of Day):

Forms: TOD {time-specification}
            TOD {P}

Examples: TOD   (display the current time and date)
            TOD 08/28/82
            23:55:40   (set the time and date)
            TOD P   (repeatedly display the time and date)

HELP (CP/M-86 Help Guide):

Form: HELP {topic} {subtopic1 subtopic2 . . . subtopic8} {[P]}

Examples: HELP   (enter the help utility)
           HELP DIR   (display information about DIR)
           HELP DIR OPTIONS   (display DIR options)
           HELP ASM86
           [P]   (display ASM86 information, but
                                    don't stop screen display every 23
                                    lines.)

STAT (Status):

Forms: STAT
           STAT d: = RO
           STAT filespec {RO RW SYS DIR SIZE}
           STAT {d:}DSK:
           STAT USR:
           STAT VAL:
           STAT DEV:

           STAT LDV: = PDV:

Examples:

STAT   (display remaining space on disk)
STAT B: (display remaining space on B: disk)
STAT MYFILE   (display information about the file)
STAT DSK: (display information about the disk drive)
STAT USR: (display information about user directories)
STAT VAL: (display possible assignments)
STAT DEV: (display current logical/physical assignments)
STAT LST: = LPT: (assign list device to line printer)

PIP (Peripheral Interchange Program):

Forms:
PIP dest-file{[GN]} = source-file{[options]}
PIP dest-file{[Gn]} = dev{[options]}
PIP dev = source-file{[options]}
PIP dev = {[options]}

Examples:

PIP B: = A:*.*	(copy all files from A: to B:)
PIP B: = MYFILE.A86	(copy file from default disk to B:)
PIP B: = MYFILE.*	(copy all file types with MYFILE name to B:)
PIP MYFILE.A86 = AXI:	(copy text from auxiliary input device to file)
PIP LST: = MYFILE.A86	(list the file)
PIP NEWFILE = OLDFILE1,OLDFILE2	(combine two files into one new file)

Additional devices:

In addition to the four logical devices, three extra device names can be used in PIP:

NUL: A source device that produces 40 hexadecimal zeros.

EOF: A source device that produces a single CTRL-Z ($\wedge$Z) CP/M end of file marker.

PRN: A preset list device (uses LST:) but sets tabs to every 8th column, numbers lines, and prints 60 lines per page.

Options:

Dn	Delete any characters past column n.
E	Echo transfer at console.
F	Filter out form-feed characters.
Gn	Get source file from user number n. (Or send file to user number n.)
H	Hex data transfer.
I	Ignore :00 records in hex file transfer.
L	Translate uppercase to lowercase.
N	Add line numbers to output file.
O	Object file transfer (ignores any $\wedge$Z characters in the file.)
Pn	Set page length to n lines.
Qs	Quit copying from source device after string s.
R	Read system (SYS) files.
Ss	Start copying source file at string s.
Tn	Expand tabs to every nth column.
U	Translate lowercase to uppercase.
V	Verify that data has been sent correctly.
W	Write over files that are set to RO.
Z	Zero the parity bit.

COPYDISK (Copy disk):

Form: COPYDISK   (perform a complete disk copy for back-up
                             purposes.)

Example: COPYDISK   (this utility prompts for input)

SUBMIT (Batch Processing)

Form: SUBMIT filespec {parameters}

Examples: SUBMIT BATCH MYFILE PZ

Batch file contains:
ASM86 $1 $$2
GENCMD $1
$1

The resulting sequence of commands would be:
ASM86 MYFILE $PZ   (assemble the source file without producing a
                           print file)
GENCMD MYFILE   (generate a command file)
MYFILE   (execute the file)

Note: Up to nine parameters are allowed.

ED (Character File Editor):

Form: ED {input-filespec} {d:{output-filespec}

Examples:
ED MYFILE.A86   (edit the file)
ED MYFILE.A86 B: (write output file to B disk)
ED MYFILE.A86 NEWFILE.A86 (write output file to B disk, but rename
                           the file)

Commands:
nA   Append n lines from file.
0A   Append file until buffer is half
                           full.
#A   Append file until buffer is full (or
                           end of file).

B, -B	Move CP to top or bottom of memory buffer.
nC, -nC	Move CP n characters forward or backward.
nD, -nD	Delete n characters before or after the CP.
E	Save the new file and return to CP/M-86 CCP level.
Fstring{∧Z}	Find character string.
H	Save the new file, then reedit without leaving ED.
I	Enter insert text mode — ∧Z to exit.
Istring{∧Z}	Insert string at CP.
Jsearch-str∧Zinsert-str∧Zdel-str{∧Z}	Juxtapose strings.
nK, -nK	Delete (kill) n lines from CP.
nL, -nL	Move CP n lines.
OL	Return to start of line.
nMcommands	Execute command string n times (macro feature).
n, -n	Move CP n lines and display that line.
n:	Move to line n.
:ncommand	execute command through line n.
Nstring{∧Z)	extended find string (search through file on disk)
O	Return to original file.
nP, -nP	Move CP 23 lines forward or backward and display them.
Q	Quit without saving edit session.
R	Read X$$$$$$$.LIB file into buffer at CP.
Rfilespec{∧Z}	Read filespec into buffer.
Sdelete string∧Zinsert string{∧Z}	Substitute string.
nT, -nT	Type n lines.
OT	Retype current line.
U, -U	Uppercase translation (on or off).
V, -V	Line numbering on or off.
OV	Display free buffer space.
nW	Write n lines to new file.

nX	Write or append n lines to X$$$$$$$.LIB.
nXfilespec{∧Z}	Write n lines to filespec or append if previous X command applies to file.
0X	Delete file X$$$$$$$.LIB.
0Xfilespec{∧Z}	Delete filespec.
nZ	Wait n seconds.

ASM86 (CP/M-86 Assembler)

Form: ASM86 filespec {$ parameters}

Parameters:
$A   Override the default drive specifier for the source file.
$H   Override the default drive specifier for the hex file.
$P   Override the default drive specifier for the print file.
$S   Override the default drive specifier for the symbol file.
$F   Override the default hex file format.

The parameters must have a subsequent letter indicating the override value. For A, H, P, and S, the valid letters are A through P, corresponding to disk drives A to P, and X, Y, and Z, corresponding to console, printer, and no output, respectively. The F parameter has two values: I and D, where I stands for Intel hex format and D stands for Digital Research format. The default is "D."

Examples: ASM86
            MYFILE   (assemble with defaults)
            ASM86
            MYFILE $PX
            SX HZ   (assemble MYFILE and send the printer output to the console, the symbol table output to the console, and suppress the hex file.)
            ASM86
            MYFILE $PZ   (assemble with defaults, but suppress the print file.)

GENCMD (Generate CMD File):

Form: GENCMD   filespec {8080 CODE[An,Bn,Mn,Xn]
                              DATA[An,Bn,Mn,Xn]
                              STACK[An,Bn,Mn,Xn]
                              EXTRA[An,Bn,Mn,Xn]
                              X1[...]
                              X2[...]
                              X3[...]
                              X4[...]}
Examples: GENCMD   MYFILE 8080
           GENCMD   MYFILE
           GENCMD   MYFILE CODE[A0100]
                     STACK[A0FF00,M0100]

Parameters:
8080   Use 8080 memory model.
CODE   Override options for code segment.
DATA   Override options for data segment.
STACK   Override options for stack segment.
EXTRA   Override options for extra segment.
X1 – X4 Optional segments.

Options:
An   Load group at absolute location n.
Bn   Begin group at address n in the hexadecimal file.
Mn   The group requires a minimum of n × 16 bytes.
Xn   The group can address up to n × 16 bytes.

DDT-86 (Dynamic Debugging Tool):

Form: DDT86 {filespec}

Commands:
As   Assemble at s.
Bs,f,s1   Compare block s (to f) with s1.
D {s{,f}}   Display memory in bytes from s to f.
DW (s{,f}}   Display memory in words from s to f.
Efilespec   Load program for execution.
Fs,f,bc   Fill memory in bytes from s to f with bc.
FWs,f,wc   Fill memory in words from s to f with wc.

G{s} {,b1} {,b2}	Execute at s, with breakpoints at b1 and b2.
Hwc1,wc2	Hexadecimal sum and difference or wc1 and wc2.
Icommand tail	Set up an input command line.
L{s{,f}}	List memory in mnemonic form from s to f.
Ms,f,d	Move memory block from s (ending at f) to d.
Rfilespec	Read a disk file into memory.
Ss	Set memory (byte) values.
SWs	Set memory (word) values.
T{n}	Trace program execution for n instructions.
TS{n}	Trace program and show registers for n steps.
U{n}	Monitor execution without trace for n steps.
US{n}	Monitor execution and show registers for n steps.
V	Show memory layout after disk read.
Wfilespec{,s,f}	Write content of block to disk from s to f.
X{r}	Examine and/or modify CPU registers.

BDOS FUNCTION CALLS

BDOS Entry Registers

CL:	Single byte function number (required)
DL:	Single byte parameter (as needed)
DX:	Word or two byte parameter (as needed)
DS:	Base address of data segment (required)

BDOS Return Registers

AL:	Byte value (usually the error code)
AX and BX:	Word or two byte value (as needed)
ES and BX:	Double-word value returned with offset address in BX and segment address in ES.

Func	Description	Entry parameters (CL = function)	Results
0	System Reset	DL = Abort code	AL = ASCII character
1	Console Input		
2	Console Output	DL = ASCII character	AL = ASCII character
3	Reader Input		
4	Punch Output	DL = ASCII character	
5	List Output	DL = ASCII character	
6	Direct Console I/O	DL = (OFFH, input) (OFEH, status) or ASCII character	AL = ASCII character or status
7	Get I/O Byte		AL = I/O byte value
8	Set I/O Byte	DL = I/O byte value	
9	Print String	DX = String offset address	
10	Read Console Buffer	DX = Buffer offset address	characters in buffer
11	Get Console Status		AL = Console status
12	Return Version Number		BX = Version number
13	Reset Disk System		
14	Select Disk	DL = Selected disk	
15	Open File	DX = FCB offset address	AL = Return code
16	Close File	DX = FCB offset address	AL = Return code
17	Search for First	DX = FCB offset address	AL = Directory code
18	Search for Next		AL = Directory code
19	Delete File	DX = FCB offset address	AL = Return code
20	Read Sequential	DX = FCB offset address	AL = Return code
21	Write Sequential	DX = FCB offset address	AL = Return code
22	Make File	DX = FCB offset address	AL = Return code
23	Rename File	DX = FCB (old name, new name)	AL = Return code
24	Return Login Vector		BX = Login vector
25	Return Current Disk		AL = Current disk
26	Set DMA		

Func	Description	Entry parameters (CL = function)	Results
	Address	DX = DMA offset address	
27	Get Addr (Alloc)		ES,BX − Alloc address
28	Write Protect Disk		
29	Get Addr (R/O Vector)		BX = R/O vector value
30	Set File Attributes	DX = FCB offset address	AL = Return code
31	Get Addr (Disk Parms)		ES,BX = DPB address
32	Set/Get User Code	DL − (0FFH, get) or usercode	AL = Current code
33	Read Random	DX = FCB offset address	AL = Return code
34	Write Random	DX = FCB offset address	AL − Return code
35	Computer File Size	DX = FCB offset address	r0, r1, r2 Set
36	Set Random Record	DX = FCB offset address	r0, r1, r2 Set
37	Reset Drive	DX = drive vector	AL = 00H
40	Write Random with Zero Fill	DX = FCB offset address	AL = Return code
50	Direct BIOS Call	DX = BIOS Descriptor	AX, BX as set by BIOS
51	Set DMA Base	DX = Base Address	
52	Get DMA Base		ES,BX − DMA address
53	Get Max Mem	DX = Offset of MCB	AL = Return code
54	Get Abs Mem	DX = Offset of MCB	AL = Return code
55	Alloc Mem	DX = Offset of MCB	AL = Return code
56	Alloc Abs Mem	DX = Offset of MCB	AL = Return code
57	Free Mem		
58	Free All Mem		
59	Program Load	DX = FCB offset address	AX = Return code or BX = Base page address

READ RANDOM RETURN CODES

Return Code	Description
0	Operation successful.
1	Not used
2	No available data block — returned when the write random command attempts to allocate a new data block, but none exist.
3	Cannot close current extent. This error occurs when an attempt was made to change extents. It is caused by either an overwritten FCB or a write-random operation on a file that hasn't been opened.
4	Not used
5	No available directory space — occurs when the write command attempts to create a new extent, but no directory space exists.
6	Random record number out of range. This error code is returned whenever byte r2 of the FCB is non-zero.

WRITE RANDOM RETURN CODES

Return Code	Description
0	Operation Successful.
1	Read an unwritten record. This error indicates that a record not previously written was being read.
2	Not used
3	Cannot close current extent. This error occurs when an attempt was made to change extents. It is caused by either an overwritten FCB or a read-random operation on a file that hasn't been opened.
4	Seek to an unwritten extent. The extent requested has not been created. This error is similar to error 1.
5	Not used
6	Random record number out of range. This error code is returned whenever byte r2 of the FCB is non-zero.

File Control Block (FCB):

	dr	f1	. . .	f7	f8	t1	t2	t3	ex	s1	s2	rc	d0	. . .	dn	cr	r0	r1	r2
decimal	00	01	. . .	07	08	09	10	11	12	13	14	15	16	. . .	31	32	33	34	35
hex	00	01	. . .	07	08	09	0A	0B	0C	0D	0E	0F	10	. . .	1F	20	21	22	23
default fcb	-5C	5D	. . .	5F	60	61	62	63	64	65	66	67	68	. . .	7B	7C	7D	7E	7F

where: dr   Drive code (0 – 16)
               0 → use default drive for file
               1 → select disk drive A
               2 → select disk drive B
               . . .
               16 → select disk drive P

f1 – f8 File name field (uppercase ASCII with bit 7 = 0)

t1 – t3 File type field (uppercase ASCII)

Bit 7 of each character (denoted as t1′, t2′, and t3′ are used as follows:

t1′ → 1 = read only file

t2′ → 1 = SYS file, 0 = DIR file

t3′ → 1 = file has been archived (not used by CP/M)

ex   Contains current extent number.

ex is normally set to zero by the user when a file is opened, but can range from 0 to 31 when in use.

s1   Reserved for internal use.

s2   Reserved for internal use.

rc   Record count in current extent;

ranges from 0 to 128.

d0 – dn File allocation blocks (used by CP/M only).

cr   current record to read or write in a sequential file operation, normally set to zero by user when the file is opened.

r0 – r2 Optional random record number in the range 0 – 65535, with overflow to r2. r0 and r1 form a 16-bit word value with r0 as the low byte and r1 as the high byte.

16 Hex	10 Dec	2 Binary	ASCII ASCII	CTRL- Char	16 Hex	10 Dec	2 Binary	ASCII
00	000	00000000	NUL		60	096	01100000	
01	001	00000001	SOH	A	61	097	01100001	a
02	002	00000010	STX	B	62	098	01100010	b
03	003	00000011	ETX	C	63	099	01100011	c
04	004	00000100	EOT	D	64	100	01100100	d
05	005	00000101	ENQ	E	65	101	01100101	e
06	006	00000110	ACK	F	66	102	01100110	f
07	007	00000111	BEL	G	67	103	01100111	g
08	008	00001000	BS	H	68	104	01101000	h
09	009	00001001	HT	I	69	105	01101001	i
0A	010	00001010	LF	J	6A	106	01101010	j
0B	011	00001011	VT	K	6B	107	01101011	k
0C	012	00001100	FF	L	6C	108	01101100	l
0D	013	00001101	CR	M	6D	109	01101101	m
0E	014	00001110	SO	N	6E	110	01101110	n
0F	015	00001111	SI	O	6F	111	01101111	o
10	016	00010000	DLE	P	70	112	01110000	p
11	017	00010001	DC1	Q	71	113	01110001	q
12	018	00010010	DC2	R	72	114	01110010	r
13	019	00010011	DC3	S	73	115	01110011	s
14	020	00010100	DC4	T	74	116	01110100	t
15	021	00010101	NAK	U	75	117	01110101	v
16	022	00010110	SYN	V	76	118	01110110	v
17	023	00010111	ETB	W	77	119	01110111	w
18	024	00011000	CAN	X	78	120	01111000	x
19	025	00011001	EM	Y	79	121	01111001	y
1A	026	00011010	SUB	Z	7A	122	01111010	z
1B	027	00011011	ESC	[	7B	123	01111011	{

1C	028	00011100	FS	\	7C	124	01111100	|
1D	029	00011101	GS	]	7D	125	01111101	}
1E	030	00011110	RS	^	7E	126	01111110	~
1F	031	00011111	US		7F	127	01111111	DEL
20	032	00100000	space		80	128	10000000	
21	033	00100001	!		81	129	10000001	
22	034	00100010	"		82	130	10000010	
23	035	00100011	‡		83	131	10000011	
24	036	00100100	$		84	132	10000100	
25	037	00100101	%		85	133	10000101	
26	038	00100110	&		86	134	10000110	
27	039	00100111	'		87	135	10000111	
28	040	00101000	(		88	136	10001000	
29	041	00101001	)		89	137	10001001	
2A	042	00101010	*		8A	138	10001010	
2B	043	00101011	+		8B	139	10001011	
2C	044	00101100	,		8C	140	10001100	
2D	045	00101101	-		8D	141	10001101	
2E	046	00101110	.		8E	142	10001110	
2F	047	00101111	/		8F	143	10001111	
30	048	00110000	0		90	144	10010000	
31	049	00110001	1		91	145	10010001	
32	050	00110010	2		92	146	10010010	
33	051	00110011	3		93	147	10010011	
34	052	00110100	4		94	148	10010100	
35	053	00110101	5		95	149	10010101	
36	054	00110110	6		96	150	10010110	
37	055	00110111	7		97	151	10010111	
38	056	00111000	8		98	152	10011000	
39	057	00111001	9		99	153	10011001	
3A	058	00111010	:		9A	154	10011010	
3B	059	00111011	:		9B	155	10011011	
3C	060	00111100	<		9C	156	10011100	
3D	061	00111101	=		9D	157	10011101	
3E	062	00111110	>		9E	158	10011110	
3F	063	00111111	?		9F	159	10011111	
40	064	01000000	@		A0	160	10100000	
41	065	01000001	A		A1	161	10100001	
42	066	01000010	B		A2	162	10100010	
43	067	01000011	C		A3	163	10100011	
44	068	01000100	D		A4	164	10100100	
45	069	01000101	E		A5	165	10100101	
46	070	01000110	F		A6	166	10100110	
47	071	01000111	G		A7	167	10100111	
48	072	01001000	H		A8	168	10101000	
49	073	01001001	I		A9	169	10101001	
4A	074	01001010	J		AA	170	10101010	
4B	075	01001011	K		AB	171	10101011	
4C	076	01001100	L		AC	172	10101100	
4D	077	01001101	M		AD	173	10101101	
4E	078	01001110	N		AE	174	10101110	
4F	079	01001111	O		AF	175	10101111	

50	080	01010000	P	B0	176	10110000	
51	081	01010001	Q	B1	177	10110001	
52	082	01010010	R	B2	178	10110010	
53	083	01010011	S	B3	179	10110011	
54	084	01010100	T	B4	180	10110100	
55	085	01010101	U	B5	181	10110101	
56	086	01010110	V	B6	182	10110110	
57	087	01010111	W	B7	183	10110111	
58	088	01011000	X	B8	184	10111000	
59	089	01011001	Y	B9	185	10111001	
5A	090	01011010	Z	BA	186	10111010	
5B	091	01011011	[	BB	187	10111011	
5C	092	01011100	\	BC	188	10111100	
5D	093	01011101	]	BD	189	10111101	
5E	094	01011110	^	BE	190	10111110	
5F	095	01011111		BF	191	10111111	
C0	192	11000000		E0	224	11100000	
C1	193	11000001		E1	225	11100001	
C2	194	11000010		E2	226	11100010	
C3	195	11000011		E3	227	11100011	
C4	196	11000100		E4	228	11100100	
C5	197	11000101		E5	229	11100101	
C6	198	11000110		E6	230	11100110	
C7	199	11000111		E7	231	11100111	
C8	200	11001000		E8	232	11101000	
C9	201	11001001		E9	233	11101001	
CA	202	11001010		EA	234	11101010	
CB	203	11001011		EB	235	11101011	
CC	204	11001100		EC	236	11101100	
CD	205	11001101		ED	237	11101101	
CE	206	11001110		EE	238	11101110	
CF	207	11001111		EF	239	11101111	
D0	208	11010000		F0	240	11110000	
D1	209	11010001		F1	241	11110001	
D2	210	11010010		F2	242	11110010	
D3	211	11010011		F3	243	11110011	
D4	212	11010100		F4	244	11110100	
D5	213	11010101		F5	245	11110101	
D6	214	11010110		F6	246	11110110	
D7	215	11010111		F7	247	11110111	
D8	216	11011000		F8	248	11111000	
D9	217	11011001		F9	249	11111001	
DA	218	11011010		FA	250	11111010	
DB	219	11011011		FB	251	11111011	
DC	220	11011100		FC	252	11111100	
DD	221	11011101		FD	253	11111101	
DE	222	11011110		FE	254	11111110	
DF	223	11011111		FF	255	11111111	

Appendix **II**

Glossary

Accumulator A register internal to the CPU that holds results of arithmetic operations.

Address Bus The portion of the system bus that carries the address of the memory or I/O port to be accessed.

Address space he address space of a computer is a function of the addressing range. If a microcomputer has a 20 bit address range, the address space may be up to one megabyte in length.

ALU Arithmetic-logic unit. The portion of the central processor that performs all arithmetic and logic operations on data in the registers of the microprocessor.

Application program Any user-written software that is run on a microcomputer, using the services of the operating system.

Argument A place holder for a number, letter, or name, that is being passed from one level of a system to another. For example, a command can have several arguments that are being passed symbolically from the command level to the command itself for option selection or decision making.

ASCII American Standard Code for Information Interchange. A standard code for representing alphabetic, numeric, and special characters on a computer.

ASCII control character A group of nonprintable ASCII character such as carriage return or line feed, used to control a peripheral device or send messages from one machine to another, such as STX (Start of Text), or ESC (Escape).

Assembler A program that reads in mnemonic instructions written for the machine level of a computer and converts them to the operation codes that the computer can execute directly.

Asynchronous data transmission A form of data transmission whereby each byte may be sent at any time, with no special timing between bytes, but with strict timing within the byte. Used mostly for low-data-rate applications such as dial-up terminals.

Attribute A file characteristic that can be either on or off. File attributes in CP/M include: DIR, SYS, RO, and RW.

Back-up A copy of a disk or a file made for safe keeping.

Batch programming A method of executing programs whereby each is read into the system in order, and they are executed sequentially—as opposed to a time-sharing or multiprogramming system, whereby multiple users have concurrent access to the system.

BDOS Basic disk operating system. The CP/M nucleus.

BIOS Basic input/output system. The CP/M basic input/output system. The customized part of CP/M-86.

Bit A single binary digit, which may be either 1 or 0.

Block An allocation unit (usually 1K byte) on disk. Disk space is allocated in blocks.

Boot-load The action of loading the operating system or monitor into the computer after cold-start power-up. Normally the boot-load program is stored in programmable read-only memory so that it is present in the system on power-up.

Bootstrap See boot-load.

Buffer A block of memory set aside to hold information.

Built-in commands Commands that are resident in the operating system and don't have to be loaded from disk when needed (as opposed to transient commands).

Byte A unit of data, 8 bits.

CCP Console command processor. The CP/M command-interpreter program.

Character string A sequence of data bytes that represent characters in ASCII or EBCDIC or some other code.

CMD See command file.

Cold start The act of starting up a computer after power-on. The computer has no programs in memory and must be loaded from scratch.

Command A sequence of characters entered at either the CP/M-86 console command processor level, or to a utility program such as DDT-86 or a user program. The command usually consists of a keyword (that tells the program what you want to do) and optional arguments.

Command file A file that contains executable machine instructions.

Compiler A program that accepts as input a series of high-level commands and converts them to machine-level instructions that the computer can execute.

Concatenate An operation that combines two or more disk files and writes the result to a third file. One option within PIP allows for file concatenation.

Console The primary input/output device. The logical console device may be connected (through the BIOS) to a physical device that may be a teleprinter or VDT (Video Display Terminal) with a keyboard and text display.

Control character ASCII or EBCDIC characters used to control the input of data (e.g., carriage return, line feed, XON).

Controller A hardware circuit that controls access to a peripheral device such as a disk drive.

CP/M Control Program for Microcomputers. An operating system written and distributed by Digital Research. CP/M-86 will operate on the 8086 and 8088 16-bit microcomputers.

CPU Central processor unit. That portion of the computer that controls all operations of the ALU and the interface between the computer the outside world.

Cross assembler A program that assembles machine instructions for a computer with a different instruction set than the one the cross assembler is running on. The output of the cross assembler is then downloaded to the target computer.

Cursor A one-character symbol that appears on the screen of the console (assuming you are using a Video Display Terminal) where the next character to be sent from the keyboard or computer will be displayed.

Data bus The portion of the system bus that carries the data that is to be read or written to the main memory or I/O ports.

Debugger A program that assist the user in testing and tracing errors in an application program.

Default drive The disk drive that has been selected as the current drive. All disk file operations are performed (or attempted) on the default drive if no disk drive specifier is included in the file name.

Delimiter A special character (such as a dollar sign) that separates different items in a command line. For example, a period separates the file name from the file type, and the dollar sign is used by the assembler to separate the command and file names from the single character options.

Device assignments Logical-to-physical assignments that allow peripheral devices to be traded as needed for an application without having to be physically disconnected and reconnected.

Direct memory access (DMA) An action performed by a peripheral device that allows it to gain direct access to the main memory of the microcomputer. When the peripheral inititates direct memory access, the microprocessor is forced to stop all bus activity while the peripheral occupies the bus. This method allows extremely high datatransfer rates, at the expense of the microprocessor.

Directory The portion of a floppy disk that contains entries for each file on the disk. The CP/M-86 DIR command will display all the entries on a particular disk.

DIR attribute This file attribute specifies that the particular directory entry will be listed as a regular file, not as a system or invisible file.

Disk file A logical grouping of information on a disk. A file may contain text, a program, or any other information in any representation.

Disk formatting A procedure that writes blank sectors of data to a disk, initializing it for later use.

Disk initialization See disk formatting.

DO loop A programming construct whereby a group of instructions can be repeated under certain conditions.

DOS Disk operating system. An operating system based primarily on disk-storage capabilities.

Downloading A way of transferring programs or data from a large computer system to a microcomputer. This allows program development or data acquisition to take place on the large computer whereas program execution may take place on the microcomputer.

Editor A utility program that creates and modifies text files. The CP/M-86 editor (ED) can be used to enter programs, but in general is not useful for large-volume text editing, because it works on a single line at a time instead of a screen page.

EPROM Erasable programmable read-only memory. Similar to PROM, but can be erased when held under a shortwave ultraviolet light.

Extent A dummy file control block used to extend the size of a disk file.

External storage Memory that is not directly accessible to the microcomputer, such as disk or tape storage.

FCB File control block. A block of data used to represent hold the name and physical attributes of a disk file. Usually stored on disk in a directory of files, but is copied to memory when the file is in use.

File name The name assigned to a file. The file name portion of the file specification usually refers to only the first 8 characters, while the file type refers to the three character extension of the file name.

File specification A unique file indentifier. Sometimes referred to as the filespec or even just filename, it includes optional file name, file type, and disk drive specifier.

File type The extension to a file specification. The file type can be from one to three characters and must be separated from the file name by a period. The file type usually tells something about the contents of the file. For example: CMD stands for "Command file"; A86 refers to "Asm-86," and so on.

Floppy disk. A flexible disk made of mylar with a magnetic coating. Disks are made in two normal sizes: 8 inches and 5.25 inches. A typical 8-inch disk can hold 250,000 bytes of information in single-density mode, 500,000 in double-density mode, and 1,000,000 bytes in double-density double-sided mode, depending on the type of disk controller and disk drives used.

Floppy-disk controller The hardware or circuit board used to interface the floppy-disk drive to the microcomputer bus.

Full Duplex A form of serial data transmission in which two data links are running side by side, one in each direction.

Half Duplex A form of serial data transmission in which only one data link is used, so each computer must take turns talking and listening.

Hard disk A type of disk made from a rigid piece of metal that can store from 5 million bytes up to about 50 million bytes, and has a much faster access time.

Hardware The physical circuitry that makes up the computer. This can include the central processor, the arithmetic unit, the main memory, disk drives, and so on.

.H86 In either CP/M or MP/M, a .HEX file contains an executable program in hex-intel format. The LOAD program can be used to convert it to a .COM file.

Hexadecimal A number system based on 16. The digits are represented as 0, 1, 2, 3, 4, 5, 6, 7, 8, 9, A, B, C, D, E, F.

Hex-Intel format A standard format for storing binary information on paper tape, disk, or magnetic tape.

Input Data going into the computer, usually from the console, or serial interface, although it can refer to any input operation on the computer.

Instruction register The internal CPU register that holds the current machine instruction to be executed.

Interface Usually the hardware that connects one piece of equipment to another, such as an RS-232 interface. Can also refer to the logical connection of two programs or data files.

Interpreter A program that accepts as input a series of high-level commands and executes them as it goes, rather than saving them as machine instructions.

Interrupt An external signal that causes the microprocessor to stop what it was doing and execute a series of instructions called the *interrupt handler*. An interrupt may be generated by a disk when an action is completed, or by an incoming character at at serial port. The use of interrupts allows the microprocessor to handle events as they come, rather than having to repeatedly "poll" or search for incoming data.

I/O Input/output.

IPL Initial program load. See *boot-load*.

Jump vector A jump or branch instruction that transfers control to a specific subroutine or function.

Kilobyte 1024 bytes or 1K byte. Since all computer addressing is done in powers of two, it is convenient to define K as 1024 rather than 1000, since 1024 is a power of two.

List Device An output-only device, such as a line printer, to which encoded characters (usually ASCII) can be sent to get hard copy printouts.

Logged in A disk drive that is "logged in" has been made known to CP/M-86. Internal tables are set by CP/M to indicate the location and amount of available space on the disk, its status (i.e., read-only), etc. A disk remains logged in from the time it is first accessed, until CTRL-C is typed to reset the disk system.

Logical device A device that is defined according to CP/M's standards. CP/M-86 has four logical devices: console, list, auxiliary input, and auxiliary output. These devices can be mapped in to physical devices such as video display terminals, printers, modems, and so on. The advantage is that all users will write software that uses the logical devices which are compatible on all implementations of CP/M-86.

Mass storage Storage external to the microcomputer such as disk or tape. Generally this term is used in reference to hard-disk technology.

Megabyte 1024 kilobytes or 1024 × 1024 (1,048,576) bytes. Rather than defining one megabyte as an even million, it is defined as the nearest power of 2 or 1,048,576, to make division by two easy. See kilobytes.

Memory Any of several forms of storage, including RAM, PROM, disk, tape, or any magnetic media.

Memory dump A list of a block of main memory, showing the data in hexadecimal or other notation, and the ASCII character representation of the data.

Microprocessor A miniature computer contained on a single integrated circuit.

Multiprogramming operating system An operating system that executes multiple programs concurrently.

Nucleus That part of an operating system that is the center of all control and resource-management activities. Whenever the application program requires service performed by a program or the operating system, but are waiting in line for a particular resource. See BDOS.

Operating system Any program or group of related programs whose purpose is to act as intermediary between the hardware and the user. The operating system's main job is to manage resources such as disk drives, printers, and other peripherals, freeing the programmer from having to rewrite commonly used functions for each application. In this way, the operating system provides a uniform, consistent means for all user-written software to access the same machine resources.

Output Data that the processor sends to a disk or some logical device such as a console or list device.

Parallel interface A peripheral interface to the CPU by way of the system bus that sends or receives data in parallel from another computer or device.

Parameter Value in a command string that provides additional information to the program being called. A required element of a command.

Peripheral Any device external to the CPU, such as input or output devices, disk drives, or tape drives.

Peripheral devices Devices that are external to the CPU. Printers, terminals, and disks are peripherals; main memory is not.

Physical devices Physical hardware attached to the computer through serial or parallel input/output ports, such as printers or terminals.

Pointer A storage location or register than contains a memory address that may point to a specific location in memory.

Program A sequence of machine instructions that the microprocessor reads and interprets to carry out arithmetic data movement and transfer of control functions.

Program counter The internal CPU register that holds the address of the current machine instruction.

PROM Programmable read-only memory. An integrated circuit that stores data when programmed with high-voltage pulses and cannot be erased.

RAM Random-access memory. Memory that can be randomly accessed as necessary to retrieve data. This is the type used for the main memory of most computers.

Random allocation A software function whereby sectors are randomly allocated to files as needed, as opposed to *sequential allocation*.

Read-only This attribute is commonly used to refer to a file or disk that has been marked by the operating system so that it can't be overwritten. The read-only attribute bit in the file control block may be set for each file on a disk. A whole disk can be set to read-only as well.

Read/write This attribute refers to a file or disk that can be read or written without any special action. The read-write bit of the file control block can be set to indicate that a file can be read or written by anyone. This is the normal state of a file control block.

Record A collection of data on a disk. A logical record in CP/M-86 is 128 bytes long. It is mapped into the physical sectors of a disk, even if sectors are longer than 128 bytes.

Register pair On the 8080 or Z80, a pair of registers such as HL, BC, DE may be treated as one 16-bit register instead of two 8-bit registers for certain operations.

RO See read-only.

ROM Read-only memory. A kind of memory circuit that can only be programmed at the factory.

RW See read/write.

Scrolling The act of moving the displayed text lines of a video display up one line, to simulate the action of a teleprinter. Usually scrolling is done on receipt of a linefeed character.

Secondary extents The space allocated to disk files when the first directory entry becomes full. Each directory entry in a randomly allocated disk-file system contains a list of sectors or blocks allocated to the file. When the directory entry is full, a second or third entry must be started. These secondary entries do not show up when the directory is listed.

Sector A portion of a track on disk. A physical sector on disk contains 128 bytes on a single-density single-sided 8-inch disk drive.

Sector mapping A method of improving disk-access time by skewing or shifting sector addresses around the disk. If the operating system reads a sector and then attempts to read the next sequential sector, the disk will generally have rotated out of position and will have to complete one revolution before it is in position again. Sector skewing involves a logical-to-physical mapping of sectors so they are offset around the disk, allowing the operating system time to process each sector before reading the next one. This saves a great deal of time because the computer need not wait through a whole revolution for each sector access.

Sector skew See sector mapping.

Sequential allocation A software function whereby sectors are sequentially allocated to disk files, rather than randomly allocated.

Serial interface A peripheral interface to the CPU by way of the system bus that sends and receives data serially from another computer or terminal.

Simulator A program that simulates the actions of the central processor, allowing a program to be stepped through, instruction by instruction, to determine where errors are occurring.

Software The program or machine isntructions that the central processor interprets to perform arithmetic and data-movement functions on the hardware.

Source file ASCII text file that contains source statements for ASM-86 or some other high-level language, such as BASIC or FORTRAN.

Stack A data structure used in most microcomputers to save registers, CPU status flags, and the program counter. When a subroutine is called, the return address is "pushed" onto the stack.

Stack pointer A CPU register that contains the address of the next available stack entry.

Subroutine A program that can be called from another program. When the subroutine is completed, control is returned to the calling program.

Subroutine library A collection of frequently referenced subroutines that can be loaded with an application program.

Synchronous data transmission A form of data transmission whereby each byte is sent in a strict sequence, with strict timing between the bytes. This form is especially useful at high data rates, because it is more resistent to these errors.

Syntax Format for entering a command.

Syntax Error An error in the format of a command line, either in the CP/M-86 command processor, DDT-86, ASM-86, ED, or any other program that accepts input commands or statements.

System attribute A file attribute that can be given to any file control block on disk. This attribute tells CP/M that the file is a system file, and that it shouldn't be displayed in a directory listing. The file itself is no different than any other file, though.

System bus The group of parallel data, address, and control lines that connect the CPU to the rest of the computer system.

System environment The hardware and software organization of a microcomputer system.

System utilities Programs that assist the user in performing certain housekeeping functions on the system.

Track Concentric circles on a disk. A typical 8-inch disk has 77 concentric tracks, each containing 26 sectors.

Transient program A program that is used only briefly or only once in a great while. A program that is not resident in the operating system.

UART Universal asynchronous receiver/transmitter. An integrated circuit that contains all circuitry required to send and recieve serial data.

USART Universal synchronous-asynchronous receiver/transmitter. An integrated circuit that contains all circuitry required to send and receive serial data either synchronously or asynchronously.

User number The number assigned to a file in the disk directory that tells CP/M which user area the file belongs to. Since up to 15 users are allowed, each user can have a separate directory display that doesn't contain the files of other users. Actually, the directory entries for all users are intermixed, but the user number lets CP/M sort them out for each user.

Utility A program that enables the user to perform commonly used operations such as copying files, deleting or editing files, and so on. They are a convenience for the users and are provided so the user doesn't have to write them all from scratch.

Video display A display device using a cathode ray tube (CRT) as the display mechanism. Used to display character and graphic information.

VDT Video display terminal. A terminal that uses a video display rather than a printer to display incoming text.

Wait state A machine cycle inserted into the normal operation of the microprocessor when it becomes necessary to slow down and wait for a slow memory of I/O device.

Warm start The act of restarting a computer after it has been running. This may be necessary because of program failure or hardware failure.

Wild card characters Special characters that match certain fields in a file name. In CP/M-86 there are two wild card characters: * and ?. The question mark (?) can be substituted for any single character in a file name or file type, and the asterisk (*) can be substituted for the file name, file type, or both. By placing wild card characters in file specifications, the user can create an ambiguous file name that can quickly reference one or more files (when using utilities that support wild cards such as PIP and DIR).

XON-XOFF protocol A standard protocol used when information is being tranferred from one computer to another. This protocol usually requires a full duplex data link. When the receiving end can no longer accept data (if it has something else to do and cannot wait for data to come to it), it can send an XOFF ASCII control character that tells the sender to wait until an XON is sent.

Appendix III

MY-DIR Listing

```
;-----------------------------------------------
;
;    This program is provided as an example.
;All (or any part) of it may be copied for
;use on any 8086/8088 microcomputer system.
;
;-----------------------------------------------
;
;    This program is almost the same as the
;built-in DIR command on CP/M-86.  It lists
;all files, but only works on the default
;disk.  It doesn't accept a command tail,
;and displays all files of a user number,
;including system files.
;It is provided as an example of how to
;write assembler programs using BDOS function
;calls.
;-----------------------------------------------
;
;
0001                    coninp  equ     1
0002                    conout  equ     2
0009                    pstring equ     9
000A                    rstring equ     10
0011                    search  equ     17
0012                    srchn   equ     18
                        ;
                        ;
000D                    cr      equ     0dh
000A                    lf      equ     0ah
                        ;
```

```
    0004                    fper_line equ   4                   ;number of file
                                                                ;names per line
                        ;
                                cseg                            ;start of code segment
                        ;
                        ;
                        ;                                       print startup message
                        ;
0000 B109                       mov     cl,pstring
0002 BA0001                     mov   · dx,offset startmsg
0005 E89900      00A1           call    bdos
                        ;
                        ;
                        ; fill fcb with question marks
                        ;
0008 8CD8                       mov     ax,ds               ;make sure ES
                                                            ;is the same as DS
000A 8EC0                       mov     es,ax
                        ;
000C BE2701                     mov     si,offset fcbqm
000F BF5C00                     mov     di,offset fcb
0012 B92300                     mov     cx,35
0015 F3A4                       rep movs al,al
                        ;
0017 C6064A0104                 mov     count,fper_line         ;initialize
                                                                ;count to 6
                        ;
                        ;                                       search for
                        ;                                       first entry
001C B111           srch:       mov     cl,search
001E BA5C00                     mov     dx,offset fcb
0021 E87D00      00A1           call    bdos
                        ;
0024 3CFF                       cmp     al,0ffh             ;test for failure
0026 7414        003C           je      error
0028 E81900      0044           call    pr_fcb              ;print it
                        ;
002B B112           snext:      mov     cl,srchn
002D BA5C00                     mov     dx,offset fcb
0030 E86E00      00A1           call    bdos                ;search for next
                        ;
0033 3CFF                       cmp     al,0ffh             ;test for failure
0035 7405        003C           jz      error
                        ;
0037 E80A00      0044           call    pr_fcb              ;print it
003A EBEF        002B           jmps    snext               ;continue
                        ;
                    error:                                  ;if here, we have
                                                            ;end of directory
003C E86500      00A4           call    prcrlf              ;new line
                        ;
003F B100           abort:      mov     cl,0
0041 E85D00      00A1           call    bdos
                        ;----------------------------------> Return to CP/M
                        ;
                        ;
                    pr_fcb:                                 ;Print the FCB
                        ;
0044 8CDB                       mov     bx,ds               ;set up es
0046 8EC3                       mov     es,bx
                        ;
                        ;
                        ;                                   on entry, al=offset
                        ;                                   into buffer
0048 B105                       mov     cl,5                ;number of shifts
                                                            ;to perform
004A D2E0                       shl     al,cl               ;al * 32
004C BA8000                     mov     dx,offset buff
```

```
004F 03D0                          add     dx,ax           ;buffer + (al*32)
                          ;
0051 8BF2                          mov     si,dx
0053 46                            inc     si              ;point to fname field
0054 BF1701                        mov     di,offset ofn   ;output area
0057 B90800                        mov     cx,8            ;8 chars
005A F3A4                          rep movs al,al          ;block move
                                                           ;SI is already set
                                                           ;from last move
005C B90300                        mov     cx,3
005F BF2001                        mov     di,offset oft   ;set up pointer
                                                           ;to output buffer
0062 F3A4                          rep movs al,al
                          ;
                          ;before printing, mask off all bit 7s
                          ;in the filename and filetype
                          ;
0064 BE1701                        mov     si,offset ofn
0067 BF1701                        mov     di,offset ofn
006A B90C00                        mov     cx,12           ;file name and
                                                           ;file type (12
                                                           ;characters)
006D AC              iter:         lods    al
006E 247F                          and     al,7fh          ;mask off top bit
0070 8805                          mov     [di],al         ;save it again
0072 47                            inc     di
0073 E2F8            006D          loop    iter            ;decrement cx, repeat
                          ;                                 now print the file spec
0075 BA1401                        mov     dx,offset oarea
0078 E81200          008D          call    pstrng
                          ;
                          ;
007B A04A01                        mov     al,count
007E FE0E4A01                      dec     count           ;count = count - 1
0082 7508            008C          jnz     done
0084 E81D00          00A4          call    prcrlf
0087 C6064A0104                    mov     count,fper_line ;if count = 0, reset it
                          done:
008C C3                            ret
                          ;
                          pstrng:                 ;we have to make our own
                                                  ;print function since
                                                  ;the standard bdos print string
                                                  ;uses a $ as the terminator.
                                                  ;(the dollar sign is a valid
                                                  ; character in the filespec)
                          ;
                          ; on entry, addr is in dx.
                          ; string should terminate with a 00h byte.
008D 8BDA                          mov     bx,dx           ;put address of
                                                           ;string in bx
008F 8A17            pstr:         mov     dl,[bx]         ;get byte at bx
0091 0AD2                          or      dl,dl           ;test for zero
                                                           ;(end of string)
0093 740B            00A0          jz      pstr2           ;end of string
0095 53                            push    bx
0096 B102                          mov     cl,conout       ;print char
0098 E80600          00A1          call    bdos
009B 5B                            pop     bx
009C 43                            inc     bx              ;point to next
                                                           ;character
009D E9EFFF          008F          jmp     pstr            ;do it again
00A0 C3              pstr2:        ret                     ;done
                          ;This is subroutine calls the bdos through
                          ;software interrupt 224.  Since all CP/M-80
                          ;programs call the bdos through location 0005H
                          ;in memory, this makes conversion of programs
                          ;easier.  Also, using a CALL is easier than
```

```
                        ;using the INT instruction.
                        ;
                        ;However, the following sequence could be used:
                        ;
                        ;bdos    equ     224
                        ;
                        ;        int     bdos
                        ;
                        ; BDOS ENTRY POINT (CALLABLE AS A SUBROUTINE)
                        ;
00A1 CDE0               bdos:   int     224
00A3 C3                         ret
                        ;
                        ;This subroutine simply displays a
                        ;carriage return and a line feed
                        ;on the logical console device.
                        ;
                        ;
                        prcrlf:                         ;go to new line
00A4 B109                       mov     cl,pstring
00A6 BA2401                     mov     dx,offset crlf
00A9 E8F5FF      00A1           call    bdos
00AC C3                         ret
                        ;
                        ;This is the beginning of the Data Segment.
                        ;
                        ;
                        ;
                                dseg
                        ;
                                org     005CH           ;This is the
                                                        ;location of the
                                                        ; default FCB.
  005C                  fcb     equ     $
005C                    drcode  rb      1
005D                    fname   rb      8
0065                    ftype   rb      3
0068                    ext     rb      1
0069                            rb      2
006B                    reccnt  rb      1
006C                            rb      16
007C                    currec  rb      1
007D                    ranrec  rw      1
007F                    ranovf  rb      1
                        ;
0080                    buff    rb      128
                        ;
                                org     0100H   ;In all programs,
                                                ;start your data area
                                                ;at 0100H.  The memory
                                                ;from DS + 0000h to
                                                ;to DS + 00FFh is used
                                                ;by CP/M-86, just as
                                                ;0000h to 00FFH
                                                ;is used by CP/M-80.
                        ;
                        ;
                        ;
0100 446972656374       startmsg db      'Directory Command'
     6F727920436F
     6D6D616E64
0111 0D0A24                      db      cr,lf,'$'
                        ;
0114 203A20             oarea   db      ' : '
0117 202020202020       ofn     db      '        '
     2020
011F 2E                         db      '.'
```

```
0120 202020          oft     db      '  '
0123 00                      db      0                      ;terminator
                     ;
0124 0D0A24          crlf    db      cr,lf,'$'      ;end of line string
                     ;
                     ;
0127 003F3F3F3F3F    fcbqm   db      0,'???????????'
     3F3F3F3F3F3F
0133                         rb      23
                     ;
014A 00              count   db      0                      ;temporary variable
                     ;
                             end
```

END OF ASSEMBLY. NUMBER OF ERRORS: 0. USE FACTOR: 5%

A>type b:my-dir.sym

```
0000 VARIABLES
0080 BUFF        014A COUNT      0124 CRLF      007C CURREC    005C DRCODE
0068 EXT         0127 FCBQM      005D FNAME     0065 FTYPE     0114 OAREA
0117 OFN         0120 OFT        007F RANOVF    007D RANREC    006B RECCNT
0100 STARTMSG

0000 NUMBERS
0001 CONINP      0002 CONOUT     000D CR        0004 FPERLINE  000A LF
0009 PSTRING     000A RSTRING    0011 SEARCH    0012 SRCHN

0000 LABELS
003F ABORT       00A1 BDOS       008C DONE      003C ERROR     005C FCB
006D ITER        00A4 PRCRLF     0044 PRFCB      008F PSTR      00A0 PSTR2
008D PSTRNG      002B SNEXT      001C SRCH
```


A>type b:my-dir.h86

```
:0400000300000000F9
:1B000081B109BA0001E899008CD88EC0BE2701BF5C00B92300F3A4C6064A0131
:1B001B8104B11BA5C00E87D003CFF7414E81900B112BA5C00E86E003CFF7466
:1B00368105E80A00EBEFE86500B100E85D008CDB8EC3B105D2E0BA800003D0ED
:1B0051818BF246BF1701B90800F3A4B90300BF2001F3A4BE1701BF1701B90C7C
:1B006C8100AC247F880547E2F8BA1401E81200A04A01FE0E4A017508E81D006E
:1B008781C6064A0104C38BDA8A170AD2740B53B102E806005B43E9EFFFC3CDA5
:0B00A281E0C3B109BA2401E8F5FFC3F7
:1B010082446972656374F727920436F6D6D616E640D0A24203A202020202099
:18011B82202020202E202020000D0A24003F3F3F3F3F3F3F3F3F3F3F4C
:01014A820032
:00000001FF
```

A>dir b:

```
B: MY-DIR    A86 : MY-DIR    LST : MY-DIR    H86 : MY-DIR    SYM
B: MY-DIR    CMD
A>
```

```
B>my-dir

Directory Command
 : MY-DIR   .A86 : MY-DIR   .LST : MY-DIR   .H86 : MY-DIR   .SYM
 : MY-DIR   .CMD
```

Appendix **IV**

Character I/O Disk Functions

INTRODUCTION

This appendix describes some sample assembler programs included in this book as public domain software. The subroutines, collectively, allow disk files to be read or written a character at a time—transparently. This means that disk files can be treated just like the console or other character-oriented devices.

Normally, disk files are manipulated a record (128 bytes) at a time. There are, however, times when it would be easier to work with a text file one character at a time, such as for search and/or filtering functions.

Figure IV.1 shows the data structures for the subroutines described in this section. Since it is likely that both read and write files will be active at the same time, two data buffers (referred to as DMA buffers) are needed. Each is 128 bytes or one record long. The pointers, RPTR and WPTR, always point to the next available character or character location in their respective buffers. RCNTR and WCNTR are counters that count down from 128 to 0 and are used to determine when the read buffer is empty (completely read) or the write buffer is full (completely written). Both read and write files also must have file control blocks. RFCB and WFCB point to the two FCBs.

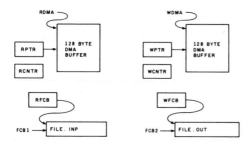

Figure IV.1: Data structures.

Figure IV.2 shows the read routine initialization procedure. The address of the FCB (supplied by the user) is entered in the DX register. RD_INIT opens the read file, checks for errors, and reads the first record into the RDMA buffer. The pointer RPTR and counter RCNTR are initialized.

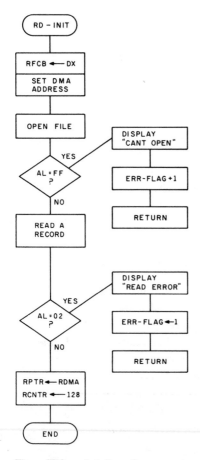

Figure IV.2: rd_init routine.

Figure IV.3 shows the write routine initialization procedure. WR_INIT also requires the user FCB address. This routine first tries to delete the old file (if one exists) and then creates a new of the same name. If the file can't be created, an error message is displayed. The WPNTR and WCNTR variables are initialized.

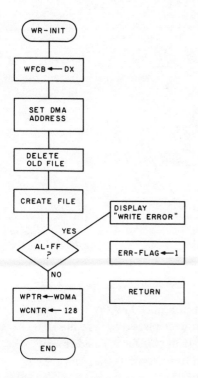

Figure IV.3:   wr_init routine.

The actual read character routine is shown in Figure IV.4 (RD_CHAR). For each call to RD_CHAR, a single character from the file is returned in the DL register. If the buffer is empty, RD_CHAR will transparently (without the user's knowledge) read a new record from disk and reset the pointer and counter values. The user is responsible for stopping the application program when an end of file character (1A in hexadecimal, 26 in decimal, or CTRL-Z) is returned.

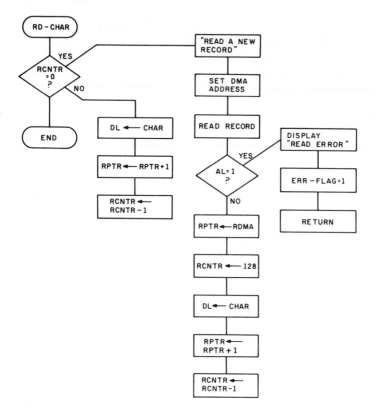

Figure IV.4: RD_CHAR.

The write character routine is shown in Figure IV.5 (WR_CHAR). For each call to WR_CHAR, a single character passed to it in the DL register will be written to the output file. If the buffer is filled (every 128 characters), the buffer will be written to the output file, and the pointer and counter will be reset.

Using these subroutines, file input and output can be viewed as sending or receiving a continuous stream of characters, with no intervening program logic to complicate things.

Listing IV.1 shows the actual character I/O subroutines. If Listing IV.1 is entered exactly as shown and stored in a file called CHARIO.LIB, any subsequent assembly program can simply insert the statement INCLUDE CHARIO.LIB just before the END directive. Note that the include statement must precede the END statement for the subroutines to work properly in the user's program.

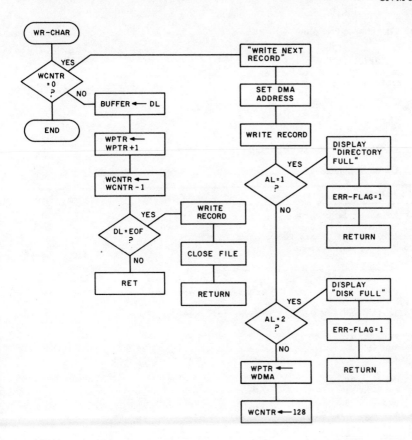

Figure IV.5: WR_CHAR.

Listing IV.1:   char-io.lib listing.

```
A>type b:chario.lib
;(This is an include file, not an
; executable program.)
;
;
;
;
;
;         Character oriented Disk I/O
;
;         by Mark Dahmke
;
;         7-24-82
;----------------------------------------------
;  This is a sample program.
;
;Any part or all of it may be used by
;the reader for any purpose.
;
;----------------------------------------------
;
          cseg    $                    ;restart the code segment.
;
;The following equates must be present for char-io to work.
;
setdma    equ     26
conout    equ     2
conin     equ     1
openf     equ     15
readf     equ     20
writef    equ     21
closef    equ     16
pstring   equ     9
makef     equ     22
deletf    equ     19
eof_char  equ     1ah
;
;
;------------------------------------------
; RD_INIT initializes the read file
; for RD_CHAR.
; Entry:  DX -> FCB
; Returns: err_flag = 0 if no error.
;
;
;
rd_init:
          push    dx
          push    cx
          push    bx
          push    ax
          mov     rfcb,dx         ;save fcb pointer
          mov     dx,offset rdma
          mov     cl,setdma
          call    bdos
;
          mov     dx,rfcb                  ;get pointer to fcb
          mov     cl,openf
          call    bdos            ;open the file
          cmp     al,0ffh         ;error?
          jz      open_err
;
          mov     rptr,offset rdma         ;load address of buffer
          mov     rcntr,length rdma        ;init counter
          mov     dx,rfcb
```

```
          mov     cl,readf
          call    bdos                      ;load the first record
;
          cmp     al,01h          ;error?
          jnz     rd_2            ;if no error, terminate normally
rd_error:
          mov     dx,offset rd_msg
          mov     cl,pstring
          call    bdos
          mov     err_flag,1                ;set error flag
rd_2:
          pop     ax
          pop     bx
          pop     cx
          pop     dx
          ret
;
open_err:
          mov     dx,offset opn_msg
          mov     cl,pstring
          call    bdos                      ;print open error
          mov     err_flag,1                ;set flag
          jmp     rd_2                      ;then terminate
;
;-----------------------------------------------------------------
;
; WR_INIT initializes the write buffer (and file) for
;WR_CHAR.
;
;Entry: DX -> FCB
;Returns: err_flag = 0 if no errors.
;
;
wr_init:
          push    dx
          push    cx
          push    bx
          push    ax
          mov     wfcb,dx         ;save entry FCB pointer
          mov     dx,offset wdma  ;set dma address
          mov     cl,setdma
          call    bdos
;
          mov     dx,wfcb         ;get pointer to fcb
          mov     cl,deletf
          call    bdos            ;first get rid of old file
;
          mov     dx,wfcb
          mov     cl,makef
          call    bdos            ;create the new file
;
          cmp     al,0ffh         ;check for error
          jz      wr_error
;
          mov     wptr,offset wdma            ;set pointer to start of buffer
          mov     wcntr,length wdma
          jmp     wr_2            ;terminate normally
;
wr_error:
          mov     dx,offset wr_msg
          mov     cl,pstring
          call    bdos
          mov     err_flag,1      ;set flag
wr_2:
          pop     ax
          pop     bx
          pop     cx
          pop     dx
          ret
```

```
;
;
;--------------------------------
;RD_CHAR returns a single character
;from the file, in the DL register.
;
;Entry: none.
;Returns: DL = character.
;          and err_flag = 0 if no errors.
;
;
rd_char: cmp    rcntr,0           ;have we exhausted the buffer?
         jz     rd_rec            ;if so, get a new record
         push   si
         mov    si,rptr           ;get pointer
         mov    dl,[si]           ;get byte
         pop    si
         inc    rptr              ;point to next byte
         dec    rcntr             ;decrement the counter
         ret
;
rd_rec:  push   dx                ;save dx
         push   cx
         push   bx
         push   ax
         mov    dx,offset rdma    ;load dma address
         mov    cl,setdma
         call   bdos
         mov    dx,rfcb ;load user fcb
         mov    cl,readf
         call   bdos              ;read the next record
         cmp    al,01h            ;error?
         jz     rd_rerr
         mov    rptr,offset rdma  ;reset the pointer
         mov    rcntr,length rdma        ;reset the counter
         pop    ax
         pop    bx
         pop    cx
         pop    dx                ;restore dx
         jmp    rd_char           ;continue with read.
rd_rerr:
         mov    dx,offset rd_msg
         mov    cl,pstring
         call   bdos
         mov    err_flag,1        ;set error flag
rd_r2:
         pop    ax
         pop    bx
         pop    cx
         pop    dx
         ret
;
;
;--------------------------------
;WR_CHAR writes a single character
;to the output file.
;
;Entry: character in DL.
;Returns: err_flag = 0 if no errors.
;
;
wr_char:
;
         cmp    wcntr,0           ;is counter zero yet?
         jz     wr_rec            ;if so, write the record
         push   si
         mov    si,wptr           ;get pointer
         mov    [si],dl           ;store the incoming byte
         pop    si
```

```
        inc     wptr                ;point to next location
        dec     wcntr               ;decrement counter
        cmp     dl,eof_char         ;have we reached end of file?
        jz      wr_rec              ;if so, write last record,
                                    ;and close file.
;
wr_ret:
        ret
;
wr_rec:
        push    dx
        push    cx
        push    bx
        push    ax
        mov     dx,offset wdma      ;get pointer to buffer
        mov     cl,setdma
        call    bdos                ;set dma to point to buffer
;
        mov     dx,wfcb
        mov     cl,writef
        call    bdos
;
        cmp     al,01h              ;check for directory full
        jz      dir_full
        cmp     al,02h              ;check for disk full
        jz      disk_full
        mov     wptr,offset wdma    ;reset pointer
        mov     wcntr,length wdma   ;reset counter
        pop     ax
        pop     bx
        pop     cx
        pop     dx
        cmp     dl,eof_char         ;check for eof character
        jz      wr_close            ;if eof, close the file.
        jmp     wr_char             ;write the character
;
wr_close:
        push    dx
        push    cx
        push    bx
        push    ax
        mov     dx,wfcb
        mov     cl,closef
        call    bdos                ;close the file
        pop     ax
        pop     bx
        pop     cx
        pop     dx
        ret
;
dir_full:
        mov     dx,offset dir_msg
        mov     cl,pstring
        call    bdos
        mov     err_flag,1          ;set error flag
        jmp     wr_rerr
disk_full:
        mov     dx,offset disk_msg
        mov     cl,pstring
        call    bdos
        mov     err_flag,1
wr_rerr:
        pop     ax
        pop     bx
        pop     cx
        pop     dx
        ret
;
abort:                              ;return control to CP/M-86.
```

```
        mov     cl,0
        call    bdos
;
;
;
;
;
bdos:   int     224
        ret
;
;--------------------------------
;
; This data segment section must be included
;for char-io to work.  Although its location is
;dependent on the previous (user program) data
;segment, it must occur AFTER 0100H for it to
;work properly.
;
;
        dseg    $                       ;restart the data segment.
;
fcb     equ     005ch                   ;user fcb is at this address
                                        ;in data segment.
;
;
;
rfcb    dw      0                       ;pointer to user fcb
rptr    dw      0                       ;pointer to dma area
rcntr   db      0                       ;counter for buffer
;
rdma    rb      128                     ;reserve buffer area
        db      0
;
wfcb    dw      0                       ;pointer to user fcb for write
wptr    dw      0                       ;pointer to dma write area
wcntr   db      0                       ;counter for write buffer
;
wdma    rb      128
        db      0
fcb2    rb      36                      ;set up second fcb area
        db      0
;
;
;
;
disk_msg db     'No space for destination file.$'
dir_msg  db     'Directory full.$'
rd_msg   db     'Read error.$'
wr_msg   db     'Write error.$'
opn_msg  db     'Can''t open the file.$'
;
err_flag db     0
;
        end
```

SOME EXAMPLES

Listing IV.2 shows a simple use for the character I/O routines—a lowercase to uppercase character translation program. This kind of program is often called a filter, because it filters characters (and perhaps alters them) on their way from the source file to the destination file. Note the include statement at the end of the listing. The include statement will be replaced by the source for the actual subroutines in the file CHARIO.LIB. Listing IV.3 shows the result of assembling Listing IV.2.

Listing IV.2: Sample—lowercase to uppercase translation.

```
A>type b:chario.a86
;
;
;
;
;
;          Character oriented Disk I/O
;
;          by Mark Dahmke
;
;          7-24-82
;-----------------------------------------------
;   This is a sample program.
;
;Any part or all of it may be used by
;the reader for any purpose.
;
;-----------------------------------------------
;
;
;
;
          cseg
          mov       ax,ds            ;make sure ES is the same as DS
          mov       es,ax
;
;
main:
;
          mov       si,offset fcb+16      ;point to second fcb
          mov       di,offset fcb2        ;destination area
          mov       cx,16                 ;move 16 bytes
          rep movs al,al
;
          mov       err_flag,0            ;reset error flag
          mov       dx,offset fcb
          call      rd_init               ;initialize the input file.
          cmp       err_flag,0            ;check for errors
          jnz       stop                  ;found?
;
;
          mov       dx,offset fcb2
          call      wr_init               ;init the output file
          cmp       err_flag,0
          jnz       stop                  ;if error, abort
;
;
          mov       bx,offset t_table  ;set up pointer to translate table
loop:     call      rd_char            ;get a char
          cmp       err_flag,0
          jnz       stop               ;if error, abort
          mov       al,dl              ;put the char in al
          xlat      bx
          mov       dl,al              ;return the tranlated char to dl
          push      bx
          push      dx
          mov       cl,conout
          call      bdos               ;display it
          pop       dx
          push      dx                 ;restore dl register
          call      wr_char
          cmp       err_flag,0
          jnz       stop               ;if error, abort
          pop       dx
          pop       bx
```

```
        cmp     dl,eof_char     ;have we reached the end yet?
        jz      stop            ;if so, terminate.
        jmp     loop
;
stop:   jmp     abort           ;this instruction allows the
                                ;use of relative jz and jnz
                                ;instructions in the above
                                ;program.
;
        dseg
;
        org     0100h
;
;
t_table db      0,1,2,3,4,5,6,7,8,9,10,11,12,13,14,15
        db      16,17,18,19,20,21,22,23,24,25,26,27,28,29,30,31
        db      ' !"#$%&'
        db      27h             ;quote character
        db      '( )*+,-./'
        db      '0123456789'
        db      ':;<=>?@'
        db      'ABCDEFGHIJKLMNOPQRSTUVWXYZ'
        db      '[\]^_`'
        db      'ABCDEFGHIJKLMNOPQRSTUVWXYZ'
        db      '{|}~'
        db      7fh                             ;delete char
;
;
; now, include the library file for character i/o functions
;
        include chario.lib
;
        end
```

Listing IV.3: The listing in IV.2 assembled.

```
                        ;
                        ;
                        ;       Lower to Upper Case Translation
                        ;
                        ;
                        ;       using character oriented Disk I/O
                        ;
                        ;       by Mark Dahmke
                        ;
                        ;       7-24-82
                        ;----------------------------------------
                        ;   This is a sample program.
                        ;
                        ;Any part or all of it may be used by
                        ;the reader for any purpose.
                        ;
                        ;----------------------------------------
                        ;
                                cseg
0000 8CD8                       mov     ax,ds           ;make sure ES is the
                                                        ;same as DS
0002 8EC0                       mov     es,ax
                        ;
                        main:
                        ;
0004 BE6C00                     mov     si,offset fcb+16        ;point to the
                                                                ;second fcb
0007 BF8C02                     mov     di,offset fcb2         ;destination
                                                                ;area
000A B91000                     mov     cx,16                 ;move 16 bytes
000D F3A4                       rep movs al,al
```

```
                              ;
000F C6060E0300              mov     err_flag,0              ;reset error
                                                            ;flag
0014 BA5C00                  mov     dx,offset fcb
0017 E84600         0060     call    rd_init                 ;initialize the
                                                            ;input file.
001A 803E0E0300              cmp     err_flag,0              ;check for
                                                            ;errors
001F 753C           005D     jnz     stop                    ;found?
                              ;
                              ;
0021 BA8C02                  mov     dx,offset fcb2
0024 E89000         00B7     call    wr_init                 ;init the
                                                            ;output file
0027 803E0E0300              cmp     err_flag,0
002C 752F           005D     jnz     stop                    ;if error,
                                                            ;abort

                              ;
                              ;
002E BB0001                  mov     bx,offset t_table  ;set up pointer to
                                                         ;translate table
0031 E8C900    00FD loop:    call    rd_char             ;get a char
0034 803E0E0300              cmp     err_flag,0
0039 7522           005D     jnz     stop                ;if error, abort
003B 8AC2                    mov     al,dl               ;put the char in al
003D D7                      xlat    bx
003E 8AD0                    mov     dl,al               ;return the tranlated
                                                         ;char to dl
0040 53                      push    bx
0041 52                      push    dx
0042 B102                    mov     cl,conout
0044 E89501    01DC          call    bdos                ;display it
0047 5A                      pop     dx
0048 52                      push    dx                  ;restore dl register
0049 E80601    0152          call    wr_char
004C 803E0E0300              cmp     err_flag,0
0051 750A      005D          jnz     stop                ;if error, abort
0053 5A                      pop     dx
0054 5B                      pop     bx
0055 80FA1A                  cmp     dl,eof_char         ;have we reached the
                                                         ;end yet?
0058 7403      005D          jz      stop                ;if so, terminate.
005A E9D4FF    0031          jmp     loop
                              ;
005D E97701    01D7 stop:    jmp     abort               ;this instruction
                                                         ;allows the use of
                                                         ;relative jz and jnz
                                                         ;instructions in the
                                                         ;above program.

                              ;
                              dseg
                              ;
                              org     0100h
                              ;
                              ;
0100 000102030405    t_table db      0,1,2,3,4,5,6,7,8,9,10,11,12,13,14,15
     060708090A0B
     0C0D0E0F
0110 101112131415            db      16,17,18,19,20,21
0116 161718191A1B            db      22,23,24,25,26,27
011C 1C1D1E1F                db      28,29,30,31
0120 202122232425            db      ' !"#$%&'
     26
0127 27                      db      27h                 ;quote character
0128 28292A2B2C2D            db      '( )*+,-./'
     2E2F
0130 303132333435            db      '0123456789'
     36373839
```

```
013A 3A3B3C3D3E3F                db          ':;<=>?@'
     40
0141 414243444546                db          'ABCDEFGHIJKLMNOPQRSTUVWXYZ'
     4748494A4B4C
     4D4E4F505152
     535455565758
     595A
015B 5B5C5D5E5F60                db          '[\]^_`'
0161 414243444546                db          'ABCDEFGHIJKLMNOPQRSTUVWXYZ'
     4748494A4B4C
     4D4E4F505152
     535455565758
     595A
017B 7B7C7D7E                    db          '{|}~'
017F 7F                          db          7fh              ;delete char
                            ;
                            ;
                            ; now, include the library file for character i/o
                            ; functions:
                            ;
  =                                 include chario.lib
  =                         ;(This is an include file, not an
  =                         ; executable program.)
  =                            ;
  =                            ;
  =                            ;
  =                            ;
  =                            ;
  =                            ;           Character oriented Disk I/O
  =                            ;
  =                            ;           by Mark Dahmke
  =                            ;
  =                            ;           7-24-82
  =                            ;-------------------------------------------
  =                            ; This is a sample program.
  =                            ;
  =                         ;Any part or all of it may be used by
  =                         ;the reader for any purpose.
  =                            ;
  =                            ;-------------------------------------------
  =                            ;
  =                                 cseg     $           ;restart the code segment.
  =                            ;
  =                         ;The following equates must be present for char-io
  =                         ;to work.
  =                            ;
  = 001A                     setdma   equ      26
  = 0002                     conout   equ      2
  = 0001                     conin    equ      1
  = 000F                     openf    equ      15
  = 0014                     readf    equ      20
  = 0015                     writef   equ      21
  = 0010                     closef   equ      16
  = 0009                     pstring  equ      9
  = 0016                     makef    equ      22
  = 0013                     deletf   equ      19
  = 001A                     eof_char equ      1ah
  =                            ;
  =                            ;
  =                            ;-------------------------------------------
  =                         ; RD_INIT initializes the read file
  =                         ; for RD_CHAR.
  =                         ; Entry:  DX -> FCB
  =                         ; Returns: err_flag = 0 if no error.
  =                            ;
  =                            ;
  =                            ;
  =                         rd_init:
```

```
=0060 52                          push    dx
=0061 51                          push    cx
=0062 53                          push    bx
=0063 50                          push    ax
=0064 89168001                    mov     rfcb,dx          ;save fcb pointer
=0068 BA8501                      mov     dx,offset rdma
=006B B11A                        mov     cl,setdma
=006D E86C01        01DC          call    bdos
=                           ;
=0070 8B168001                    mov     dx,rfcb          ;get pointer to fcb
=0074 B10F                        mov     cl,openf
=0076 E86301        01DC          call    bdos             ;open the file
=0079 3CFF                        cmp     al,0ffh          ;error?
=007B 742A          00A7          jz      open_err
=                           ;
=007D C70682018501                mov     rptr,offset rdma         ;load address
=                                                          ; of buffer
=0083 C606840180                  mov     rcntr,length rdma        ;init counter
=0088 8B168001                    mov     dx,rfcb
=008C B114                        mov     cl,readf
=008E E84B01        01DC          call    bdos             ;load the first record
=                           ;
=0091 3C01                        cmp     al,01h           ;error?
=0093 750D          00A2          jnz     rd_2             ;if no error,
=                                                          ;terminate normally
=                           rd_error:
=0095 BAE002                      mov     dx,offset rd_msg
=0098 B109                        mov     cl,pstring
=009A E83F01        01DC          call    bdos
=009D C6060E0301                  mov     err_flag,1       ;set error flag
=                           rd_2:
=00A2 58                          pop     ax
=00A3 5B                          pop     bx
=00A4 59                          pop     cx
=00A5 5A                          pop     dx
=00A6 C3                          ret
=                           ;
=                           open_err:
=00A7 BAF902                      mov     dx,offset opn_msg
=00AA B109                        mov     cl,pstring
=00AC E82D01        01DC          call    bdos             ;print open error
=00AF C6060E0301                  mov     err_flag,1       ;set flag
=00B4 E9EBFF        00A2          jmp     rd_2             ;then terminate
=                           ;
=                           ;-----------------------------------------
=                           ;
=                           ; WR_INIT initializes the write buffer (and file) for
=                           ;WR_CHAR.
=                           ;
=                           ;Entry: DX -> FCB
=                           ;Returns: err_flag = 0 if no errors.
=                           ;
=                           ;
=                           wr_init:
=00B7 52                          push    dx
=00B8 51                          push    cx
=00B9 53                          push    bx
=00BA 50                          push    ax
=00BB 89160602                    mov     wfcb,dx          ;save entry FCB pointer
=00BF BA0B02                      mov     dx,offset wdma   ;set dma address
=00C2 B11A                        mov     cl,setdma
=00C4 E81501        01DC          call    bdos
=                           ;
=00C7 8B160602                    mov     dx,wfcb          ;get pointer to fcb
=00CB B113                        mov     cl,deletf
=00CD E80C01        01DC          call    bdos             ;first get rid of old
=                                                          ;file
=                           ; .
```

```
=00D0 8B160602                      mov     dx,wfcb
=00D4 B116                          mov     cl,makef
=00D6 E80301      01DC              call    bdos            ;create the new file
=                              ;
=00D9 3CFF                          cmp     al,0ffh         ;check for error
=00DB 740E        00EB              jz      wr_error
=                              ;
=00DD C70608020B02                  mov     wptr,offset wdma      ;set pointer to
=                                                                 ;start of buffer
=00E3 C6060A0280                    mov     wcntr,length wdma
=00E8 E90D00      00F8              jmp     wr_2            ;terminate normally
=                              ;
=                          wr_error:
=00EB BAEC02                        mov     dx,offset wr_msg
=00EE B109                          mov     cl,pstring
=00F0 E8E900      01DC              call    bdos
=00F3 C6060E0301                    mov     err_flag,1      ;set flag
=                          wr_2:
=00F8 58                            pop     ax
=00F9 5B                            pop     bx
=00FA 59                            pop     cx
=00FB 5A                            pop     dx
=00FC C3                            ret
=                              ;
=                              ;
=                              ;------------------------------
=                              ;RD_CHAR returns a single character
=                              ;from the file, in the DL register.
=                              ;
=                              ;Entry: none.
=                              ;Returns: DL = character.
=                              ;         and err_flag = 0 if no errors.
=                              ;
=                              ;
=00FD 803E840100   rd_char: cmp     rcntr,0         ;have we exhausted the
=                                                   ;buffer?
=0102 7411        0115              jz      rd_rec          ;if so, get a new
=                                                           ;record
=0104 56                            push    si
=0105 8B368201                      mov     si,rptr         ;get pointer
=0109 8A14                          mov     dl,[si]         ;get byte
=010B 5E                            pop     si
=010C FF068201                      inc     rptr            ;point to next byte
=0110 FE0E8401                      dec     rcntr           ;decrement the counter
=0114 C3                            ret
=                              ;
=0115 52          rd_rec: push      dx              ;save dx
=0116 51                            push    cx
=0117 53                            push    bx
=0118 50                            push    ax
=0119 BA8501                        mov     dx,offset rdma  ;load dma address
=011C B11A                          mov     cl,setdma
=011E E8BB00      01DC              call    bdos
=0121 8B168001                      mov     dx,rfcb ;load user fcb
=0125 B114                          mov     cl,readf
=0127 E8B200      01DC              call    bdos            ;read the next record
=012A 3C01                          cmp     al,01h          ;error?
=012C 7412        0140              jz      rd_rerr
=012E C70682018501                  mov     rptr,offset rdma   ;reset the pointer
=0134 C606840180                    mov     rcntr,length rdma      ;reset the
=                                                                  ;counter
=0139 58                            pop     ax
=013A 5B                            pop     bx
=013B 59                            pop     cx
=013C 5A                            pop     dx              ;restore dx
=013D E9BDFF      00FD              jmp     rd_char         ;continue with read.
=                          rd_rerr:
=0140 BAE002                        mov     dx,offset rd_msg
```

```
=0143 B109                      mov     cl,pstring
=0145 E89400      01DC          call    bdos
=0148 C6060E0301                mov     err_flag,1      ;set error flag
=                       rd_r2:
=014D 58                        pop     ax
=014E 5B                        pop     bx
=014F 59                        pop     cx
=0150 5A                        pop     dx
=0151 C3                        ret
=                       ;
=                       ;
=                       ;------------------------------------
=                       ;WR_CHAR writes a single character
=                       ;to the output file.
=                       ;
=                       ;Entry: character in DL.
=                       ;Returns: err_flag = 0 if no errors.
=                       ;
=                       ;
=                       wr_char:
=                       ;
=0152 803E0A0200                cmp     wcntr,0         ;is counter zero yet?
=0157 7416      016F            jz      wr_rec          ;if so, write the
=                                                       ;record
=0159 56                        push    si
=015A 8B360802                  mov     si,wptr         ;get pointer
=015E 8814                      mov     [si],dl         ;store the incoming
=                                                       ;byte
=0160 5E                        pop     si
=0161 FF060802                  inc     wptr            ;point to next location
=0165 FE0E0A02                  dec     wcntr           ;decrement counter
=0169 80FA1A                    cmp     dl,eof_char     ;have we reached
=                                                       ;end of file?
=016C 7401      016F            jz      wr_rec          ;if so, write last
=                                                       ;record, and close
=                                                       ;the file.
=                       wr_ret:
=016E C3                        ret
=                       wr_rec:
=016F 52                        push    dx
=0170 51                        push    cx
=0171 53                        push    bx
=0172 50                        push    ax
=0173 BA0B02                    mov     dx,offset wdma  ;get pointer to buffer
=0176 B11A                      mov     cl,setdma
=0178 E86100      01DC          call    bdos            ;set dma to point to
=                                                       ;buffer
=                       ;
=017B 8B160602                  mov     dx,wfcb
=017F B115                      mov     cl,writef
=0181 E85800      01DC          call    bdos
=                       ;
=0184 3C01                      cmp     al,01h          ;check for directory
=                                                       ;full
=0186 742D      01B5            jz      dir_full
=0188 3C02                      cmp     al,02h          ;check for disk full
=018A 7439      01C5            jz      disk_full
=018C C70608020B02              mov     wptr,offset wdma        ;reset pointer
=0192 C6060A0280                mov     wcntr,length wdma       ;reset counter
=0197 58                        pop     ax
=0198 5B                        pop     bx
=0199 59                        pop     cx
=019A 5A                        pop     dx
=019B 80FA1A                    cmp     dl,eof_char             ;check for eof
=                                                               ;character
=019E 7403      01A3            jz      wr_close                ;if eof, close
=                                                               ;the file.
=01A0 E9AFFF     0152           jmp     wr_char                 ;write the
=                                                               ;character
```

```
-                           wr_close:
-01A3 52                            push    dx
-01A4 51                            push    cx
-01A5 53                            push    bx
-01A6 50                            push    ax
-01A7 8B160602                      mov     dx,wfcb
-01AB B110                          mov     cl,closef
-01AD E82C00      01DC              call    bdos              ;close the file
-01B0 58                            pop     ax
-01B1 5B                            pop     bx
-01B2 59                            pop     cx
-01B3 5A                            pop     dx
-01B4 C3                            ret
-                           dir_full:
=01B5 BAD002                        mov     dx,offset dir_msg
=01B8 B109                          mov     cl,pstring
=01BA E81F00      01DC              call    bdos
=01BD C6060E0301                    mov     err_flag,1        ;set error flag
=01C2 E90D00      01D2              jmp     wr_rerr
-                           disk_full:
=01C5 BAB102                        mov     dx,offset disk_msg
=01C8 B109                          mov     cl,pstring
=01CA E80F00      01DC              call    bdos
=01CD C6060E0301                    mov     err_flag,1
-                           wr_rerr:
=01D2 58                            pop     ax
=01D3 5B                            pop     bx
=01D4 59                            pop     cx
=01D5 5A                            pop     dx
=01D6 C3                            ret
-                           ;
-                           abort:                           ;return control
-                                                            ;to CP/M-86.
=01D7 B100                          mov     cl,0
=01D9 E80000      01DC              call    bdos
-                           ;
-                           ;
-                           ;
-                           ;
-                           ;
=01DC CDE0                 bdos:    int     224
=01DE C3                            ret
-                           ;
-                           ;-------------------------------
-                           ;
-                           ; This data segment section must be included
-                           ;for char-io to work.  Although its location is
-                           ;dependent on the previous (user program) data
-                           ;segment, it must occur AFTER 0100H for it to
-                           ;work properly.
-                           ;
-                           ;
-                                    dseg    $                ;restart the data
-                                                             ;segment.
-                           ;
-  005C                     fcb      equ     005ch            ;user fcb is at
-                                                             ;this address
-                                                             ;in data segment.
-                           ;
=0180 0000                  rfcb     dw      0                ;pointer to user fcb
=0182 0000                  rptr     dw      0                ;pointer to dma area
=0184 00                    rcntr    db      0                ;counter for buffer
-                           ;
=0185                       rdma     rb      128              ;reserve buffer area
=0205 00                             db      0
-                           ;
=0206 0000                  wfcb     dw      0                ;pointer to user fcb
-                                                             ;for write
```

```
=0208 0000              wptr    dw      0               ;pointer to dma
=                                                       ;write area
=020A 00                wcntr   db      0               ;counter for
=                                                       ;write buffer
=                               ;
=020B                   wdma    rb      128
=028B 00                        db      0
=028C                   fcb2    rb      36              ;set up second fcb area
=02B0 00                        db      0
=                               ;
=                               ;
=                               ;
=                               ;
=02B1 4E6F20737061      disk_msg db     'No space for destination file.$'
      636520666F72
      206465737469
      6E6174696F6E
      2066696C652E
      24
=02D0 446972656374      dir_msg db      'Directory full.$'
      6F7279206675
      6C6C2E24
=02E0 526561642065      rd_msg  db      'Read error.$'
      72726F722E24
=02EC 577269746520      wr_msg  db      'Write error.$'
      6572726F722E
      24
=02F9 43616E277420      opn_msg db      'Can''t open the file.$'
      6F70656E2074
      68652066696C
      652E24
=                               ;
=030E 00                err_flag db     0
=                               ;
                                end
                        ;
                                end
```

```
END OF ASSEMBLY.   NUMBER OF ERRORS:   0.  USE FACTOR:  6%
0000 VARIABLES
02D0 DIRMSG       02B1 DISKMSG     030E ERRFLAG     028C FCB2        02F9 OPNMSG
0184 RCNTR        0185 RDMA        02E0 RDMSG       0180 RFCB        0182 RPTR
0100 TTABLE       020A WCNTR       020B WDMA        0206 WFCB        0208 WPTR
02EC WRMSG

0000 NUMBERS
0010 CLOSEF       0001 CONIN       0002 CONOUT      0013 DELETF      001A EOFCHAR
005C FCB          0016 MAKEF       000F OPENF       0009 PSTRING     0014 READF
001A SETDMA       0015 WRITEF

0000 LABELS
01D7 ABORT        01DC BDOS        01B5 DIRFULL     01C5 DISKFULL    0031 LOOP
0004 MAIN         00A7 OPENERR     00A2 RD2         00FD RDCHAR      0095 RDERROR
0060 RDINIT       014D RDR2        0115 RDREC       0140 RDRERR      005D STOP
00F8 WR2          0152 WRCHAR      01A3 WRCLOSE     00EB WRERROR     00B7 WRINIT
016F WRREC        01D2 WRRERR      016E WRRET
```

Since the include file has its own code and data segments, it is necessary to use the forms CSEG $ and DSEG $ in the include file, so these segments will append to the end of the application program's segments. Your program must have both code and data segments, even if the data segment has no statements following it before the include directive.

Listing IV.4:   Input and output examples of Listing IV.3.

```
A>

A>type b:test.in

This is a test file for char-io.

ABCDEFGHIJKLMNOPQRSTUVWXYZ

0123456789

!@#$%^&*( )_-=+[]{};:'`""~,./<>?

abcdefghijklmnopqrstuvwxyz



A>type b:test.txt

THIS IS A TEST FILE FOR CHAR-IO.

ABCDEFGHIJKLMNOPQRSTUVWXYZ

0123456789

!@#$%^&*( )_-=+[]{};:'`""~,./<>?

ABCDEFGHIJKLMNOPQRSTUVWXYZ

A>
```

Listing IV.4 shows sample input and output files used with the program in Listing IV.3. The first file is called TEST.IN and contains the input for the RD_CHAR subroutine. The second file is called TEST.TXT and is the output from WR_CHAR after the program was run. The only difference is that all lowercase characters in the input file have been translated to uppercase in the output file.

ANOTHER EXAMPLE

Listing IV.5 shows the FIND program. This program requires an input file name on the command line and will prompt you on the console for a search string. The program will read through the entire input file searching for every occurrence of the string. When found, the text line (from the last line to the next carriage return) is displayed on the console. No output file was written in this example, but it would not be difficult to add.

In summary, these examples are intended to show how RD_CHAR and WR_CHAR can be used for simplified disk file input and output.

Listing IV.5: Sample of the find program.

```
                           ;
                           ;
                           ;
                           ;
                           ;
                           ;          String search program
                           ;
                           ;          by Mark Dahmke
                           ;
                           ;          7-24-82
                           ;-------------------------------------------
                           ;  This is a sample program.
                           ;
                           ;Any part or all of it may be used by
                           ;the reader for any purpose.
                           ;
                           ;-------------------------------------------
                           ;
                           ;
                           ;          title    'FIND - String Search Program'
                           ;
                           ;
                           ;
 000D                      cr       equ      0dh                      ;carriage
                                                                      ;return
 000A                      lf       equ      0ah                      ;line-feed
 000A                      rstring  equ      10                       ;read console
                           buffer
                                                                      ;bdos function
                           ;
                           cseg
 0000 8CD8                 mov      ax,ds                    ;make sure ES is the
                                                             ;same as DS
 0002 8EC0                 mov      es,ax
                           ;
                           ;
                           main:
                           ;
                           ;
 0004 C606B20B00           mov      err_flag,0               ;reset error
                                                             ;flag
 0009 BA5C00               mov      dx,offset fcb
 000C E87C00      008B     call     rd_init                  ;initialize
                                                             ;the input
                                                             ;file.
 000F 803EB20B00           cmp      err_flag,0               ;check for
                                                             ;errors
 0014 7572        0088     jnz      stop                     ;found?
                           ;
                           ;
 0016 BA030A               mov      dx,offset str_msg        ;display
                                                             ;prompt
 0019 B109                 mov      cl,pstring
 001B E8E901      0207     call     bdos
                           ;
 001E BA0001               mov      dx,offset in_buff        ;point to
                                                             ;input buffer
 0021 B10A                 mov      cl,rstring               ;read the
                                                             ;search string
 0023 E8E101      0207     call     bdos
                           ;
 0026 803E000100           cmp      buff_len,0               ;check for zero case
 002B 745B        0088     jz       stop                     ;if zero, abort.
                           ;
                           srch:                             ;begin the search.
 002D E83400      0064     call     rd_line                  ;read in a text line
                                                             ;from the input file.
```

```
0030 8CD8                    mov      ax,ds             ;set es to overlap ds
0032 8EC0                    mov      es,ax             ;(DI always uses
                                                        ;ES for) addressing
                                                        ;memory.
0034 B80202                  mov      ax,offset line    ;point to start of
                                                        ;text line
0037 A30002                  mov      line_ptr,ax       ;store start position
                    ;
                    srcha:                              ;this is the inner
                                                        ;search loop.
003A 8B360002                mov      si,line_ptr       ;point to start
                                                        ;of text line
003E BF0101                  mov      di,offset buff_st ;point to start
                                                        ;of string
0041 B500                    mov      ch,0              ;make sure
                                                        ;cx = buff_len
0043 8A0E0001                mov      cl,buff_len       ;first byte of in_buff
                                                        ;contains string
                                                        ;length
                                                        ;(returned by bdos
                                                        ;call)
0047 F3A6                    repz     cmps al,al        ;string compare
                                                        ;instruction
0049 740A        0055        jz       equal             ;zero flag will be set
                                                        ;if a match was found.
004B FF060002                inc      line_ptr          ;increment the
                                                        ;line pointer
                                                        ;and try again.
004F 807C010D                cmp      byte [si],cr      ;if we have reached
                                                        ;the end of the
                                                        ;text line,
                                                        ;then abort the search
                                                        ;and get a new line.
0053 74D8        002D        je       srch
                    equal:                              ;if equal, print the
                                                        ;line.
0055 E80300       005B       call     pr_line
0058 E9D2FF       002D       jmp      srch              ;and get the next line
                    ;
                    ;
                    ;
                    pr_line:
005B B109                    mov      cl,pstring
005D BA0202       0207       mov      dx,offset line    ;point to text line
0060 E8A401                  call     bdos
0063 C3                      ret
                    ;
                    rd_line:                            ;this routine reads a
                                                        ;text line from the
                                                        ;disk file and stores
                                                        ;it in the
                                                        ;buffer called "line."
0064 BB0202                  mov      bx,offset line
                    rd_loop:
0067 E8BE00       0128       call     rd_char           ;get a character
006A 803EB20B00              cmp      err_flag,0
006F 7517        0088        jnz      stop              ;any errors?
0071 80FA0A                  cmp      dl,lf             ;if it is a line-feed
                                                        ;character, ignore it.
0074 74F1        0067        jz       rd_loop
                    ;
0076 8817                    mov      [bx],dl           ;save the character
                                                        ;in the line buffer
0078 43                      inc      bx                ;increment the buffer
                                                        ;pointer
```

```
0079 80FAOD                      cmp     dl,cr             ;was it a cr?
007C 75E9           0067         jnz     rd_loop           ;if not, get next
                                                           ;character

007E C647010A                    mov     byte [bx],lf      ;if so, then terminate
                                                           ;the line with a line-
                                                           ;feed and a dollar
                                                           ;sign (for
                                                           ;the pstring function)
0082 43                          inc     bx
0083 C6470124                    mov     byte [bx],'$'
0087 C3                          ret
                          ;
                          ;
0088 E97701         0202 stop:   jmp     abort             ;this instruction
                                                           ;the use of relative
                                                           ;jz and jnz
                                                           ;instructions in the
                                                           ;above program.

                          ;
                                  dseg
                          ;
                                  org     0100h
                          ;
                          ;
   0100                   in_buff equ     $
0100 00                   buff_len db     0                 ;length of string
                                                            ;set by the bdos)
                                                            ;in the read string
                                                            ;function)
0101                      buff_st rb      254               ;set aside some extra
                          buffer space
01FF 00                           db      0
                          ;
0200 0000                 line_ptr dw     0
                          ;
0202                      line    rb      2048              ;reserve space for
                                                            ;text line.
                          ;
0A02 00                           db      0
                          ;
0A03 506C65617365        str_msg db       'Please enter the search string: $'
     20656E746572
     207468652073
     656172636820
     737472696E67
     3A2024

                          ;
                          ;
                          ;Now, include the library file for character i/o
                          ;functions:
                          ;
-                                 include chario.lib
-                         ;(This is an include file, not an
-                         ; executable program.)
-                         ;
-                         ;
-                         ;
-                         ;
-                         ;
-                         ;       Character oriented Disk I/O
-                         ;
-                         ;       .by Mark Dahmke
-                         ;
-                         ;       7-24-82
-                         ;-------------------------------------
-                         ; This is a sample program.
-                         ;
```

```
    =                            ;Any part or all of it may be used by
    =                            ;the reader for any purpose.
    =                            ;
    =                            ;------------------------------------------
    =                            ;
    =                                     cseg    $              ;restart the code
    =                                                            ;segment.
    =                            ;
    =                            ;The following equates must be present for char-io to
    =                            ;work.
    =                            ;
    =   001A                     setdma   equ    26
    =   0002                     conout   equ    2
    =   0001                     conin    equ    1
    =   000F                     openf    equ    15
    =   0014                     readf    equ    20
    =   0015                     writef   equ    21
    =   0010                     closef   equ    16
    =   0009                     pstring  equ    9
    =   0016                     makef    equ    22
    =   0013                     deletf   equ    19
    =   001A                     eof_char equ    1ah
    =                            ;
    =                            ;
    =                            ;---------------------------------------
    =                            ; RD_INIT initializes the read file
    =                            ; for RD_CHAR.
    =                            ; Entry:  DX -> FCB
    =                            ; Returns: err_flag = 0 if no error.
    =                            ;
    =                            ;
    =                            ;
    =                            rd_init:
    =008B 52                             push    dx
    =008C 51                             push    cx
    =008D 53                             push    bx
    =008E 50                             push    ax
    =008F 8916240A                       mov     rfcb,dx        ;save fcb pointer
    =0093 BA290A                         mov     dx,offset rdma
    =0096 B11A                           mov     cl,setdma
    =0098 E86C01       0207              call    bdos
    =                            ;
    =009B 8B16240A                       mov     dx,rfcb        ;get pointer
    =                                                           ;to fcb
    =009F B10F                           mov     cl,openf
    =00A1 E86301       0207              call    bdos           ;open the file
    =00A4 3CFF                           cmp     al,0ffh        ;error?
    =00A6 742A         00D2              jz      open_err
    =                            ;
    =00A8 C706260A290A                   mov     rptr,offset rdma       ;load address
    =                                                                   ;of buffer.
    =00AE C606280A80                     mov     rcntr,length rdma      ;init counter
    =00B3 8B16240A                       mov     dx,rfcb
    =00B7 B114                           mov     cl,readf
    =00B9 E84B01       0207              call    bdos                   ;load the
    ;next record
    =                            ;
    =00BC 3C01                           cmp     al,01h         ;error?
    =00BE 750D         00CD              jnz     rd_2 .         ;if no error,
    =                                                           ;terminate normally
    =                            rd_error:
    =00C0 BA840B                         mov     dx,offset rd_msg
    =00C3 B109                           mov     cl,pstring
    =00C5 E83F01       0207              call    bdos
    =00C8 C606B20B01                     mov     err_flag,1     ;set error flag
    =                            rd_2:
    =00CD 58                             pop     ax
    =00CE 5B                             pop     bx
    =00CF 59                             pop     cx
```

```
=00D0 5A                          pop     dx
=00D1 C3                          ret
=                         ;
=                         open_err:
=00D2 BA9D0B                      mov     dx,offset opn_msg
=00D5 B109                        mov     cl,pstring
=00D7 E82D01          0207        call    bdos              ;print open error
=00DA C606B20B01                  mov     err_flag,1        ;set flag
=00DF E9EBFF          00CD        jmp     rd_2              ;then terminate
=                         ;
=                         ;------------------------------------------------------
=                         ;
=                         ; WR_INIT initializes the write buffer (and file) for
=                         ;WR_CHAR.
=                         ;
=                         ;Entry: DX -> FCB
=                         ;Returns: err_flag = 0 if no errors.
=                         ;
=                         ;
=                         wr_init:
=00E2 52                          push    dx
=00E3 51                          push    cx
=00E4 53                          push    bx
=00E5 50                          push    ax
=00E6 8916AA0A                    mov     wfcb,dx           ;save entry FCB
=                                                           ;pointer
=00EA BAAF0A                      mov     dx,offset wdma    ;set dma address
=00ED B11A                        mov     cl,setdma
=00EF E81501          0207        call    bdos
=                         ;
=00F2 8B16AA0A                    mov     dx,wfcb           ;get pointer to fcb
=00F6 B113                        mov     cl,deletf
=00F8 E80C01          0207        call    bdos              ;first get rid of old
=                                                           ;file
=                         ;
=00FB 8B16AA0A                    mov     dx,wfcb
=00FF B116                        mov     cl,makef
=0101 E80301          0207        call    bdos              ;create the new file
=                         ;
=0104 3CFF                        cmp     al,0ffh           ;check for error
=0106 740E            0116        jz      wr_error
=                         ;
=0108 C706AC0AAF0A                mov     wptr,offset wdma       ;set pointer
=                                                                ;to start of
=                                                                ;buffer
=010E C606AE0A80                  mov     wcntr,length wdma
=0113 E90D00          0123        jmp     wr_2              ;terminate normally
=                         ;
=                         wr_error:
=0116 BA900B                      mov     dx,offset wr_msg
=0119 B109                        mov     cl,pstring        '
=011B E8E900          0207        call    bdos
=011E C606B20B01                  mov     err_flag,1        ;set flag
=                         wr_2:
=0123 58                          pop     ax
=0124 5B                          pop     bx
=0125 59                          pop     cx
=0126 5A                          pop     dx
=0127 C3                          ret
=                         ;
=                         ;
=                         ;-------------------------------------------
=                         ;RD_CHAR returns a single character
=                         ;from the file, in the DL register.
=                         ;
=                         ;Entry: none.
=                         ;Returns: DL = character.
=                         ;         and err_flag = 0 if no errors.
```

```
=
=
=0128 803E280A00      rd_char:  cmp     rcntr,0             ;have we exhausted the
=                                                           ;buffer?
=012D 7411     0140             jz      rd_rec              ;if so, get a new
=                                                           ;record
=012F 56                        push    si
=0130 8B36260A                  mov     si,rptr             ;get pointer
=0134 8A14                      mov     dl,[si]             ;get byte
=0136 5E                        pop     si
=0137 FF06260A                  inc     rptr                ;point to next byte
=013B FE0E280A                  dec     rcntr               ;decrement the counter
=013F C3                        ret
=                         ;
=0140 52              rd_rec:   push    dx                  ;save dx
=0141 51                        push    cx
=0142 53                        push    bx
=0143 50                        push    ax
=0144 BA290A                    mov     dx,offset rdma  ;load dma address
=0147 B11A                      mov     cl,setdma
=0149 E8BB00     0207           call    bdos
=014C 8B16240A                  mov     dx,rfcb ;load user fcb
=0150 B114                      mov     cl,readf
=0152 E8B200     0207           call    bdos                ;read the next record
=0155 3C01                      cmp     al,01h              ;error?
=0157 7412     016B             jz      rd_rerr
=0159 C706260A290A              mov     rptr,offset rdma  ;reset the pointer
=015F C606280A80               mov     rcntr,length rdma        ;reset the
=                                                                 ;counter
=0164 58                        pop     ax
=0165 5B                        pop     bx
=0166 59                        pop     cx
=0167 5A                        pop     dx                  ;restore dx
=0168 E9BDFF     0128           jmp     rd_char             ;continue with read.
=                      rd_rerr:
=016B BA840B                    mov     dx,offset rd_msg
=016E B109                      mov     cl,pstring
=0170 E89400     0207           call    bdos
=0173 C606B20B01               mov     err_flag,1        ;set error flag
=                      rd_r2:
=0178 58                        pop     ax
=0179 5B                        pop     bx
=017A 59                        pop     cx
=017B 5A                        pop     dx
=017C C3                        ret
=                         ;
=                         ;-----------------------------------
=                         ;WR_CHAR writes a single character
=                         ;to the output file.
=                         ;
=                         ;Entry: character in DL.
=                         ;Returns: err_flag = 0 if no errors.
=                         ;
=                         ;
=                      wr_char:
=                         ;
=017D 803EAE0A00                cmp     wcntr,0             ;is counter zero yet?
=0182 7416     019A             jz      wr_rec              ;if so, write the
=                                                           ;record
=0184 56                        push    si
=0185 8B36AC0A                  mov     si,wptr             ;get pointer
=0189 8814                      mov     [si],dl             ;store the incoming
=                                                           ;byte
=018B 5E                        pop     si
=018C FF06AC0A                  inc     wptr                ;point to next
=                                                           ;location
=0190 FE0EAE0A                  dec     wcntr               ;decrement counter
```

```
=0194 80FA1A                    cmp     dl,eof_char     ;have we reached end
=                                                       ;of file?
=0197 7401      019A            jz      wr_rec          ;if so, write last
=                                                       ;record,
=                                                       ;and close file.
=                       ;
=                       wr_ret:
=0199 C3                        ret
=                       ;
=                       wr_rec:
=019A 52                        push    dx
=019B 51                        push    cx
=019C 53                        push    bx
=019D 50                        push    ax
=019E BAAF0A                     mov     dx,offset wdma  ;get pointer to buffer
=01A1 B11A                      mov     cl,setdma
=01A3 E86100     0207           call    bdos            ;set dma to point to
=                                                       ;buffer
=                       ;
=01A6 8B16AA0A                  mov     dx,wfcb
=01AA B115                      mov     cl,writef
=01AC E85800     0207           call    bdos
=                       ;
=01AF 3C01                      cmp     al,01h          ;check for directory
=                                                       ;full
=01B1 742D       01E0           jz      dir_full
=01B3 3C02                      cmp     al,02h          ;check for disk full
=01B5 7439       01F0           jz      disk_full
=01B7 C706AC0AAF0A             mov     wptr,offset wdma  ;reset pointer
=01BD C606AE0A80              mov     wcntr,length wdma  ;reset counter
=01C2 58                        pop     ax
=01C3 5B                        pop     bx
=01C4 59                        pop     cx
=01C5 5A                        pop     dx
=01C6 80FA1A                    cmp     dl,eof_char     ;check for eof
=                                                       ;character
=01C9 7403       01CE           jz      wr_close        ;if eof, close
=                                                       ;the file.
=01CB E9AFFF     017D           jmp     wr_char         ;write the
=                                                       ;character
=                       ;
=                       wr_close:
=01CE 52                        push    dx
=01CF 51                        push    cx
=01D0 53                        push    bx
=01D1 50                        push    ax
=01D2 8B16AA0A                  mov     dx,wfcb
=01D6 B110                      mov     cl,closef
=01D8 E82C00     0207           call    bdos            ;close the file
=01DB 58                        pop     ax
=01DC 5B                        pop     bx
=01DD 59                        pop     cx
=01DE 5A                        pop     dx
=01DF C3                        ret
=                       ;
=                       dir_full:
=01E0 BA740B                    mov     dx,offset dir_msg
=01E3 B109                      mov     cl,pstring
=01E5 E81F00     0207           call    bdos
=01E8 C606B20B01               mov     err_flag,1       ;set error flag
=01ED E90D00     01FD           jmp     wr_rerr
=                       disk_full:
=01F0 BA550B                    mov     dx,offset disk_msg
=01F3 B109                      mov     cl,pstring
=01F5 E80F00     0207           call    bdos
=01F8 C606B20B01               mov     err_flag,1
=                       wr_rerr:
=01FD 58                        pop     ax
```

```
-01FE 5B                    pop     bx
-01FF 59                    pop     cx
-0200 5A                    pop     dx
-0201 C3                    ret
-                           ;
-                   abort:                          ;return control to
-                                                   ;CP/M-86.
-0202 B100                  mov     cl,0
-0204 E80000      0207      call    bdos
-                           ;
-                           ;
-                           ;
-                           ;
-                           ;
-0207 CDE0         bdos:    int     224
-0209 C3                    ret
-                           ;
-                           ;------------------------------
-                           ;
-                           ; This data segment section must be included
-                           ;for char-io to work.  Although its location is
-                           ;dependent on the previous (user program) data
-                           ;segment, it must occur AFTER 0100H for it to
-                           ;work properly.
-                           ;
-                           ;
-                           dseg    $               ;restart the data
-                                                   ;segment.
-                           ;
-     005C          fcb     equ     005ch           ;user fcb is at this
-                                                   ;offset within
-                                                   ;data segment.
-                           ;
-                           ;
-                           ;
-0A24 0000         rfcb     dw      0               ;pointer to user fcb
-0A26 0000         rptr     dw      0               ;pointer to dma area
-0A28 00           rcntr    db      0               ;counter for buffer
-                           ;
-0A29             rdma     rb      128             ;reserve buffer area
-0AA9 00                   db      0
-                           ;
-0AAA 0000         wfcb     dw      0               ;pointer to user fcb
-                                                   ;for write
-0AAC 0000         wptr     dw      0               ;pointer to dma write
-                                                   ;area
-0AAE 00           wcntr .  db      0               ;counter for write
-                                                   ;buffer
-                           ;
-0AAF             wdma     rb      128
-0B2F 00                   db      0
-0B30             fcb2     rb      36              ;set up second
-                                                   ;fcb area
-0B54 00                   db      0
-                           ;
-                           ;
-                           ;
-0B55 4E6F20737061  disk_msg db     'No space for destination file.$'
      636520666F72
      206465737469
      6E6174696F6E
      2066696C652E
      24
-0B74 446972656374  dir_msg db      'Directory full.$'
      6F7279206675
      6C6C2E24
```

```
=0B84 526561642065      rd_msg   db        'Read error.$'
      72726F722E24
=0B90 577269746520      wr_msg   db        'Write error.$'
      6572726F722E
      24
=0B9D 43616E277420      opn_msg  db        'Can''t open the file.$'
      6F70656E2074
      68652066696C
      652E24
=                       ;
=0BB2 00                err_flag db        0
=                       ;
                             end
```

END OF ASSEMBLY. NUMBER OF ERRORS: 0. USE FACTOR: 8%

Appendix **V**

CP/M-86 Error Messages

BDOS ERRORS

Error message	**Meaning**

BDOS err on d:

> This message can have many meanings. It can occur if no disk is in the drive, if the disk is improperly formatted, if the disk drive door is open, or if some other mechanical problems occur that aren't directly under the control of CP/M-86. "d:" is the disk drive the error occurred on.
>
> **Remedy:** type CTRL-C to try again.

BDOS err on d: bad sector

> This error can occur if an improperly formatted disk is used or if the disk is worn. "d:" is the disk drive the error occurred on.
>
> **Remedy:** type CTRL-C to retry.

BDOS err on d: select

> This error occurs when a nonexistant disk drive "d:" has been specified.
>
> **Remedy:** type CTRL-C to retry.

BDOS err on d: RO

This error occurs when disk drive "d:" has been set to read/only status or the disk in the drive has been changed since the last warm-start operation.

Remedy: type CTRL-C to retry.

Command name?

If CP/M-86 can't find the command (.CMD file) you specified, it returns the command name followed by a question mark. The possible cause is that the file was not on the default disk or that the file name was misspelled.

Remedy: check file name spelling and file location on disk. Try again.

File exists

The file you have asked CP/M-86 to create already exists on disk.

Remedy: choose a different file name than the one that exists or delete the existing file.

File not found

The file you specified cannot be found by CP/M-86 on the specified disk.

Remedy: check that the desired file is on the specified disk, or check the spelling of the file name.

No file

The specified file could not be found on the specified disk.

Remedy: check that the desired file is on the specified disk, or check the spelling of the file name.

STAT **ERRORS**

Error message   **Meaning**

Bad Directory d:
Space allocation conflict:
User n d:filename.typ

> The STAT utility has detected a space allocation
> problem on disk "d:". One data block on disk has
> been assigned to more than one file at the same
> time.
>
> **Remedy:**   erase the file (or files) listed after the
> error. If you do not, the error could repeat itself.

Invalid assignment

> An invalid device was specified in a STAT device
> assignment command.
>
> **Remedy:**   use the STAT val: command to view
> the possible device assignments.

Use: [size] [ro] [rw] [sys] or [dir]

> An invalid file attribute was specified in a "set file
> attributes" command.
>
> **Remedy:**   check the list of attributes entered to
> make sure they match those in the above list.

Use: STAT d: = RO

> An invalid drive assignment was given in a STAT
> command. The only valid drive assignment is RO
> (read only).
>
> **Remedy:**   reenter the command with the RO op-
> tion, if needed.

PIP **ERRORS**

Error message   **Meaning**

DESTINATION IS R/O, DELETE (Y/N)?

The destination file specified in the PIP command exists and is marked as read only.

Remedy: typing Y in response to the message will cause the file to be overwritten. Typing N will abort the command.

ERROR: BAD PARAMETER

An illegal parameter has been entered in a PIP command.

Remedy: check for spelling errors, or consult the user's manual for a list of valid parameters.

ERROR: CLOSE FILE {filespec}

An output file cannot be closed. It is possilbe that the wrong disk is in the drive or that the disk is write protected.

Remedy: check for the correct disk and for read-only status. Reenter the command.

ERROR: DISK READ - {filespec}

The input file (filespec) could not be read properly. It is possible that the file is empty.

Remedy: Check the file name, or check for an empty input file.

ERROR: DISK WRITE - {filespec}

A disk-write operation could not be performed. It is possible that the disk is full.

Remedy: check that there is sufficient space on the output disk, and if necessary delete some files.

ERROR: FILE NOT FOUND - {filespec}

The input file has not been specified.

Remedy: check that the file exists on the specified disk.

ERROR: HEX RECORD CHECKSUM - {filespec}

A hex record checksum error was found in the input file.

Remedy: check the input file, or recreate the file by reassembling the program.

ERROR: INVALID DESTINATION

The destination specified by the PIP command is not valid.

Remedy: check that you haven't specified an input device as the destination. Check spelling, or refer to the manual for a list of destination devices.

ERROR: INVALID FORMAT

The format of the PIP command is illegal.

Remedy: check the manual for proper formats.

ERROR: INVALID HEX DIGIT - {filespec}

An invalid hexadecimal digit has been found while PIP was reading an input hex file.

Remedy: try recreating the hex file.

ERROR: INVALID SEPARATOR

An invalid character has been placed between two input file names as a separator.

Remedy: check the manual for proper PIP command format.

ERROR: INVALID SOURCE

The source device or file specified in the PIP command is not allowed. It is possible that you have used an output device as a source device.

Remedy: check that you have used a valid source device, or refer to the manual for further information.

ERROR: INVALID USER NUMBER

The user number specified in a PIP command is greater than 15.

Remedy: make sure that the user number ranges from 0 to 15.

ERROR: NO DIRECTORY SPACE

No empty directory entries are available to create the output file.

Remedy: erase a file, or use a different disk.

ERROR: QUIT NOT FOUND

The Q (quit) command string argument could not be found in the input file.

Remedy: check to make sure that the string does exist (check spelling) and resubmit the command.

ERROR: START NOT FOUND

The S (start) parameter string argument could not be found in the input file.

Remedy: check the file to make sure the string exists, and resubmit the command.

ERROR: UNEXPECTED END OF HEX FILE - {filespec}

An end of file was encountered prior to the termination of the hex record.

Remedy: reassemble the hex file to make sure it is valid. Then resubmit the PIP command.

ERROR: USER ABORTED

PIP has been aborted by the user.

Remedy: none.

ERROR: VERIFY - {filespec}

The file being copied with a V or verify parameter has been found to have an error. This usually is the cause of a failed disk or disk drive.

Remedy: try the copy operation again, and if the error occurs, run a disk diagnostic program (if available). Otherwise, assume that the disk is bad and try a different one.

DDT-86 ERRORS

Error message   **Meaning**

Ambiguous operand

An attempt was made to assemble an instruction with an ambiguous operand.

Remedy: precede the instruction with the prefix BYTE or WORD.

Cannot close

The disk file written by DDT-86 (with the W command) cannot be closed. DDT-86 will terminate.

Remedy: check that the correct disk and drive were specified, and that the disk is not marked as read only. Then reenter DDT-86 and try again.

Disk read error

The disk file specified in the R command could not be read properly.

Remedy: it is possible that an end of file was detected before the actual end. Check the input file for errors.

Disk write error

The disk file specified in the W command could not be written. The probable cause is a full disk.

Remedy: erase a file on the output disk and try again. Make sure that enough space is available for the file.

Memory request denied

A request for memory during an R command because eight memory allocations have already been done.

Remedy: none.

Insufficient memory

There is not enough memory to load the file requested by the E or R commands.

Remedy: cut down the program size or add more memory.

No file

The file specified in an E or R command could not be found on the specified disk.

Remedy: check to make sure the file is on the disk.

No space

No space is available in the output disk directory for a file being written by a W command.

Remedy: erase a file on the output disk and try again.

Verify error at s:o

The value placed in memory by a fill, set, move, or assemble command could not be read back correctly. The probable cause is no memory at the location, bad memory at the location, or a ROM (read-only memory) at the location.

Remedy: display the memory at that location to see if it contains data or is empty.

ASM-86 ERRORS

Error message   **Meaning**

Cannot close

An output file can't be closed. This error causes ASM-86 to terminate.

Remedy: make sure the correct disk is in the drive, and check that the disk has not been write protected.

Directory full

There isn't enough directory space for new output files.

Remedy: erase some files on the output disk or use a new disk. Reenter the assembly command.

Disk full

The output disk is full. No room exists for the LST, H86, or SYM files.

Remedy: erase some files on the output disk or use a new disk. Reenter the assembly command.

Disk read error

A source or include file could not be read. The most likely cause is an unexpected end of file.

Remedy: check the source files for obvious errors in the length of the file.

Double defined variable

An identifier used as the name of a variable has been defined twice.

Remedy: check the program for repeated variable names.

Double defined label

An identifier used as the name of a label has been used twice.

Remedy: check the program for repeated labels.

Double defined svmbol—treated as undefined

The identifier in an EQU directive was used somewhere else in the program.

Remedy: check the program for repeated use of a symbol.

Error in codemacro building

Either a codemacro contains an invalid statement, or a codemacro directive was found outside a codemacro.

Remedy: check the program codemacros for errors.

File name syntax error

The file name in an include directive is not formed properly.

Remedy: check the spelling and format of the include directive.

Garbage at end of line—ignored

Additional text was found after an end of line was expected. ASM-86 ignores it.

Remedy: although ASM-86 will run correctly without correcting the error, it would be wise to check the source program for missing semicolons (comment delimiters) or other errors.

Illegal expression element

An expression is improperly formed.

Remedy: check the source program for errors in mathematical expressions.

Illegal first item

The first item on a source line is not a valid identifier, directive, or mnemonic.

Remedy: check the source program for errors at the beginning of the source line. Refer to the ASM-86 manual for help.

Illegal IF operand—IF ignored

Either the expression in an IF statement is not numeric, or it contains a forward reference (to a cônstant).

Remedy: refer to the ASM-86 manual for help.

Illegal pseudo instruction

The identifier in front of a pseudo instruction is missing, or an identifier appears before a pseudo instruction that doesn't allow identifiers.

Remedy: refer to the ASM-86 manual for help.

Illegal pseudo operand

The operand in a directive is invalid. For example, a string is not enclosed in quotes.

Remedy: check the ASM-86 manual for more information.

Instruction not in code segment

An instruction appears in a segment other than the code segment (CSEG).

Remedy: make sure that a CSEG directive occurs before any assembly instructions.

Label out of range

The label referred to in a call, jump, or loop instruction is out of range. It is possible that the label was defined in a segment other than the one containing the instruction. It is also possible that a conditional jump instruction referred to a label that is outside the -127 to $+128$ byte range of conditional jumps.

Remedy: in the case of an unconditional jump to another segment, change the instruction to a jump far instruction. In the case of a conditional jump outside of -127 to $+128$ bytes, first jump to an unconditional jump instruction.

Missing instruction

A prefix on a source line is not followed by an instruction. For example, REP was placed on a line by itself.

Remedy: check the program for prefixes occurring by themselves.

Missing pseudo instruction

The first item on a source line is a valid identifier and the second item is not a valid directive that can be preceded by an identifier.

Remedy: check the ASM-86 manual for details.

Missing segment information in operand

The operand in a CALLF or JMPF instruction (or an expression in a DD directive) does not contain segment information.

Remedy: make sure that the CALLF or JMPF or DD directive includes a segment reference, as described in the ASM-86 manual.

Missing type information in operand(s)

Either one or the other operand in an instruction does not contain enough type information.

Remedy: make sure that the instruction contains a byte or word prefix to define the type of the instruction.

Nested IF illegal—IF ignored

The maximum IF statement nesting level permitted by ASM-86 has been exceeded.

Remedy: try to combine some of the IF statement levels.

Nested INCLUDE not allowed

An include directive was found within a file already included in the source.

Remedy: combine some of the INCLUDE levels.

No file

The requested source or include file could not be found on the specified drive.

Remedy: check the spelling of all file names and try again. Also, one of the include files may not exist.

No matching IF for ENDIF

An ENDIF statement was encountered without a matching IF statement.

Remedy: check the source program. The starting IF statement was probably left out by accident.

Operand(s) mismatch instruction

Either an instruction has the wrong number of operands, or the types of the operands don't match.

Remedy: check with the ASM-86 manual for the allowable operands of the instruction.

Parameter error

A parameter in the command tail of the ASM-86 command was entered incorrectly.

Remedy: check the parameter list for obvious errors or mistyping. Then resubmit the command.

Symbol illegally forward referenced—neglected

The indicated symbol was forward referenced in an ORG, RS, EQU, or IF statement.

Remedy: move the symbol equate so that it occurs before it is needed.

Symbol table overflow

Insufficient memory exists for the symbol table.

Remedy: reduce the number of or length of symbols, or reassemble on a system with more memory.

Undefined element of expression

An identifier used as an operand is not defined or is illegally forward referenced.

Remedy: make sure that all identifiers are defined before they are needed.

Undefined instruction

The item following a label on a source line is not a valid instruction.

Remedy: check for typing errors in the instruction field. Refer to the ASM-86 manual for a list of valid instructions.

Appendix **VI**

References and Further Reading

An Introduction to CP/M Features and Facilities. Pacific Grove, CA: Digital Research. 1978.

CP/M-86 Operating System—Programmer's Guide. Pacific Grove, CA: Digital Research, 1981.

CP/M-86 Operating System—System Guide. Pacific Grove, CA: Digital Research, 1981.

CP/M-86 Operating System—User's Guide. Pacific Grove, CA: Digital Research, 1981.

Dahmke, Mark. "Introduction to Multiprocessing," *Programming Techniques*, Vol. 4. Peterborough, NH: BYTE Books, 1979.

Dahmke, Mark. "Introduction to Multiprogramming," *BYTE*. Sept. 1979.

Dahmke, Mark. *Microcomputer Operating Systems*. Peterborough, NH: BYTE Books, 1982.

Davis, Williams. *Operating Systems*. Reading, MA: Addison-Wesley, 1977.

Tannenbaum, Andrew. *Structured Computer Organization*. Englewood Cliffs, NJ: Prentice-Hall, 1976.

Index

ABOUT THE AUTHOR

Mark Dahmke is a contributor for both *BYTE* and *Popular Computing* magazines. He had a monthly column called "Telecomputing" in *Popular Computing* and as a computer consultant has designed operating systems and installed CP/M for several different computers. He is the author of *Microcomputer Operating Systems*.